THE INTERNET AND THE CUSTOMER-SUPPLIER RELATIONSHIP

Stefano Ronchi obtained his Masters degree in Management and Industrial Engineering with honours at Politecnico di Milano; during which he studied for one year at the University of Birmingham, UK. In January 2002 he gained a Doctoral degree in Management, Economics and Industrial Engineering at Politecnico di Milano. He defended his dissertation in the area of supply chain management and the Internet adoption in customer-supplier relationships. During the program, the author spent five months at the Center for Transportation Studies, MIT, working within the 'Integrated Supply Chain Management Program'. He is now Assistant Professor at Politecnico di Milano in Business Management and Administration, Project Management and Supply Chain Management. He has participated in several research and consulting projects in Italy and abroad in the area of process management and supply chain management, and is the author or co-author of over 20 journal and international conference papers.

The Internet and the Customer-Supplier Relationship

160401

STEFANO RONCHI
Politecnico di Milano, Italy

ASHGATE

Published by
Ashgate Publishing Limited
Gower House
Croft Road
Aldershot
Hants GU11 3HR
England

Ashgate Publishing Company
Suite 420
101 Cherry Street
Burlington, VT 05401-4405
USA

Ashgate website: http://www.ashgate.com

British Library Cataloguing in Publication Data
Ronchi, Stefano
The Internet and the customer-supplier relationship
1. Business logistics - Data processing 2. Electronic commerce 3. Customer relations - Data processing
I. Title
658.5'002854678

Library of Congress Cataloging-in-Publication Data
Ronchi, Stefano, 1974-
The internet and the customer-supplier relationship / Stefano Ronchi.
   p. cm.
Includes bibliographical references and index.
ISBN 0-7546-3746-8
   1. Industrial procurement. 2. Industrial procurement--Data processing. 3. Electronic commerce--Management. I. Title.

HD39.5.R66 2003
658.7'2'02854678--dc21

2003050264

ISBN 0 7546 3746 8

Printed and bound in Great Britain by Biddles Ltd, *www.biddles.co.uk*

Contents

List of Figures

List of Tables

Preface

Companies today are increasingly competing in the marketplace on the basis of their supply chain capabilities. These capabilities are reflected in many ways – getting products to market faster, at a lower cost, and/or at higher levels of quality or customization for the customer. Interestingly, these capabilities that drive a firm's competitiveness are no longer solely the results of the firm's internal operations; they are now more often a function of work across the firm's boundaries, largely the result of unique interactions and relationships with customers and suppliers. This applies to both collaborative relationships, where the concept of integrated supply chain management is exemplified, and to more traditional arm's length relationships with other parties in the supply chain. To create unique supply chain capabilities, companies must rely on a complex supply network of industrial relationships that collectively contribute to a competitive offering in the marketplace.

One of the most significant changes occurring in industrial relationships in recent years has been the expansion of information and communication technology, and specifically in the supply chain area, the introduction of Internet-based tools. Aside from the hubris and unrealistic optimism at the outset and that quickly tempered with the March 6, 2000 NASDAQ market crash and the subsequent business-to-consumer (B2C) dot.com fallout, practitioners and academics are recognizing some practical and tangible benefits that are being derived from the business-to-business (B2B) relationships with Internet technologies. This trend has been highlighted by continuous developments and innovations in electronic auctions, electronic catalogs, Internet-based collaborative tools and environments, and new Internet-based intermediaries.

This book explores a related important issue, Internet adoption in industrial relationships, in some depth. Despite the proliferation of contributions in literature regarding this topic, it is difficult to find a comprehensive treatment interpreting such a complex phenomenon. Moreover, in this field it is also difficult to find publications based on a solid and reliable research methodology. Given this, the book provides a useful contribution as it brings together several different research studies and contributions in developing a conceptual framework for Internet tools adoption in customer-supplier relationships. Furthermore, the author analyzes critical issues based on significant empirical evidence and a well designed research methodology. The result is a well-defined synthesis of existing knowledge and practice.

While the book will hopefully be of interest to executives who are concerned with the complex and interrelated issues associated with managing Internet-based relationships, its primary audiences are academics in the field of Supply Chain Management and the Internet adoption. In particular, PhD students and researchers might benefit from the general framework of the subject as well as from studying concrete applications of Internet-based tools in customer-supplier relationships. Additionally, Master students might benefit from the book for deep and specialized courses in Supply Chain Management, and for reference support during their Master thesis as well. The text might be appropriate for use also in methodological courses for PhD students and young researchers, as the research methodology is quite complex and deeply described in the book.

Overall, it is an honor and a pleasure to introduce this useful text, a product of Dr. Ronchi's research efforts (conducted at both MIT and at Politecnico di Milano) and his keen insight.

James B. Rice, Jr.
Director, Integrated Supply Chain Management Program
Center for Transportation and Logistics
Massachusetts Institute of Technology

Introduction

In recent years, a great attention has been paid to the potentialities related to the Internet adoption within business processes. Firstly, the introduction of web-based technologies led to the e-commerce paradigm: companies started to adopt the new technologies in order to enter new markets, to enhance revenues in existing ones and to supply better customer services to the final consumer. Soon the e-commerce became e-business due to the interaction of the new technologies with all processes within the company. As a matter of fact, processes going beyond the boundaries of the firm are also influenced by this trend and in particular the relationships among companies within the supply chain are changing in order to face new threats and opportunities.

As far as the relationships across the supply chain are concerned, the Internet seems supporting two apparently contrasting trends. On the one hand, standardization and market mechanisms are emphasized through electronic catalogs, auctions and liquid exchanges. On the other hand, there is the opportunity to enhance the value added with higher customization and to improve supply chain performances with close relationships through new technologies, which make integrable different companies' information systems. At a first glance, it could be hypothesized that the first trend should support indirect or MRO (Maintenance, Repairs and Operations) materials purchases; while the second trend should support direct or customized materials procurement.

In reality, the consequences of the introduction of the new technologies are rather complex and, although they do not change dramatically traditional business concepts, their influence on supply chain management and companies' relationships is not easy to analyze. The Internet changes the nature of traditional relationships and leads to new possible configurations. Those changes are allowed by the technology, but its introduction will not be worthwhile if it is not supported by an integrated analysis within the company and beyond it, upstream and downstream in the supply chain. This implies the reengineering of processes, organizations and managerial configurations. Performances of processes across the supply chain are strongly influenced by these interactions between new managerial and organizational configurations and new technologies. There is not a deterministic one-way impact of one of these two areas on the other, but their development is mutually fostered and supported by each other.

Within such context, the aim of this research study is to analyze and to understand clearly what are the main implications related to new technologies on vertical relationships between companies along the supply chain. In particular, three main objectives are addressed in the work.

The first main objective of the research is to clarify what are the motivations that should stimulate companies to adopt web-based technologies within their relationships with suppliers.

The second objective is to identify what are the appropriate Internet tools companies should adopt according to their specific goals.

Finally, the most relevant objective is to explain what are the implications on customer-supplier relationships related to the Internet adoption.

In order to answer these research questions, all the study has been based on a wide literature review and systematization, which mainly concern three research streams: supply chain management, customer-supplier relationships, and Internet tools adoption within inter-enterprise relationships. Literature analysis supported the clear definition of the research questions and the formulation of preliminary research assumptions. The overall empirical methodology has then followed three subsequent stages. The first stage is exploratory in nature and consists of case analyses and qualitative interviews. The second stage is explanatory in nature and consists of survey analysis. Finally, the third stage is descriptive in nature and consists of web sites analysis. Along the entire research process, the unit of analysis has been the customer-supplier relationship.

The exploratory stage aims at identifying main variables explaining and influencing the Internet adoption in procurement relationships. Evidence has been collected from four case studies of companies adopting the Internet in some of their relationships with suppliers. In addition, a wider inquiry has been carried out over the Internet and with academics, consultants, and experts in the field in order to gather further information about general trends in such context.

The outcome of this first stage is the formulation of preliminary answers to previously mentioned research questions, thus stating clear hypotheses underlying such answers.

Subsequently, the explanatory stage aims at testing formulated answers and related underlying hypotheses through a survey analysis. Such survey is based on a questionnaire sent out in the period July-August 2001 to a sample of 1.500 North American companies, randomly selected from a 15.000 firms database, which resulted from data provided by three American purchasing associations. Valid responses are 162 out of 185 respondents (response rate of 12.3 per cent). Collected data were analyzed through different statistics methods; as far as the testing purpose of the analysis is concerned, factor analysis, logit and multiple regression models, and analysis of variance techniques have been adopted.

Finally, as research hypotheses were proved, an Internet research has been performed in order to collect and analyze further data about emergent supply chain services offered on web, thus providing a detailed description of web-portals supporting coordination and collaboration between customers and suppliers. The main results of the research can be summarized as follows.

The research has clarified and systematized what are the main motivations driving companies to the adoption of the Internet in customer-supplier relationships; such motivations are different, but not mutually exclusive. Firstly, web-based technologies provide the opportunity to increase the supply process efficiency, both in terms of internal activities and in terms of external activities with the suppliers. Increased efficiency means, for example, lead times reduction, operational procedures costs reduction, and inventory costs reduction. Secondly, new technologies might allow reducing procurement costs by increasing market efficiency in terms of suppliers' search and selection, contract negotiation, and purchase price. Finally, the Internet adoption might increase supply process effectiveness in terms of quality, degree of innovation, time-to-market, and service level to the final consumer.

The second result is related to the second research question. In order to pursue the previously described objectives, according to the acquired material, companies still have to choose among different tools. Electronic catalogs are suited for low criticality materials where the firm pursues mainly internal process efficiency. Electronic auctions are powerful tools to increase competitiveness among suppliers for high volume purchases, thus significantly reducing procurement costs. Web EDI and team working tools surely support supply process efficiency and effectiveness, but they might increase procurement costs.

These are only some examples of the results related to the specific web-based tools; however, an interesting evidence shows that companies, regardless of their motivations, mostly adopt private exchanges rather than consortia initiatives or independent ones.

Finally, the most important result is related to the influence of the Internet adoption in customer-supplier relationships. Both case studies and survey evidences prove a clear divergence between arm's length relationships and more collaborative alliances. On the one hand the Internet provides higher transparency and standardization, thus increasing market efficiency. On the other hand, it supports higher levels of coordination and collaboration among trading actors. Such divergence opens the space for a new typology of relationship, which is referred to as *collaborative market* in this work.

A collaborative market relationship occurs where companies choose trading partners through a market-oriented approach, but new technologies allow them to reach high level of coordination and collaboration without big investments. These are short-term relationships with low initial costs, and therefore low switching costs: if the relation is not worthwhile any more trading companies can give it up and find someone else on the market. Collaborative markets are characterized by a set of collaboration services between customers and suppliers that might be classified as operational services, on the one hand, and technological services, on the other.

Although some barriers to collaborative market environments are still in place, the existence of such relationships should allow companies to compete on their businesses by leveraging their dynamic collaborating networks.

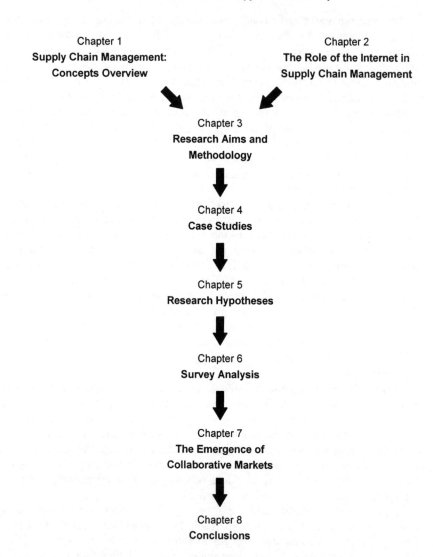

Figure 1 Book structure

The structure of the book essentially follows the methodological path previously described (see Figure 1).

Chapter 1 collects and systematizes relevant contributions deriving from a literature review in the supply chain management research stream. In particular, in addition to external supply chains and networks of companies issues, customer-supplier relationships are deeply discussed.

Chapter 2 provides a general collection of contributions related to the Internet phenomenon and then focuses deep attention on the role of the Internet in supply chain management.

After analyzing main literature contributions related to the research topic, in Chapter 3 clear research questions are formulated and the research methodology adopted to address such questions is described.

Chapter 4 provides the analyses of the four selected case studies; in particular, the Grapes, Chemics, Smart Technologies and Gias cases are discussed. Due to privacy concerns, the names of these real cases are fictitious.

In Chapter 5, the preliminary answers to research questions are formulated basing on empirical evidence collected in the explorative stage of the research. In addition, also hypotheses underlying such answers are stated.

Chapter 6 presents the details of the survey methodology and analyses aimed at testing the research hypotheses formulated in Chapter 5.

In Chapter 7, on the basis of formulated and tested research hypotheses, the emergence of *collaborative market* relationship is envisaged. Such relationship is deeply described also through the analysis of some web initiatives offering collaborative services on the web. The analysis also provides a discussion of main barriers that are still in place.

Finally, Chapter 8 draws the main conclusions of the research.

Chapter 1

Supply Chain Management: Concepts Overview

1.1   Origin and Definitions

Although the term *Supply Chain Management* appeared for the first time in literature only in 1982 with the contribution of Oliver and Webber, the underlining concepts find their roots in the stream concerning physical distribution in the early 1960s. An example of this first stage is provided by the National Council of Physical Distribution Management (NCPDM) in 1962, which defines physical distribution as:

> A term employed in manufacturing and commerce to describe the broad range of activities concerned with efficient movement of finished products from the end of the production line to consumer, and in some cases includes the movement of raw materials from the source of supply to the beginning of the production line.

Fourteen years later, the same Council revised the definition including the manufacturing activities in order to coordinate better the inbound and outbound product movements:

> Physical distribution management is the term describing the integration of two or more activities for the purpose of planning, implementing and controlling the efficient flow of raw materials, in-process inventory and finished goods from point of origin to point of consumption.

According to this latter definition, during the 1970s and the 1980s the first physical distribution stage embedded also manufacturing, procurement and order management functions leading to the Logistics era. The Council of Logistics Management proposed in 1986 its own definition of integrated logistics:

> Logistics management is the process of planning, implementing, and controlling the efficient, cost-effective flow and storage of raw materials, in process-inventory, finished goods, and related information flow from point of origin to point of consumption for the purpose of conforming to customer requirements.

At this time, information sharing starts to appear as an important issue beside materials handling; Oliver and Webber (1982), Houlihan (1984), Jones and Riley (1985), Stevens (1989) and other researchers conveyed in defining the internal supply chain as the integration of the functions involved in the flow of materials and information, from inbound to outbound ends of the business.

The scope of the issue goes definitively beyond the company's boundaries with Hayes and Wheelwright (1984) who described a commercial chain including all the actors from raw materials producers to the final consumers (Figure 1.1); the roots of this trend are in the industrial dynamics studies started with Forrester (1961) and Burbidge (1961).

Figure 1.1   An inter-business supply chain (adapted from Hayes and Wheelwright, 1984)

The studies in the last ten years have lead to the Integrated Supply Chain era in which supply chain management is seen as the management of activities including the supplier, the supplier's supplier, the customer and the customer's customer.

In this period, researchers, managers and consultants have addressed the topic using many different terms, some examples are network sourcing, supply pipeline management, network supply chain, supply base management, value chain management, and value stream management (Croom et al., 2000). In this landscape, Table 1.1 shows a set of the main definitions of Supply Chain Management provided in the last two decades.

Table 1.1 Main definitions of Supply Chain Management

Year	Author	Definition
1982	Oliver and Webber	Management of the internal supply chain that integrates business functions involved in the flow of materials and information from inbound to outbound ends of the business.
1985	Jones and Riley	An integrative approach to dealing with the planning and control of the materials flow from suppliers to end-users.
1991	Ellram	A network of firms interacting to deliver product or service to the end customer, linking flows from raw material supply to final delivery.
1992	Christopher	Network of organizations that are involved, through upstream and downstream linkages, in the different processes and activities that produce value in the form of products and services in the hands of the ultimate consumer.

Year	Author	Definition
1992	Lee and Billington	Networks of manufacturing and distribution sites that procure raw materials, transform them into intermediate and finished products, and distribute the finished products to customers.
1994	Berry et al.	Supply chain management aims at building trust, exchanging information on market needs, developing new products, and reducing the supplier base to a particular OEM (original equipment manufacturer) so as to release management resources for developing meaningful, long term relationship.
1994	The International Center for Competitive Excellence (ICFCE)	Supply chain management is the integration of business processes from end user through original suppliers that provides products, services and information that add value for customers.
1995	Saunders	External chain is the total chain of exchange from the original source of raw material, through the various firms involved in extracting and processing raw materials, manufacturing, assembling, distributing and retailing to ultimate end customers.
1997	Kopczak	The set of entities, including suppliers, logistics services providers, manufacturers, distributors and resellers, through which materials, products and information flow.
1997	Lee and Ng	A network of entities that starts with the suppliers' suppliers and ends with the customers' customers, dealing with the production and delivery of goods and services.
1998	Tan et al.	Supply chain management encompasses materials/supply management from the supply of basic raw materials to final product (and possible recycling and re-use). Supply chain management focuses on how firms utilize their suppliers' processes, technology and capability to enhance competitive advantage. It is a management philosophy that extends traditional intra-enterprise activities by bringing trading partners together with the common goal of optimization and efficiency.

Year	Author	Definition
1998	Metz	Integrated Supply Chain Management (ISCM) is a process-oriented, integrated approach to procuring, producing, and delivering products and services to customers. ISCM has a broad scope that includes sub-suppliers, suppliers, internal operations, trade customers, retail customers, and end users. ISCM covers the management of material, information, and funds flows.
2000	Global Supply Chain Management Forum (former ICFCE)	Supply chain management is the integration of key business processes from end user through original suppliers that provides products, services and information that add value for other customers and other stakeholders (customer relationship management, customer service management, demand management, order fulfillment, manufacturing flow management, procurement, product development and commercialization, returns).
2000	Ballou et al.	The supply chain refers to all those activities associated with the transformation and flow of goods and services, including their attendant information flows, from the sources of raw materials to end users. Management refers to the integration of all these activities, both internal and external to the firm.
2000	Lambert and Cooper	The management of multiple relationships across the supply chain. It is not a chain of business with one-to-one, business-to-business relationships, but a network of multiple businesses and relationships.

Although the definitions are slightly different (in some cases pretty different) and each one of those provides its own contribution; it is quite clear the step forward from a pure logistics perspective to a more holistic one. This step is explainable by identifying three main concepts recurring in the definitions and underpinning the research done in the supply chain management field (see Figure 1.2).

Process oriented approach
The authors all agree on thinking the supply chain management as a way to integrate all the activities performed across the different companies with a process perspective. This entails a strong focus both on the final consumer and on the immediate downstream customer. In this aspect there is a clear inheritance from the process organization literature (Hammer, 1990; Davenport, 1993; Hammer and Champy, 1993): supply chain management goes beyond and implies not only the process integration among functions within a company, but the integration of activities realized in different companies is also perceived as a competitive factor. This perspective refers

to all the processes creating value for the end consumer, from the new product development to the reverse logistics and returns management.

Products, information and funds
Most of the authors see supply chain management dealing with products, information and funds flow. Such aspect is directly related to the previous one. Products mean not only physical materials (raw materials, work in progress and finished products) but also services (Fine, 2001). All the relevant information needed to pursue efficiency and effectiveness across the supply chain must be shared among participants. Finally, an important issue in transactions is surely money and how it is transferred.

Network of companies
The last important factor concerns the actors involved: in order to manage efficiently and effectively all flows across the chain, from the beginning to the end consumption, more companies need to interact. The presence of organizations with different and conflicting objectives makes finding the best supply chain strategy a significant challenge (Simchi-Levi et al., 2000). Coordination and collaboration across the network open the discussion to concepts like trust and partnership, themes which many authors have coped with (only few recent examples are Handfield et al., 2000; Simchi-Levi et al., 2000; Mentzer et al., 2000; Manrodt and Fitzgerald, 2001).

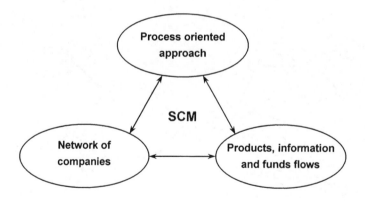

Figure 1.2 Concepts underpinning supply chain management research

Due to its multidimensional complexity, the supply chain management theme has been analyzed by different disciplines: the industrial economics literature, the organization literature, the operational research literature, the strategy literature and finally by the operations management literature. The different contributions

coming from all these disciplines can be related to different areas of interest, which
have been evolved as follows (Figure 1.3):

- internal supply chains;
- customer-supplier relationships;
- external supply chains;
- networks of companies.

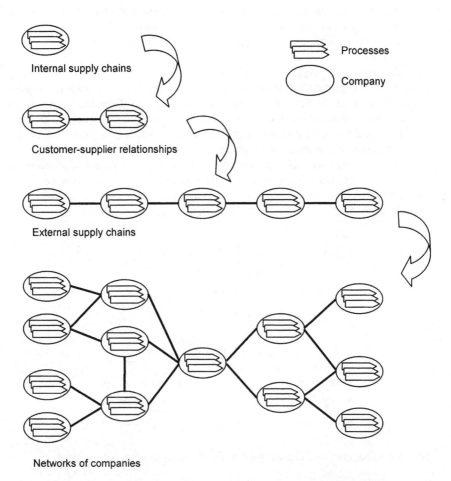

Figure 1.3 Areas of interest in supply chain management literature

Due to the aim and the scope of the research, this work addresses the state of the
art in literature and practices from the operations management perspective and
focuses the attention particularly on dyadic relationships, although some

considerations on external supply chains and networks of companies are provided. Focusing the attention on customer-supplier relationship is a first necessary step in studying supply chain management. However, such perspective surely does not highlight important issues such as upstream and downstream multi-tier supply chain management, and relationships portfolio strategy in managing a network of companies.

Nevertheless, some relevant contributions from other main disciplines will also be explored (especially from industrial economics and strategic literature).

1.2 Customer-Supplier Relationships

The evolution of relationships among companies within the supply chain has been an interesting and important issue for researchers and managers in the last years and will continue to be important in the future. The increasing market turbulence and competition (both in terms of quality, cost and service level), the product life-cycles reduction, the increased variety of products and services and technology evolution have lead companies to search for a higher flexibility, both in terms of mix, volume, products and technologies. Because of the difficulty to preside and manage all different technologies and competencies, the consequence of this evolving scenario is the outsourcing of some non-core activities.

Frequently, a company may find it more effective to use other firms with specialized resources and technical knowledge to perform these business functions. Even if a firm has the resources to realize a particular task, another company could be better suited to perform that task simply because of its location, its resources, its expertise or its possibility to exploit economies of scale, thus reducing costs.

In literature, specific attention has been paid to analyse the advantages of strategic outsourcing (Quinn and Hilmer, 1994; Quinn, 1999). The opportunities stand both at the operational and the strategic level. The main benefits deriving from outsourcing are: increasing flexibility, especially in purchasing rapidly developing technologies; decreasing design-cycle time, because the suppliers work simultaneously on individual components of the system; spreading the company's risks for components and technology development among a number of suppliers; concentration of key competencies; and improvement of the efficiency and quality of processes. On the other hand, the main risks are the loss of critical skills or the development of the wrong ones, the loss of cross-functional skills, the loss of control over a supplier, especially when its priorities are not aligned with the buyer's ones.

For all these reasons, the customer-supplier relationship has become an important topic on managers' and scholars' agendas.

In order to understand the different typologies of possible relationships between customer and supplier, this section provides an overview of contributions regarding coordination mechanisms between firms; among those coordination mechanisms, it addresses the connection between markets and vertical alliances and the kind of purchase; and finally, it provides a classification framework for alliances based on the literature review.

Coordination Mechanisms

This work refers to the definition of coordination mechanisms with the acceptation that Williamson provided for governance structures: 'the institutional framework within the integrity of a transaction is decided' (Williamson, 1979).

There are basically two major business activities coordination mechanisms: market and hierarchy. On the one hand, in the market a number of economic actors (both firms and final users) coordinate each other in order to sustain the exchange of goods or services among themselves. On the other hand, hierarchy implies production resources ownership and authority exercising from one single entity that imposes its own decisions through a system of awards and punishments.

The fundamental roots of the choice between those coordination mechanisms used to manage a transaction can be found in the industrial economics literature, and in particular in the transaction costs literature, initially developed in the 1930s (Commons, 1934; Coase, 1937) and further expanded starting from Williamson in the 1970s and then Grossman and Hart with the incomplete contracts theory in the 1980s (Williamson, 1975, 1979, 1983; Grossman and Hart, 1986). This approach emerges as opposition to the neoclassical theory, which considered markets as the most efficient mechanism in allocating resources, in order to explain the existence of firms controlling and coordinating internally part of the economic activities.

The hub of this approach is the transaction, that could be defined as the conveyance of a good or a service in exchange for a transfer of values between parties.

Table 1.2   Main transaction costs components (adapted from Watson et al, 2000)

Search and selection costs	Research costs	Collecting information regarding potential suppliers
	Information costs	Collecting information from specific suppliers regarding the transaction
Negotiation and evaluation costs	Negotiation costs	Communication and negotiation process with suppliers
	Decision costs	Evaluation of different options and contracting
Transaction management costs	Control costs	Control of shipment and billing, payment, quality control, ...
	Contentious costs	Management of possible compliance or breach of contract

Williamson identified three main aspects characterizing any transaction: bounded rationality (Simon, 1977), opportunism, and transaction specific investments. According to the bounded rationality theory, any 'economic man' is characterized by having limited and not perfect information and low procedural capabilities. Most of these actors are also opportunistic, they pursuit their self-interests even in an egoistic way. Finally, transactions often require specific investments that lose their value outside the relation between the two parties.

The presence of one of those specific aspects causes some costs associated with the transaction, these are called transaction costs. Table 1.2 briefly summarizes the nature of transaction costs characterizing any transaction.

Such transaction costs can be reduced through hierarchy; although this solution maintains other kinds of costs caused by the coordination within its internal bureaucratic structure (e.g. managerial decision making, accounting, planning and control).

In addition to transaction costs, each transaction is also characterized by the production costs that represent the expenses related to the acquisition of the specific good or service purchased.

In each situation, the coordination mechanism minimizing the sum of these two kinds of costs (transaction and production costs) will be chosen.

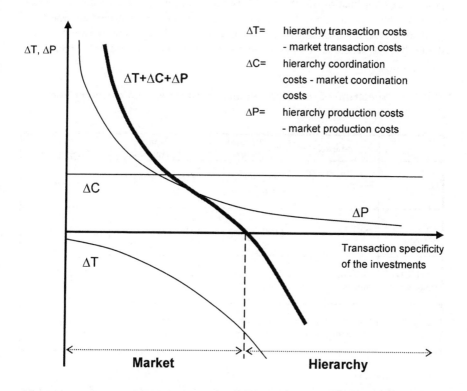

Figure 1.4 Impact of transaction specific investments on market/hierarchy choice (adapted from Mariotti, 2000)

Figure 1.4 shows how transaction specific investments, one of the three main aspects characterizing any transaction, impacts on the choice between market and hierarchy. Such choice can be based on the analysis of three cost components. The difference between hierarchy and market transaction costs is negative for transactions characterized by low specific investments (transaction costs equal zero in the case of hierarchy as they become coordination costs), and it further decreases for more idiosyncratic investments, due to the high specificity of the efforts the actors should face. Coordination costs can be considered as constant in the case of hierarchy and zero in the case of market (as they become transaction costs). Finally, the difference between hierarchy and market production costs is very high for transactions characterized by low specific investments, due to the efforts in internalizing the activity, and it tends to set at zero for more idiosyncratic investments, as those efforts are comparable to the high price obtainable on the market. As a result, for transactions characterized by low specific investments, the market is the most efficient coordination mechanism; vice versa, for transactions characterized by high specific investments, the hierarchy is the most efficient one.

As a matter of fact, the industrial economics literature identifies a third typology of coordination mechanism between firms within the spectrum market-hierarchy. This is the so called hybrid, quasi-market or intermediate mode of organization. It implies some efforts in activities integration between actors, without having recourse to hierarchic model (through, for example, merger or acquisition).

Table 1.3   Spectrum of coordination mechanisms between customer and supplier

	Market	**Vertical Alliance**	**Equity Partnership**	**Vertical Integration**
Goals	Different	Some of them are equal	Most of them are equal	All the same
Time horizon	Short	Medium-long	Medium-long	Long
Proprietary structure	Two different entities	Two different entities	Equity sharing	Ownership
Main feature	Competitive arm's length relationship	Collaborative relationship	High level of risk-sharing	One totally integrated activity

There are many contributions in literature that define those kind of relationships. Lamming, Ellram, and De Maio and Maggiore call them partnerships, in which the transaction entails also efforts in cooperating and collaborating together to improve both actors' performances (Lamming, 1993; Ellram, 1995a, 1995b, De Maio and Maggiore, 1992). A similar concept is provided by Simchi-Levi, who calls them strategic alliances (Simchi-Levi et al., 2000). In such a relation, many drivers push companies towards collaboration (see for example the games theory and win-win situations between companies).

In reality, a sort of continuum of relationships can be seen in practice. Ellram identifies four levels of coordination between market and hierarchy: short-term contract, long-term contract, joint venture and equity interest (Ellram, 1991). Macbeth and Ferguson write about product life relationship, shared destiny, minority share-holding, strategic alliance and joint venture as intermediate types of relationship (Macbeth and Ferguson, 1994).

Analyzing the main contributions found in literature, a general framework of coordination mechanisms between customer and supplier could be drawn (Table 1.3). This framework presents a spectrum of relationships between market and vertical integration.

Market

This is the traditional arm's length transaction. A company needs a specific product or service, and it simply purchases that on the market from the best bidder. Of course, the goals and the objectives of the two actors involved in the transaction might not match; for this reason the relationship is not exclusive, the buyer could find other suppliers and the seller could find other customers. As a consequence its time horizon is often short.

Vertical Alliance

This is typically a multi-dimensional and goal-oriented relationship between two firms in which both risks and rewards are shared. Companies with similar objectives decide to collaborate either on inventory management or on new product development or on marketing activities; and these are only a few examples. Due to the goals commonality and the kind of information shared, this relationship presents typically a medium-long term commitment. Such a commitment and collaboration often lead to strategic benefits for both partners. With regard to this kind of relationship, one of the main and most critical themes debated in literature is surely trust between the companies.

Equity Partnership

This is a relationship in which the level of commitment is even higher than in the previous case. Goals and objectives of the two companies are so similar that the financial structure of the relationship changes, the two actors start sharing equity interests and they are not two completely separate entities anymore. For this reason collaboration and integration become even stronger and the firms share their destiny. Some examples can be found in subsidiaries, joint ventures and equity interests cases.

Vertical Integration

Finally, vertical integration deals with mergers and acquisitions. This solution provides full control over all the activities performed and the objectives become all the same. The costs of acquiring or merging another company could be very high and the efforts in making the two cultures compatible could be very high as well. Due to the characteristics of this relationship, the time-horizon is very long because the switching costs related to the integration are relevant.

It is important to note that in literature, authors often speak indifferently about strategic or vertical alliances and partnerships meaning the same concept; in any case, those contributions have been studied to describe the kind of relationship which is referred to as vertical alliance in this book.

The material analyzed within this work is related to the choice between the first two typologies of relationships within a transaction situation: market and vertical alliance. This is due to the fact that equity partnership and vertical integration also entails financial and equity issues which are out of the scope of the research.

Market or Vertical Alliance?

Substantial contributions have been written about the choice between markets and vertical alliances in different situations; they mainly refer to the object of the transaction and the environment as two key drivers.

Again, the first contribution can be found in the industrial economics literature, even if it properly refers to the market-hierarchy dilemma. In the previous paragraph the effect of transaction specific investments on that choice has already been shown (Figure 1.4). In particular, Williamson identifies three main factors describing the transaction and determining the choice:

- transaction specific investments;
- frequency of the transaction;
- environment uncertainty.

The higher those factors, the more likely vertical integration would be the best solution (Williamson, 1979). Assuming that a certain level of uncertainty always exists, he suggests different ways of coordinating in different situations, considering also the so called intermediate modes of organization (Figure 1.5). Underpinning such relationships, he then develops the hostages theory: a hostage is anything that has a low value for the party which is holding it, but a great value for the party bestowing it (Williamson, 1983). The exchange of hostages between firms could prevent possible opportunistic behaviors. On the one hand, the hostage can be seen as equity participation in case of partnerships; on the other hand it can be represented by transaction specific investments on both sides or trust and reputation issues in case of vertical alliances.

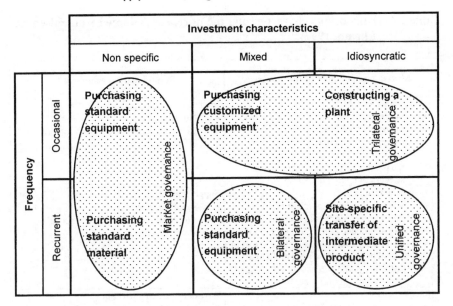

Figure 1.5 Transaction dimensions and governance structures (adapted from Williamson, 1979)

In 1983, Kraljic adds other two dimensions to specific investments, frequency and uncertainty in order to better characterize the transaction: importance of the purchase and complexity of the supply market (Kraljic, 1983). His framework is then slightly changed and further developed by Olsen and Ellram (Olsen and Ellram, 1997) and takes cue from the previous work done by Fiocca (Fiocca, 1982): they are both oriented towards a portfolio approach in managing relationships, but Fiocca refers his study to downstream relationships with customers, whereas Kraljic is concerned about supplier relationships.

Olsen and Ellram define the strategic importance (or relevance) of the purchase by describing those factors internal to the firm that characterize the purchase itself. On the contrary, the complexity of the supply market derives from factors external to the company, which make the purchase require more efforts to be managed. In Table 1.4 the dimensions characterizing the purchase are summarized.

By using these factors, it is possible to classify the different purchases of a company. In particular there are four sets of purchases: non-critical, bottleneck, leverage and strategic (Figure 1.6).

Non-critical purchases have a low strategic importance and are easy to manage. The key issue here is to reduce administrative costs by standardizing and consolidating as much as possible the purchases. In this situation, the buyer could concentrate the purchases from few suppliers among the best bidders; the relationships with these suppliers are mainly at arm's length based as the supply market characteristics allow that.

Table 1.4   Dimensions characterizing the purchase (adapted from Olsen and Ellram, 1997)

Strategic importance of the purchase	Supply market complexity
Competence factors • the extent to which the purchase is part of the firm's core competencies • the purchase improves knowledge of buying organization • the purchase improves technological strength of buying organization	Product characteristics • Novelty • Complexity (number of parts and process difficulties)
Economic factors • volume or value of purchases • the extent to which the purchase is part of a final product with a great value added • the extent to which the purchase is part of a final product with a good profitability • criticality of the purchase to get leverage with the supplier for other buys	Supply market characteristics • suppliers' power • suppliers' technical and commercial competence
Image factors • supplier critical image/brand name • potential environmental/safety concerns	Environmental characteristics • Risk • Uncertainty

Bottleneck purchases are characterized by low strategic importance, but they are difficult to manage. The supply market complexity stimulates the company to try to standardize the purchase or find some substitutes. The buyer should find reliable relationships focusing on practices like concurrent engineering and value analysis in order to lower the costs of operations.

Leverage purchases have a high strategic importance and they are easy to manage. The company should leverage volumes across product lines and suppliers to lower the materials costs. Medium-term contracts and two-way relationships with reliable suppliers should be established to maintain the quality of the product and to lower the total costs as much as possible.

Finally, the strategic purchases are the most critical to manage as they are relevant and the supply market is complex. The company should build close relationship with the most reliable supplier establishing an alliance and focusing on improving both parties' performances. The supplier should be viewed as a natural extension of the company.

A further step in the analysis of the company's purchases portfolio is to identify the right suppliers' attractiveness and the strength of the relationships according to the typology of acquired material. The attractiveness describes the factors that make a company choose a specific supplier: some examples could be represented by economic and financial factors, performances, technological capabilities, organizational, cultural and strategic issues. The strength of the relationship considers factors as economic exchange volumes, cooperation between the two companies, cultural, technological and geographic distance. By comparing the typology of the purchase with the supplier's attractiveness and the strength of the relationship it is possible to develop action plans in order to improve the matching between what the purchase would require and how it is actually managed.

		Strategic importance of the purchase	
		Low	High
Supply market complexity	High	**Bottleneck** • concurrent engineering • control of vendors	**Strategic** • focus on quality performance • long-term supply relationships *(Alliance)*
	Low	**Non-critical** • product standardization and consolidation • administrative costs reduction *(Market)*	**Leverage** • exploitation of purchasing power • vendors selection

Figure 1.6 Classification of purchases (adapted from Kraljic, 1983)

Malone, Yates and Benjamin, and De Maio and Maggiore add another dimension characterizing the purchase: external or product description complexity, which indicates the amount of information needed to describe all the features of the object of the transaction. They then provide the link between this dimension and the transaction specific investments (or product specificity) (Malone, Yates and Benjamin, 1987; De Maio and Maggiore, 1992). They argue that with the increasing of these two dimensions characterizing the purchase, the most suited relationship shifts from market towards vertical integration (Figure 1.7). They also found that the development of information and communication technology potentially reduces the external product complexity and that advanced practices as flexible automation, CAD-CAM integration and lean production potentially reduce transaction specific investments. In De Maio and Maggiore's minds these factors open new opportunities for vertical alliances between customers and suppliers.

Summarizing the contributions analyzed in this section, it is possible to infer that there are six main factors characterizing the purchase and influencing the choice between market and vertical alliance:

- the presence of transaction specific investments;
- the frequency of the purchase;

- the risk and uncertainty related to the environment;
- the strategic relevance of the purchase;
- the supply market complexity;
- the complexity of product description.

The higher these factors, the more the relationship should shift from a market towards a vertical alliance.

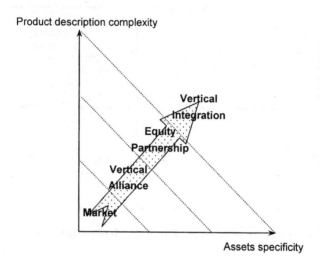

Figure 1.7   Impact of product description complexity and specificity on the typology of relationship

Features of a Vertical Alliance

A lot of material and contributions have been produced and published about customer-supplier alliances, often called partnerships in literature (Nassimbeni, 1996); defining what is exactly a vertical alliance is not easy though, due to its multi-dimensional aspects.

Mentzer provides a nice metaphor describing an alliance as a 'marriage' opposed to 'dating': 'It takes a lot of work to build a relationship and keep it active and keep it vibrant [...] Once the commitment is made, you do not throw it away after a couple of years' (Mentzer et al., 2000). The authors think of an alliance as characterized by the sharing of information, knowledge, risk, and profits.

Ellram defines an alliance as:

> ... an ongoing relationship between two organizations which involves a commitment over an extended time period, and a mutual sharing of the risks and rewards of the relationship [...] By definition, a partnership relationship is a two-

way relationship involving a mutual exchange of ideas, information, and benefits. (Ellram, 1995)

Vertical alliances do not concern only a small part of the organization, but they must be strongly supported by the top management and all the actors involved in the transaction, which is not a pure economical transaction any more, but becomes a real source of competitive value for both parties in the long run. Walton proposes a graphical model to compare a traditional arm's length transaction to an alliance (Cooper et al., 1997). On the one hand, in a 'bow-tie' situation, only few persons belonging respectively to sales and purchasing come into contact; they constitute a double filter for the information exchange between the actual organizations (Figure 1.12). On the other hand, in a 'diamond' situation, all the functions involved in the transaction communicate with each other and share more specific information building a sort of multi-channel communication (Figure 1.8). This model has been implemented for the first time in the relationship between Wal-Mart and Procter & Gamble with the so called 'mirror teams'.

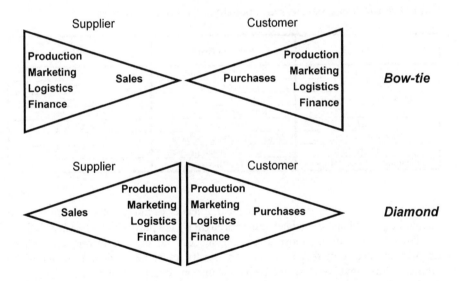

Figure 1.8 Market vs. Alliance relationship (adapted from Walton in Cooper et al., 1997)

Enablers, barriers, risks and benefits of a vertical alliance have been widely studied in literature (only few examples are: Lamming, 1993; Ellram, 1995a, 1995b; Handfield et al., 2000; Mentzer et al., 2000; Dyer et al., 2001).

Enablers
Customer and supplier must share common goals and interests to ensure their ongoing commitment, this entails also expectations from each other be clear and different organizational cultures be compatible. It must be clear then how the allies share both profits and losses coming from the relationship. Shared goals and benefits are necessary conditions to provide the right inducements to collaborate from both parties.

Top management support is another key issue; both parties should present a strong top management commitment providing strategic direction in the alliance in order to induce people to effectively collaborate. A significant top management commitment might be represented, for example, by the existence of a 'strategic alliances function' (Dyer et al., 2001). This function would have four major roles: improving knowledge and practices management among alliances, increasing external visibility of the firm, providing internal coordination to mobilize internal resources to invest into alliances and to align internal objectives, and, finally, facilitating intervention and accountability in alliances management.

Table 1.5 Enablers, barriers and benefits of vertical alliances

Enablers	Barriers/Risks	Benefits
Shared goals	Lack of any enabler	Costs
Shared benefits	High efforts	Time
Top management support	Switching costs	Quality
Roles	Knowledge diffusion	Innovation
Trust	Inconsistency	Risk sharing
Personal attitude	Market and strategic changes	
High interaction	Distance	
Planning and monitoring	Conflicts	

Roles within the relationship must be clear; a leader to move collaboration forward should be present and the added values brought by the parties must be specified.

Trust is one of the most important success factors supporting an alliance debated in literature; this basic human quality must be evident throughout the whole actors involved in the relationship, at every management level and functional area.

Personal attitudes and relationships are also crucial; people must openly discuss their practices and processes; a climate of mutual help, adjustment and joint collaboration should be created. It is possible to enhance some of these factors by specific training in partnering methods of people involved in the relationship.

Of course, to solve problems together, a high level of two-way interaction between parties is needed; that means early supplier involvement, frequent meetings and visits at both sites and multiple contacts management. As a consequence, in order to pursue that effectively, a company cannot be allied with many others. A recent study shows that the top 500 global companies have 60 major strategic alliances on average (Dyer et al., 2001), which can be considered not much compared to their sizes.

Finally, it is necessary to plan actions within the relationship and to create a performance measurement system to monitor continuously the alliance and to share benefits.

Barriers and risks

The first threat for an alliance is, of course, the lack of any of the previous mentioned enablers.

Collaboration takes time and a lot of hard work, and to keep the relationship collaborative, even more efforts are required. To get people the necessary efforts, they have to be clearly shown what the expected benefits are. Furthermore, if the wrong allied has been chosen, those efforts make switching the relationship very costly.

Surely, the risk of know-how diffusion exists, especially in those relationships in which the two firms collaborate on new technologies or products development. The loss of reputation and trust among other companies, however, can be a deterrent for adopting an opportunistic behavior.

Inconsistency is also an impediment for the alliance: bases for a relationship could be set properly, but there is always a natural resistance to change any *modus operandi* as, for example, conventional accounting practices, which focus on determining the value for a single firm rather than measuring cross-company values. People could have a restricted view only about their activities, without interfacing effectively with the other party.

Significant market changes can induce in modifying strategic directions, therefore possibly mining an established alliance as well. Moreover, also strategic changes (e.g. change of ownership) could mine the relationship.

Also physical distance can be seen as an obstacle for collaboration to take place and keep going efficiently and effectively.

Finally, unresolved conflicts, maybe due to the absence of effective conflict resolution mechanisms, could mine an already established alliance.

Benefits

Establishing an alliance and focusing on the company's core competence presents some benefits. The first observed benefit is total cost reduction, both in terms of inventory reduction, internal processes efficiency, more efficient use of human resources and production costs.

Surely, time performance can be improved: time to market of new product development can be reduced due to collaboration with suppliers and their early involvement in the designing process; also throughput lead time can be reduced through a better synchronization of operational processes. This leads to a better service level to the final customer.

Quality standards can be improved by both parties' competencies working together and the access to each other's technology capabilities can foster innovation.

Finally, also risk sharing is perceived as a benefit in case of new products launch or market downturns.

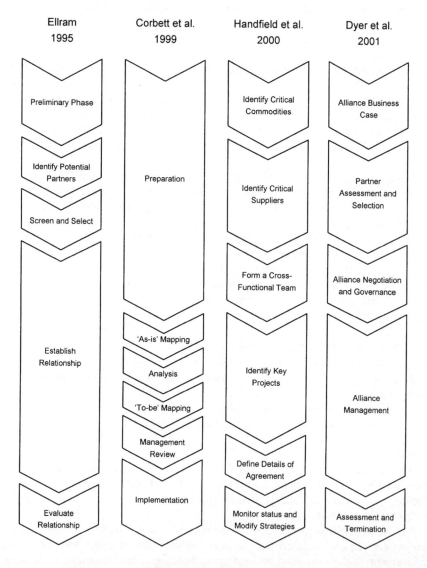

Figure 1.9 Comparison of some proposed methodologies to build a vertical alliance

On the base of those main enablers and barriers, some contributions provide also methodological guidelines and possible tools in order to establish and manage a vertical alliance (Ellram, 1995a; Corbett et al., 1999; Handfield et al., 2000; Dyer et al., 2001). In Figure 1.9 those proposed methodologies are compared. The main recurrent aspects are the identification of the critical purchased items (for example through some of the previously described classifications), the screening and selection of the supplier (again, through some of the previous contributions), the establishment of the relationship (defining objectives, people involved and key projects), the implementation, and, finally, the evaluation of the alliance itself. Within the alliance building process, a crucial role is played by the evaluation of supplier performances. This theme opens a wide literature on vendor rating systems (Nassimbeni, 2000).

In the establishment of any vertical alliance, a further crucial point is to identify exactly what is the object of the coordination and collaboration. Spina identifies two dimensions of collaboration (Spina in De Maio and Maggiore, 1992):

- *Operational Integration*: the two companies collaborate and coordinate each other on main operations processes related to physical flows. The main objectives pursued in this kind of relationship are the reduction of lead time, the reduction of production and transportation costs, the quality improvement and final customer service level improvement. This entails, for example, inventory management, production planning, transportation scheduling, forecasting, and logistics.
- *Technological Integration*: the two companies collaborate and coordinate each other on research and technology development issues. The main objectives pursued in this kind of relationship are the reduction of time-to-market, the reduction of development and designing costs and quality and innovation enhancement. This entails, for example, research and development projects, new product development projects, and new processes implementation.

By combining the extent to which companies collaborate on these two dimensions, it is possible to define four kinds of relationships (Figure 1.10).

Market relationships are essentially traditional relations managed through price mechanisms without any form of collaboration. Co-design relationships are those where customer and supplier do not operationally integrate themselves, probably due to low volumes exchanges, but cooperate in designing together products or processes. Just in Time relations consist of integrated activities in terms of small jobs, high frequency shipments, production planning synchronization, and production and quality continuous improvement. Finally, partnerships are those relationships where both technological and operational integration is pursued; the main aim of this kind of relationships is to introduce new products into the market the quickest as possible, both in terms of development and in terms of logistical pipeline fulfillment.

Within the area of collaborative design, Spina and Leandro identify different typologies of co-design. The classification is based on the fact that customer and supplier could design together either the component or the process, and the decision making process could be either joint or separated (Spina and Leandro, 1998).

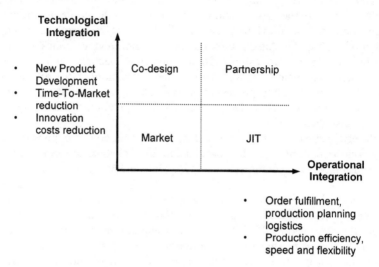

Figure 1.10   Operational and Technological Integration (adapted from Spina in De Maio and Maggiore, 1992)

De Toni and Nassimbeni (De Toni and Nassimbeni, 1999) provide a similar classification. The authors distinguish between *design link*, which consists of the involvement of suppliers in customer's product development activities (Clark, 1989; Clark and Fujimoto, 1991; Turnbull et al., 1992), *logistics link*, which essentially consists of JIT implementation (Schonberger and Gilbert, 1983; Ansari and Modarress, 1987 and 1990), and, finally, *quality link*, which occurs when customer and supplier exchange information concerning quality issues.

Temkin provides another interesting framework to describe collaboration (Temkin, 2001). He deals with dynamic collaboration, defined as a win-win partnership that share business activities; he identifies three levels of synchronization and states that firms can select increasingly higher level of collaboration:

- *Monitor:* this level involves just a one-way transfer of data; such a visibility enables companies to share critical information as available-to-promise and order status.
- *Manage:* this level involves at least one feed-back loop between partners; the companies develop common sets of business rules to coordinate each other's business activities like demand forecasting.

• *Optimize:* this level involves the analysis of bottlenecks, suggests optimal courses of action, and redirects tasks to best fit the current capabilities of participants.

Based on the previous considerations, a proposal of a possible classification of alliances is presented in Figure 1.11.

Scope of the alliance

		Operational	Technological	Complete
Depth of the alliance	Decision Making	**Operations collaboration**	**Development collaboration**	**Full collaboration**
	Information Sharing	**Operations visibility**	**Development visibility**	**Full visibility**

Figure 1.11 Classification of vertical alliances

The first dimension characterizing the relationship is the *scope of the alliance,* which entails Spina's contribution. The scope could be operational, technological or both of them.

The second dimension is the *depth of the alliance,* which considers the extent to which decision processes of the two companies are shared. In the *information sharing* case, supplier and customer share only information about each others' processes; some examples could be inventory visibility, production schedules sharing, product specifications and drawings, and process mapping. In the *decision making* case, the two parties really share also the decision making processes and define together their decisions; some examples could be collaborative planning, collaborative forecasting, and joint development. In these situations the real collaboration occurs between the two parties (Rice and Ronchi, 2001). Of course, this second level of integration requires more involvement and increases the decision making time, due to the presence of two different entities which should deeply share common goals.

1.3   External Supply Chains

One of the most important streams identified in literature concerns the integrated vision of the overall supply chain in which processes integration goes beyond the traditional boundaries of the company and the dyadic relationship. Intra-functional, inter-functional and inter-organizational coordination must merge together to compete in the market (Ballou, Gilbert, Mukherjee, 2000). All main definitions of supply chain mentioned in Section 1.1 (Figure 1.2) properly refer to this vision of supply chain.

When integrating their external supply chains, companies recognize the fact that optimizing single local processes within each enterprise leads to just a sub-optimal solution for the entire supply chain. Supply chain integration pursues the best systemic solution for the final consumer at the end of the value chain, regardless of local reduction in performances (Cooper et al., 1997; Metz, 1998). The best solution for the consumer might be both in terms of effectiveness and efficiency, and it is strictly related to the typology of product.

In 1997 Fisher identifies a strong relationship between products and the overall supply chain, sustaining that for functional products an *efficient* supply chain is suitable, whereas innovative products require a *responsive* supply chain (Fisher, 1997). Three years later Christopher provides an even stronger distinction between *lean* supply chains and *agile* supply chains sustaining that in turbulent and volatile markets an agile chain adopting postponement and modularization is much more efficient and effective (Christopher, 2000).

By integrating their processes, companies involved in the supply chain might find together the right balance between push and pull policies (Christopher, 2000; Holmstrom et al., 2000). The order de-coupling point is not defined within internal boundaries in each company any more, but it becomes the whole supply chain de-coupling point. Such higher coordination supports postponement policies and mass-customization practices at a supply chain level.

Of course, realizing such an integrated and coordinated supply chain is not easy; Lee and Billington (1992) identify common pitfalls in managing supply chain inventory: lack of common and consumer oriented performance measures along the whole chain, extremely different and not integrated firms' databases, low coordination among actors constituting the value chain, different objectives organization by organization, and superficial materials management policies.

In order to overcome such obstacles and pursue an effective supply chain integration, some authors agree on a sort of evolutionary path (Stevens, 1989; Hewitt, 1997; Cooper et al., 1997; Scott and Westbrook, 1997). Each company should firstly focus on internal processes integration; the following step is integrating also most relevant first tier customers and suppliers. Once reached complete coordination within the company and outside with strategic customers and suppliers, it is possible to enlarge integration to the whole supply chain, both upstream and downstream.

A strong evidence of the inter-relations among the members of a chain is provided by the bullwhip effect (Figure 1.12): the demand variability increases in the upper stages of the supply chain, this leads of course to higher costs and lower service levels. Forrester in 1961 illustrates this effect and points out that this is due to time varying behaviors of industrial organizations (Forrester, 1961); in 1989 Sterman reports evidence of the bullwhip effect in the 'beer distribution game' and he interprets the phenomenon as a consequence of players' systematic irrational behaviors (Sterman, 1989).

Demand

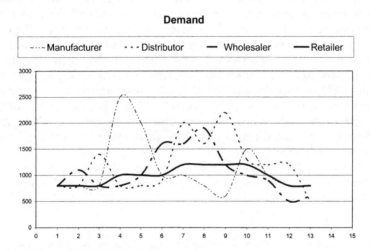

Figure 1.12 The Bullwhip effect

In 1997 Lee, Padmanabhan and Whang demonstrated that the bullwhip effect is not a consequence of varying behaviors and irrationality, but it is due to demand forecast updating, order batching, price fluctuations and rationing and shortage gaming (Lee, Padmanabhan and Whang, 1997a and 1997b). These factors lead to excessive inventories, poor customer service, lost revenues, misguided capacity plans, ineffective transportation, and missed production schedules. The authors also suggest possible remedies based on information sharing, channel alignment, and operational efficiency. With information sharing, demand information is transmitted as timely as possible along all the tiers of the supply chain. Channel alignment is the coordination of pricing, transportation, inventory planning, and ownership between upstream and downstream sites in the supply chain. Finally, operational efficiency refers to activities that improve performance, such as reduced costs and lead times.

As far as analytic models and operational research are concerned within the supply chain theme, Thomas and Griffin (Thomas and Griffin, 1996) provide a brilliant literature review on the existing models in supply chain planning; they distinguish operational and strategic planning models. The former concern buyer-vendor, production-distribution and inventory-distribution coordination; the latter are predominantly methodological works, case studies or discussion of strategic issues.

1.4   Networks of companies

Theory about networks of companies developed since the early 80s from the idea that the firm needs to look outside its boundaries to find all the resources and competencies required in order to produce its products/services. While some generic definitions of network are simply based on the presence of relations among persons, groups, or bodies (Aldrich and Dubini, 1989), more specific ones distinguish networks as the place for long term relations among actors involved (Thorelli, 1986), and specifically the already described intermediate organizational form between market and hierarchy (Thorelli, 1986; Grandori, 1989; Miles and Snow, 1992). The basic mechanism that characterizes network relationships is collaboration, that is the willingness to share goals, information, and technologies (see also Section 1.2.3).

In literature, different names have been adopted to describe networks of companies; the most frequent are *supply networks, extended manufacturing enterprises,* and *virtual enterprises.*

Supply Networks
Supply networks can be defined as sets of supply chains, describing the flow of goods and services from original sources to end consumers (Harland, 1996). The relatively recent incorporation of the term 'network' into supply chain management research represents an attempt to make the concept wider and more strategic by harnessing the resource potential of the network in a more effective way.

Another definition of supply network is the following (AA.VV., 2001): a body of advanced relations defined by integrated strategy and management policy which the focal company maintains with a limited number of suppliers. Three distinctive features are included in this definition: the existence of partnership relations between customer and supplier, a systemic view of supplier relationships, and the definition of integrated strategies and management policies for the overall network. According to this conceptualization, supply network theory is the evolution of the theory of partnership.

Fujimoto describes the Japanese supply network systems named 'keiretsu', and the main mechanisms of information sharing, performance improvement, and development of suppliers' knowledge (Fujimoto, 1997).

An initial classification of supply networks has been given by Lamming (Lamming et al., 2000); he distinguishes between supply networks aimed at producing *innovative-unique* products and those aimed at producing *functional* products.

Another interesting classification of supply networks based on literature review distinguishes between *tiered networks* and *learning networks* (Cagliano et al., 1999). *Tiered networks* are supply networks organized in 'tiers', that is levels of suppliers. The first tier is formed by main subcontractors, which are responsible for the supply of a complete product or subassembly, and thus have to manage a group of second tier suppliers. This is the typical model for Japanese supply networks (Dyer and Ouchi, 1993; Ellram, 1995; Fujimoto, 1997) and it is generally suited for high levels of systemic interactions among final product's components. *Learning networks* model has been proposed by Stuart (Stuart et al., 1998) as opposed to tiered networks. In such form of networks, competencies, know-how, and experience on operational practices are shared among members, which often operate at different levels of the value chain. The aim is to increase the overall knowledge within the network. This typology is suited when the production is characterized by the presence of high technological or operational commonalities.

Stuart et al. (Stuart et al., 1998) highlight the specific competitive advantages of a learning network compared to tiered networks. In a tiered network, without supplier association, there is a one-to-one relationship between buyer and supplier, and the focus is optimizing it. In a learning network, the interactions are among suppliers and the focus is on learning and developing world-class practice.

Of course, tiered networks and learning networks might also co-exist; thus creating *strategic networks* (Cagliano et al., 1999).

Extended Manufacturing Enterprises

Extended Manufacturing Enterprises (EME) are defined by Busby and Fan as a way of combining manufacturing operations that is alternative both to pure market and to pure hierarchical structures (Busby and Fan, 1993). In the EME each company specialized in the production of specific goods or services continues operating divided in different firms, in distinct legal and organizational entities, even if collaborating to obtain a final product. Firms combine their activities for periods that greatly exceed the lead times associated to the specific transactions. This persistence means that they can build channels among themselves through which information and knowledge can be exchanged, information and knowledge that extends far beyond the traditional exchange of specifications, drawings and contracts.

As a consequence, the extended enterprise is characterized by the information channels and by the sharing of knowledge, which allow customers and suppliers to adapt readily to changing needs and circumstances (Busby and Fan, 1993). Clearly, information exchange and sharing mechanisms are central to this organizational form. Davis and O'Sullivan (Davis and O'Sullivan, 1998 and 1999) provide a panoramic view of IT supports to the EME and Lillehagen and Dag Karlsen (Lillehagen and Dag Karlsen, 2001) provide some solutions of knowledge management in the EME.

Stock et al. define the extended enterprise as a globally dispersed collection of strategically aligned organizations (Stock et al., 2000). The EME concept has brought new attention to how organizations coordinate the flows of information and materials across their supply chains. The authors explore and develop the concept of enterprise logistics as a tool to integrate the logistics activities both within and among the strategically aligned organizations constituting the extended enterprise.

Childe (Childe, 1998) highlights that the concept of EME has something additional to the concept of supply networks. The EME is described in terms of manufacturing companies that cooperate closely together to maximize the benefits of the business they are involved with. In this idea, suppliers are considered as part of the principal company.

Basing on these considerations, it is possible to conclude that the concept of EME is: i) more centered on pooling manufacturing resources, also among partners working at the same stage within the supply chain, and ii) focused on mechanisms of operational integration to integrate information and materials flows.

Virtual Enterprises

Many conceptualizations have been provided concerning the *virtual enterprise* (e.g. Davidow and Malone, 1992; Seidel and Mey, 1994; the holonic-virtual enterprise of Merli and Saccani, 1994; the frachised factory by Dean and Carrie, 1996; the fractal company by Warnecke, 1993; the holonic manufacturing by Nakane and Hall, 1991). These organizational models are based on geographically dispersed modular units, which are specialized on particular competencies that are joined together for a definite period of time to satisfy specific market needs.

The virtual enterprise has fuzzy boundaries (Davidow and Malone, 1992), and it is an opportunistic alliance putting together complementary competencies, owned by separate units (Goldman et al., 1995). The geographical separation among units often amplifies the need for advanced IT tools to support information and knowledge exchange and to work as a unique company (Upton and Mcafee, 1996).

Again, the virtual enterprise is a similar concept to supply networks and extended enterprises. However, this model focuses on: i) the temporary and short-to-medium term of the relation, ii) the physical separation among companies, and iii) the autonomy and complementary nature of the units participating in the network.

The advantages gained by firms in developing networks, generally speaking, are widely recognized in literature and are similar to the advantages generally quoted for collaboration. Such advantages can be summarized in three categories (AA.VV., 2001).

- *Improved efficiency of inter-company processes.* Above all, the management of the network leads to greater integration of processes, avoiding redundancy and duplication, providing a more efficient exchange of information and, consequently, eliminating wastage of resources and misunderstandings, and easing planning. Moreover, the costs of coordinating the various units involved in the processes are reduced (e.g. transaction costs including partners searching, negotiation, administration and opportunistic behaviors) (Frohlich and Westbrook, 2001; De Maio and Maggiore, 1992).

- *Access to external resources beyond the company.* Networks of companies reduce the cost of access to the production, technological, financial, and relational resources of other firms by creating an environment for the exchange of such complex assets, in particular those which are intangible (Harland, 1996; Quinn, 1999; Quinn and Hilmer, 1994).
- *Integration and exchange of know-how.* Networks give greater opportunities to access specialized know-how different from the one internal to the company itself. This determines considerable advantages in terms of growth, learning, differentiation, and service. Networks are a rapid means of access to external knowledge, even in cases of tacit knowledge which is difficult to codify and transfer (Cohen and Levinthal, 1990; Esposito, 1996; Stuart et al., 1998).

In this first Chapter, main contributions found in literature dealing with inter-company process management have been explored. Both scholars and practitioners in the supply chain management field have progressively shifted their attention from company's internal processes to processes crossing the boundaries of the firm. In order to follow this trend, also organizational structures and management practices are changing, and aim at creating more and more links among trading partners.

Within this context, technology, and in particular Information and Communication Technology (ICT), plays a big role. A strong, effective, and efficient technological infrastructure is required to support high communication, designed organizational structures, and management practices. This work focuses on this topic, and in particular it analyses the role of the Internet technology in supporting customer-supplier relationships.

Chapter 2

The Role of the Internet in Supply Chain Management

2.1 History and Principles of the Internet

The Internet finds its origin between the 1960s and the 1970s. In that period characterized by the 'cold war', the United States Department of Defense was developing a telecommunication network to connect the most strategic decisional centers across the country; communication had to be guaranteed even in case of a nuclear war. In 1969 the ARPAnet (Advanced Research Projects Agency, from the name of the agency that created it) was built. It was based on the redundancy principle: it presented the structure of a web connecting multiple nodes in which communication was enabled also in case of some nodes destruction. That was a new structure compared to the previous hub and spoke model which presented one central hub connected to several peripheral nodes.

During the 1970s, the Internet was extended to the academic society in order to allow faster communication among different research centers. The FTP (File Transfer Protocol) was developed to support the files transfer on the net. By the beginning of the 1980s the Department of Defense separated the military network from the academic one. In the same years, electronic mail began to be available to the most important universities; this was a real breakthrough in the communication landscape. Furthermore, in 1983 the TCP/IP (Transmission Control Protocol / Internet Protocol) started to establish itself as a standard de facto for communication on the net.

In 1986, the National Science Foundation established NSFNET based on the ARPAnet technology; NSFNET is today the main backbone of the Internet with a communication speed of 155 Mbps (through optical fibers).

Finally, in 1989, Tim Berners-Lee from CERN of Geneva established the World Wide Web as a public available standard interface between users and applications.

Today, the Internet is a set of networks controlled by multiple actors, private organizations, government entities and universities among others. By 2003, a project called Internet2 should result in connecting 140 research centers across the world with backbones able to transfer data at 2,4 Gbps.

The Internet can be defined as a communication medium among different computers that allows rapid, two-way, secure communication (Chopra et al., 2001). In order to establish communication, computers need to share the same communication protocol; simplifying, they need to reach each other and to speak the same language. The main established protocols are: TCP/IP (Transmission Control Protocol / Internet Protocol) at the transmission level, HTTP (Hyper Text Transfer Protocol) at the application level, and HTML (Hyper Text Markup Language) at the visualization level.

The TCP/IP is a seven levels protocol able to packet information in different parts, send them to the right destination across the Web and to compose the information again once arrived at final destination. In particular, the TCP manages the splitting of the file into packets and the final reassembling, and the IP manages the identification, research and localization of the final destination of the message. As a matter of fact, the IP is a numeric address made of four numeric fields (each field contains a number between 0 and 255). To make easier the connection for the user, a system translating numeric addresses into textual addresses has been created: the Domain Name System (DNS), whose identification lists has been decentralized involving many authorities across the world.

HTTP is a protocol with the lightness and speed necessary for a distributed collaborative hypermedia information system. It is a stateless object-oriented protocol, which defines how messages are formatted and transmitted, and what actions Web servers and browsers should take in response to various commands. A feature of HTTP is the negotiation of data representation, allowing systems to be built independently of the development of new advanced representations and technologies.

Finally, HTML covers the definition of the structure and layout of a Web document by using a variety of tags and attributes. It is the most used language to create documents on the World Wide Web. In reality many other and more powerful languages to develop Web documents exist; an example is given by the XML (eXtensible Markup Language).

There are different ways for a computer to be connected to the internet. Firstly it is necessary to distinguish between a permanent connection and a temporary connection. In the former case, the machine becomes a permanent node of the network (also called gateway, router or bridge depending on the specific function carried out), connected through a dedicated line, which is attributed a specific IP address and a DNS name registered to the national network manager. In the latter case, the machine is temporarily connected to the network through a server, a Point Of Presence (POP) or an Internet Service Provider (ISP). The computer can be attributed either a static or a dynamic IP address registered to the point of access.

Secondly, the medium used for the connection could be either telephone cables, coaxial cables, optical fibers or satellite communications. Today, the speed of connection ranges from 56 Kbps or less with normal telephone connections to 5 Gbps with optical fibers; research and development in optical fibers is moving rapidly up this upper bound.

The Internet supports a series of services, the major ones are the World Wide Web, the information server, the e-mail and the Internet relay chat. These services were previously exploitable through different applications, but since 1994 a unique tool called 'web browser' has been allowing to access them all.

World Wide Web
It is a distributed hypermedia system, a vast collection of interconnected documents, spanning the world. The access to this hypermedia data is viable through hyperlinks. It can be seen as a web of servers in which clients exploit services as research engines, web portals and documents visualization. The main protocols used for connections are the ones previously illustrated (TCP/IP, HTTP, HTML).

Information server
Information servers are applications that manage information transfer among computers, those information are mainly in textual form. It is possible either to emulate another distant computer (through Telnet applications) or to transfer data through protocols like Gopher, FTP (File Transfer Protocol) and NNTP (Network News Transfer Protocol), and systems like WAIS (Wide Area Information Server) and UseNet containing databases and different kinds of information.

Electronic mail
This is a system that allows messages and files codified as ASCII text to be sent in an efficient and effective way for the user. It is based both on SMTP (Simple Mail Transfer Protocol) to send messages and on POP3 or IMAP to receive messages.

Internet Relay Chat
This tool allows the users to exchange textual information in real time establishing 'virtual chat'. In some cases, also team-working tools have been developed to make possible the distant working on documents or even drawings.

The Internet can be seen as the 'net of the nets' as it is the union of many different permanent servers and networks across the world. These servers make possible the previous mentioned services. Not all those networks are public though; there are many private networks whose access is limited to few authorized actors through the use of login-names and passwords. To protect private networks from undesired accesses many security and cryptography systems have been developed. Private networks use exactly the same Internet technologies and protocols described so far, and assume different names depending on their geographical covering:

• LAN (Local Area Network) for distances shorter than 10 Km;
• MAN (Metropolitan Area Network) for distances between 10K m and 50 Km;
• WAN (Wide Area Network) for distances longer than 50 Km.

This classification is based on distances regardless who or what entity is actually connected.

Intranet, Extranet and Virtual Private Network

In the previous paragraph, a classification of private networks has been provided based on the distance covered by the network itself. Talking about private networks in the business world, a more appropriate classification could be drawn as follows: Intranet, Extranet and Virtual Private Network (VPN).

Intranet

In literature, many definitions of Intranet have been provided, only some examples follow. Guengerisich defines it as the union of a company's network protected by a proper firewall and the set of applications that are run exploiting Internetworking technologies (Guengerisich et al., 1997). Umar defines it as a TCP/IP network used by a company that exploits Web technologies within its own business (Umar, 1997). Etnoteam considers it as a private network, based on TCP/IP and other Internet technologies (Web servers, browsers, firewalls, ...), which is used to run and make available some applications exclusively within the company (Etnoteam, 1999). Finally, IDC defines it as a private network, based on Internet and Web standards, which allows users to access different applications resident on servers through a web browser (IDC, 2000).

It is possible to conclude that an Intranet is a private network whose objective is to share information and computational resources among people within a specific company. Furthermore, it can also support team-working through groupware or workplace tools for videoconferencing, documents and knowledge management systems. The Intranet could be a set of either local, metropolitan or wide area networks connected together.

The Intranet is usually connected to the public Internet through a computer called gateway; the gateway contains some correlated security applications that control and verify every access both from the public network to the Intranet and from internal users to the Internet. Such applications constitute the firewall.

Extranet

Also the Extranet has been widely defined in literature. Baker defines it as an Intranet that allows actors, which are external to the company, a controlled and selective access (Baker, 1997). Wolak stresses the collaborative aspect and considers the Extranet as a network resulting from different private sites whose access is made possible for a limited number of external actors with the aim of collaborating and exchanging information with them (Wolak, 1998). A quite different perspective comes from Gartner Group which defines the Extranet as the union of two or more Intranets via a secure link made possible through Web applications (Gartner Group, 1999). Finally, Bayles provides a very similar definition to Gartner's while stressing the commercial purpose of those links (Bayles, 1998).

In this work, the Extranet will be considered as a private network, based on Internet technologies, aimed at sharing information, collaborating and performing transactions with actors external to the company (customers, suppliers, partners, and other stakeholders). It can include part or all of the company's Intranet information. Data and Information sharing among different entities through the Extranet and XML has been the natural evolution from EDI (see also Section 2.3).

Given the access possibility of different entities besides company's employees, the security issue in this case is even more critical than for the Intranet.

Virtual Private Network (VPN)

An example of definition of Virtual Private Network is provided by Covill, who refers to it as a different technological solution from the Extranet, but with exactly the same functionality (Covill, 1998).

A Virtual Private Network is any kind of private network, either Intranet or Extranet, that exploits the public telecommunication infrastructure. From a logical perspective, it is exactly a private network, the difference lies in the technological infrastructure. It allows data security through tunneling protocols and different security procedures (codification of both messages and addresses). Of course, this solution is much cheaper for the company than a real privately owned network; for this reason, this is the most commonly adopted solution in Extranets realizations.

2.2   The Internet and the Firm: e-Business Opportunities

In the last three decades information technology has penetrated companies' processes with the aim of increasing efficiency and effectiveness by boosting productivity, reducing costs and lead times. Firms installed systems as MRP (Material Requirement Planning), MRP II (Manufacturing Resource Planning), DRP (Distribution Requirement Planning), and, later, ERP (Enterprise Resource Planning). Web-based technologies are a further step in this evolution. In this section a brief description of the Internet adoption within business activities is provided.

The Internet Adoption

In order to understand the evolution of the Internet adoption by companies, it is necessary to analyse two compelling factors: the technology evolution and the turbulence of the competitive environment.

In the previous section, the evolution of the Internet and telecommunications technologies has been described. This trend has been followed by two other extremely important ones: the pervasive computing and the knowledge digitalization (Venkatraman, 2001). The former one consists of a cumulative process of innovations, which make possible the creation of numerous 'intelligent interacting objects'. The latter consists of a continuous evolution of multimedia technologies (text, audio, video, ...) which make the electronic communication richer and richer. The interaction of these three phenomena leads to the so called *convergence of technologies*. Such convergence has brought a huge potentiality for the introduction of technology into the business.

As far as the competitive environment is concerned, it is well recognized that in the last years competition has been increasingly harder for many reasons (Bartezzaghi et al., 1999). The globalization phenomena and the creation of new markets has lead to an even more aggressive landscape, in which companies compete on quality, costs and service. To face this hard competition, the focus on customers has been stressed, leading to higher personalization and complexity of the products. As described in the first chapter, outsourcing strategies and supply relationships management have become a very relevant issue in determining the competitive position of each firm. Finally, the continuous evolution in the legislation (e.g. environment issues, anti-trust, ...) pushes companies to be more flexible to changes.

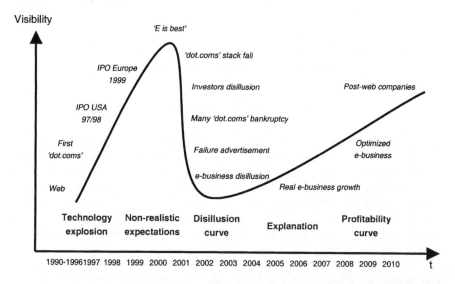

Figure 2.1 E-business evolution (adapted from Gartner Group 2000)

The union of technology potentiality and competitive needs, led companies to assume that technology was the solution of every problem. In the period between 1995 and 2000, many research organizations (e.g. International Data Corporation, Gartner Group, AMR Research, Yankee Group, Morgan Stanley's, Forrester Research) have elaborated forecasts of the adoption of the Internet, all of which presented exponential growths. The term 'New-economy' was coined to indicate the *new-way* of doing business on the Internet and the financial markets performed as venture capitalists in funding any kind of business initiatives based on the internet.

The out-of-control growth of the Internet symbolically ended on March the 6th 2000, with the NASDAQ dramatic slump. Since then, an atmosphere of disillusionment about the Internet potentialities has begun across all the industries. This evolution is well represented by Figure 2.1.

Today a more rational conviction is emerging. The Internet is only an enabling technology to be exploited in doing business, and the attractiveness of each initiative is evaluated through the traditional economic fundamentals: profitability and cash flows (*'the economic value for a company is nothing more than the gap between price and cost'*, Porter, 2001). Of course, the Internet opens new broad opportunities to increase efficiency and effectiveness, but its introduction must be matched and supported by appropriate organization structures, processes and managerial configurations (Venkatraman, 2001). The key challenge is to find the right balance between the *technology-push* attitude, in which technology evolution forces its own adoption into business processes, and the *organization-pull* one, in which companies and businesses needs drive the direction of technology innovation and development.

The Influence of the Internet on Existing Businesses

Another diffuse conviction concerns the two main possible areas of Internet adoption (McKinsey, 2000; PWC, 2000): the technology can be exploited either to create a new emerging business (e.g. Amazon, MP3, Autobytel, Vitaminic, e-steel, Bravo-build, Click4talent) or to support existing businesses (e.g. Barnes & Noble, Dell, Carpoint, Cisco, Mitsubishi, Sainsbury's, Wal-Mart). This work is focused on the second area, therefore the aim of this brief section is to introduce some of the contributions regarding the effect of the use of web-based technologies into existing businesses.

In order to explore this issue, the two fundamental factors that determine the profitability of any business can be analysed (Porter, 2001): the industry structure, which indicates the profitability of the average competitor, and the sustainable competitive advantage, which allows a company to outperform the average competitor.

Examining the effect of the web-based technologies on the well-known five forces of competition, Porter explains how the Internet will erode profitability across all industries mainly by standardizing products and capabilities, reducing barriers to entry, and shifting power to customers. Also win-win collaboration strategies among companies to improve industry economics will not solve the situation: partnering within and across different industries and outsourcing practices will only contribute to enhance standardization and reduce barriers to entry.

The collapse of long-lasting partnerships and the increasing of standardization would lead to the *e-lance economy* (Malone and Laubacher, 1998). In the past it was worthwhile to manage large organizations centrally, which provided companies with economies of scale in manufacturing, marketing, distribution and management activities. Today, because information can be shared instantly and inexpensively among many people in many locations, the value of centralized decision making and expensive bureaucracies decreases (*'Big was good... small becomes good'*, Malone and Laubacher, 1998). Industries would be highly fragmented and characterized by many small flexible organizations coordinating each other through the *invisible hand of the market*. Remaining big corporations will have the role to establish rules, standards and cultures for these network organizations (Malone and Laubacher, 1998; Brynjolffson et al., 1993).

The tool proposed by Porter to examine how competitive advantage is created by a company is the value chain: the set of activities through which a product or service is created and delivered to the customers. Because every activity involves the creation, processing, and communication of information, information and communication technologies and the Internet have a pervasive influence on the value chain and on the integration among activities. In the past, information technology worked against strategy, as packaged software applications were hard to customize according to the specific needs of the company, and firms had often to change their way of performing activities in order to conform to the 'best practices' embedded in the software. Internet architecture and new software architectures have turned technology into a far more powerful tool for developing strategy; today it is much easier to customize Internet applications to a company's unique strategic processes and positioning.

To summarize, Internet would have a critical influence on the structure of all industries, but it is a powerful complement to traditional businesses to improve processes efficiency and effectiveness, therefore improving competitive advantage.

Table 2.1 The domains of e-business opportunities

Domains of Internet adoption		
e-operations	**e-marketing**	**e-services**
• Improvement and integration of core business processes • Supply chain integration • Leverage electronic buying • Automation of administrative processes • Learning practices across SBUs	• Better understanding of customer needs • Enhancing the selling process (effective market targeting and product description) • Making the product easier to buy or better matched to customer needs	• Provision of knowledge of all relevant providers • Negotiation and construction of customer requirements and desired options (personalization) • Providing support services over the whole product life cycle

Opportunities

The improvement of competitive advantage can be read and understood more deeply by analysing three main domains of e-business opportunities: e-operations, e-marketing and e-services (Feeny, 2001). E-operations opportunities consist in web-based initiatives that improve the creation process of existing products; e-marketing opportunities consist in web-based initiatives that improve the marketing of existing products; and e-services opportunities consist in web-based initiatives that provide customer affiliated services (Table 2.1).

Given the fact that e-business opportunities can be exploited only if strongly related to existing activities, the capability to match existing assets with the use of the Internet is becoming more and more crucial in order to build a sustainable competitive advantage. Digital activities will not cannibalize physical ones, but should complement them and improve the overall performance of the company (Gulati and Garino, 2000; Venkatraman, 2001; Short, 2001; Porter, 2001).

In order to determine the right 'bricks-and-clicks' strategy, Gulati and Garino suggest examining four business dimensions - brand, management, operations, and equity – and analysing the degree of physical and digital integration that makes sense along each of these four (Table 2.2).

Brand
Extending a well recognized and respected brand to the Internet activities gives instant credibility to the initiative; this will make easier generating business both in the consumer and industrial markets. Furthermore, the physical and digital channel could create a virtuous cycle both sending on-line customers to the stores and traditional customers on-line; this will contribute to build the brand continuously.
On the other hand, the integration could cause a loss of flexibility; the company could be forced to offer the same products at the same prices to avoid customers confusion and distrust. This would also lead to the extreme difficulty in targeting different market segments and practicing dynamic pricing (Sheffi, 2001; Simchi-Levi, 2001).

Management
An integrated team could easily align strategic objectives, find and exploit synergies, and share knowledge both on practices, products and market segments.
On the other hand, separate teams could focus more sharply on their own specific activities and run their business models without contaminating or limiting each other. This would also allow to innovate more freely, without many organizational constraints.

Operations
The choice regarding operations integration should be based on the strength of a company's existing production facilities, distribution and information systems and their transferability to the web. Activities integration could

generate significant cost savings and compelling informative sites through economies of scales and scope.

On the other hand, activities separation would allow a company to develop state-of-the-art and customized systems and facilities without the flaws of the older ones.

Equity

Equity and ownership integration allows the current company to get the entire value of the Internet initiative, and to retain complete control over the activities.

On the other hand, separation could attract new and talented managers, provide easier access to outside capital (e.g. Initial Public Offering), and could also offer greater flexibility in partnering with other companies.

Of course, the degree of physical and digital integration depends on the specific company and industry characteristics; that kind of choice is not a 'black-or-white' decision, but many integration and separation balances could exists in each of the four areas. KB Toys coined the KBKids.com name, leveraging the existing brand without limiting its scope to toys; furthermore, they only integrated the purchasing staff while separating the other functions. From the operations perspective, distribution systems are separated, but buying power is shared and on-line customers can return toys bought on-line to physical stores. On the Equity side, KBKids is the result of a joint venture between KB Toys and BrainPlay.

Table 2.2 The effects of physical and digital integration/separation

	Brand	Management	Operations	Equity
Integration	• Credibility • Virtuous cycle between channels	• Strategic objectives alignment • Synergies • Knowledge sharing	• Costs reduction through economies of scale and scope	• Capturing the entire value of the Internet activities • Complete control
Separation	• Products and prices flexibility • Targeting different market segments	• Higher focalization • Higher innovation	• Ad hoc state-of-the-art solutions	• New and talented management • Easier access to outside capital • Greater flexibility in partnerships

2.3   The Role of the Internet in Supply Chain Management

All main aspects highlighted in the previous pages are useful to introduce the topic concerning the role of the Internet in Supply Chain Management. The concept of flexible organizations, the potentialities offered by the technology, its adoption in different areas of the company, the balance between current and web-based activities and the right matching of information technology on one side and organization structure, processes and managerial configuration on the other side, are all factors that can be found in literature analysing the *e-SCM*.

As a matter of fact, information transfer, frictionless transactions and Metcalfe's law[1] (i.e. 'The value of a network is equal to the square of its participants') make the Internet a powerful tool to improve, among the other processes, also supply chain performances (Cross, 2000). A recent study (Lancioni et al., 2000) shows that about 90 per cent of companies adopt the Internet in some part of their SCM program; however, this result should be viewed with much caution due to the self-selection bias related to the data collection. In addition, such questionnaire was more related to internal supply chain activities rather than to relations with suppliers. Actually, applications used mainly, emerged to be order processing, transportation management tools, and some electronic catalogs (see below).

In reality, in the last years companies have still been trying to understand the real potentialities and effects of the Internet adoption. Some authors highlighted the disintermediation/reintermediation effect (Malone et al., 1989; Voss, 2000; Chopra et al., 2000; Moakley, 2000; Kahl and Berquist, 2000). On the one hand, the new information and communication technologies provide the possibility to communicate and interact directly in an efficient and effective way with customers, thus making possible disintermediation. This possibility opens a wide interesting area, which however is outside the scope of this work, for both researchers and practitioners in the field of B2C logistics: *the last mile*. Companies selling directly to final consumers have big problems in handling shipments, and therefore try different strategies: logistics postponement, dematerialization, resource exchange, leveraged shipment, clicks and mortar, consumer direct, leverage stores (Lee and Whang, 2001; Kopczak, 2001). On the other hand, the availability of transparent information and the increasing customers' need to compare suppliers open opportunities for the creation of a new kind of intermediaries: the information intermediaries or infomediaries (Carr, 2000).

Overall, in adopting the Internet in supply chain management activities, companies have to deal with the choice of the proper tools to manage such activities, according to their specific objectives. All existing Internet relationships and the relative used tools can be classified along two dimensions:

- the interaction model;
- the scope and objectives of the Internet adoption.

---

[1] Named after Robert Metcalfe, inventor of Ethernet and founder of 3COM.

Interaction Models

Besides the specific web-based tools, which will be analysed in the following
sections, a prime concern for companies is the choice of the best suited interaction
model with customers and suppliers (Whitaker et al., 2001). There are two main
classes of models: *private* and *public* (Figure 2.2).

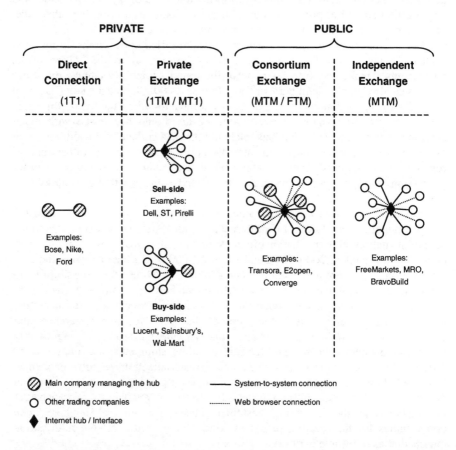

Figure 2.2 B2B Interaction Models

A private model sits on the boundary between a company and its trading parties; it
is directly used by the company itself and it provides an external interface to
internal information systems. Private models might be either a series of one-to-one
(1T1) connections (*direct connections*) or one-to-many (1TM) connections,
simultaneously connecting all the actors through a central Internet hub (*private
exchange*). Private exchanges could be either sell-side, when the company builds it

to interact with customers, or buy-side, when the company builds it to interact with suppliers.

On the contrary, public models are initiatives outside the boundaries of the company, where many-to-many (MTM) interactions are supported. These kinds of initiatives could be run either by a consortium of big players within a specific industry (*consortium portal*) or by an independent entity starting-up its business as an intermediary (*independent portal*). Of course, also such kind of initiatives might be either sell-side, buy-side, or even neutral (see the paragraph below *General Considerations about Virtual Marketplaces'*). In the case of consortium portals, literature often highlights also the concept of few-to-many (FTM), as few players, usually in the same tier of the supply chain, collect their needs to build an initiative improving their supply chains. In most of the cases, such consortia aim at lowering purchase prices by aggregating demands.

As mentioned before, this classification sets aside the typology of tools used through the Internet; it focuses only on the possible kinds of interaction models. Within each model, there are a number of services that can be used: from pure transactional services to more information sharing and collaborative ones (see following sections).

Moreover, the boundaries among these classifications is becoming more and more fuzzy, as independent and consortium exchanges are more and more providing companies with the possibility of creating their own *virtual private exchanges* or *private annexes* (Temkin, 2001). In those cases relevant privacy and security issues of course arise, but the interaction model is much closer to a private exchange.

As a matter of fact, it has been noted by some authors (Whitaker, 2001; Rangone, 2001) that companies are preferring private exchange solutions in order to conduct their supply chain activities. This is mainly due to the fact that private exchanges offer three important advantages (Whitaker, 2001): greater privacy and security, superior collaborative capabilities, and the opportunity to extend or establish a competitive advantage.

As far as the first aspect is concerned, many companies consider their procurement activities to be a competitive secret, and are thus willing to hide their supplier base, volumes, and requirements from direct competitors or even suppliers themselves. In addition, firms also want secure and monitored access to their systems and information.

The second aspect refers to the increasing need for integration among certain companies. Many organizations already collaborate for transaction processing (see Section 1.2), private exchanges will serve as an enabler to build collaborative capabilities sooner than later. Such collaboration might be simply made of information sharing and visibility along the supply chain, or even real collaboration in activities like designing, planning, and forecasting.

Finally, a private exchange might be a source of competitive and distinguished advantage. Increased efficiency and effectiveness in supply chain activities lead to value creation for the final consumer. Wal-Mart, for example, believes it has a competitive advantage in supplier collaboration and has opted not to join a public exchange, but create its own private portal (e.g. Retail-link).

There are however a few potential drawbacks to creating and operating private exchanges. First of all, the creating and operating costs will be at operator's expense. Such costs cannot be leveraged over a base of many actors, as is the case for public exchanges. Secondly, operators may choose to focus primarily on their own needs at the expense of the participants. Finally, the operator will selectively choose the participants, which may lead to criticism that this exclusivity is an attempt to slow competition and fix prices through greater contractual power.

Considering all these aspects, companies with exclusive products, processes, or market position are the best candidates for creating a private exchange (Whitaker, 2001).

Scope and Objectives of the Internet Adoption

In delineating the Internet supply chain strategy, companies should be aware of the real benefits deriving from the Internet adoption and of their portfolio of products (Chopra and Mieghen, 2000; Smeltzer and Carter, 2001).

Chopra and Mieghen highlight how web-based technologies and associated managerial policies, as most of innovations, increase effectiveness and efficiency in supply chain activities. On the one side, some examples of effectiveness and value increment consist of direct communication between parties both in sales and purchases, information sharing about products features, and prices and services customization. On the other side, some evidence of efficiency increment could be related to inventory costs reduction through postponement and centralization strategies, or collaborative practices, information processing, and prices reduction through transparency on the market.

Smeltzer and Carter, on their own, state that in adopting new technologies to pursue such objectives, companies should have clearly in mind when and where to use which tool. In particular, they suggest a four-step methodology, similar to the ones analysed in Chapter 1, in order to identify the proper tools to be used in procurement activities: spend analysis, segmentation and classification, infrastructure assessment, and supply strategy selection.

In any case, in delineating the proper Internet supply chain strategy, it has been widely recognized that companies have to align it with current and existing practices, and to coherently match the organizational structure, IT infrastructure, and employees capabilities (Smeltzer and Carter, 2001; Handfield, 2001).

All the topics mentioned so far come from different studies dealing with the role of the Internet in supply chain management, each of them contributing to the state of the art in a quite isolated fashion. A simpler and more comprehensive way of identifying potential opportunities offered by the Internet in B2B activities, and in particular in customer-supplier relationships, is thinking at the nature of the relationship itself. The first basic activity underlying each interaction is transaction management; a second basic activity is matching demand and supply; and finally, the third and most demanding one is coordinating and collaborating between parties (Chopra et al., 2001). The evolution of web-based tools in supply chain management has followed the same path (Kalakota, 2000).

In 1987, Malone, Yates and Benjamin already envisaged three basic information technology effects that would have deeply influenced customer-supplier relationships in the three mentioned activities (Malone et al., 1987; Malone et al., 1989). The first effect is termed *electronic communication effect*, which means that information technology can decrease dramatically the costs of communication, therefore facilitating transaction management. The second is named *electronic brokerage effect*, which means that standards and protocols of an electronic market can enhance transparency within a market. This leads to the increase of the number of alternatives that can be considered, the increase of quality of the selected alternative, and the decrease of the entire selection process cost, therefore facilitating demand-supply matching. Finally, the third effect is called *electronic integration effect*, which means the possibility to integrate customer and supplier's information systems, therefore facilitating coordination and collaboration.

These three effects of the Internet make it a support respectively to the procurement process, to market efficiency, and to collaboration. In the following sections, those three sets of scopes and objectives will be highlighted.

The Internet Supporting the Procurement Process: e-Procurement

The first generation B2B phenomenon started with buy-side *electronic catalogs* implemented by software companies like Ariba, SAP, Microsoft Market, Intelisys, and CommerceOne. Many authors refers to this generation with the term *e-procurement* (Chopra et al., 2001; Kalakota, 2000; Croom, 2000). The Internet could streamline inefficient procurement processes by removing the manual, paper-based, administrative and bureaucratic elements inherent in traditional purchasing systems. In this way, many of the transaction costs presented in Chapter 1 could be reduced.

This kind of solution essentially aggregates a pre-selected group of suppliers and builds an integrated catalog containing different items. Any employee can browse the customized catalog, choose the goods or services, and then send an electronic purchase order over the Internet. Where management approval is needed, an appropriate workflow automatically routes the order through the proper channels.

At the heart of all the system there is a central supply database. This database typically contains information relating to process issues such as authority levels for orders placement, suppliers' details, items details, and pricing agreements. The location and maintenance of such a central database may reside either within the customer or the supplier for each category of procurement. Generally, large companies manage their own database internally, while small firms outsource it directly to their suppliers. It is possible to find mixed situations in which some categories are managed internally and others externally.

Many benefits derive from adopting e-procurement tools (Table 2.3). First of all, the elimination of labor-intensive, paper-based requisition systems allows purchasing agents to focus on strategic procurement and supplier relationships. A second evident benefit is related to the elimination of the so called *maverick buying* effect; such practice occurs when employees buy certain items off-contract because of the need to streamline administrative activities with usual and approved suppliers or simply because of their ignorance about a consolidated supplier contract. As known, off-contract buying results in the proliferation of orders and fragmentation of purchases, leading to extra-costs. Related to maverick buying reduction is the possibility of consolidating and therefore increasing the purchasing power with selected suppliers, which usually offer lower prices for higher volumes. A fourth concrete opportunity is related to the possibility of reducing order processing time and costs, by exploiting real-time processing and electronic data retrieval. Recent researches show how it is possible to save about 70 per cent of the total order processing costs with an expected return on investments of 300 per cent (Croom, 2000; Bowles, 1999). Order lead-time reduction allows also reducing the average inventory of purchased materials. The availability of real-time electronic data allows monitoring the stage reached by the order (order tracking in that precise moment and order tracing in the past). Moreover, electronic data availability allows the continuous control of expenditures on the one hand, and suppliers' performances in terms of quality and service level on the other. Finally, many companies exploit e-procurement adoption to start a process of supply base rationalization, which leads to suppliers selection and better coordination with them.

Table 2.3 Benefits of e-procurement

Purchasing function focuses on more strategic issues
Maverick buying reduction
Purchasing consolidation
Order processing time and costs reduction
Average inventory reduction
Order tracking and tracing
Expenditures monitoring
Suppliers monitoring
Supply base rationalization

Companies using EDI (Electronic Data Interchange) already had achieved some of the highlighted benefits. However, given the high setup and operating costs, and the proprietary nature, EDI has only allowed set up links with largest suppliers, while the Internet, with its open access and lower participation costs, allows all players the opportunity to reduce transaction costs. For a detailed discussion about the differences between EDI and the Internet, see Section 2.3.

As far as the characteristics of such electronic catalogs are concerned, they have mostly been used for low volumes and high frequency MRO (Maintenance, Repair and Operating materials) items procurement. Moreover, rather high levels of standardization and low description complexity characterize these items. Such items include things like office supplies, spare parts, airline tickets and various services. For these items, the procurement process cost often overcomes the purchase cost itself, for this reason companies adopt e-procurement in order to streamline and make more efficient such a process. On the other hand, high volumes of direct materials, as shown below, need tools allowing either higher price savings or higher collaboration.

The Internet Supporting Market Efficiency: e-Sourcing

Internal efficiency in the procurement process is only the first and most simple opportunity realized through web-based technologies. Malone, Yates, and Benjamin, describing the effect of information and communication technology on two dimensions characterizing the transaction, assert an overall shift of business relationships from hierarchies towards markets (Malone et al., 1987; Malone et al., 1989). Analogous considerations can be drawn for the Internet itself (Figure 2.3).

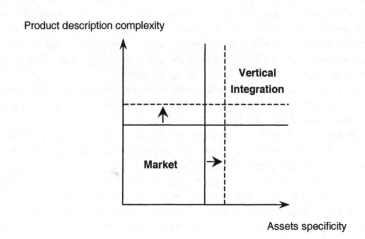

Figure 2.3 Impact of ICT on business relationships (adapted from Malone et al., 1987)

The two dimensions have been already described in Chapter 1: *product description complexity* and *assets specificity*. Web based technologies can handle and communicate complex, multidimensional product descriptions much more easily than traditional modes of communication. Therefore, the horizontal line in the figure shifts upward, indicating that some items considered complex before, are now easier to describe. The vertical line undergoes a similar change, not simply due to the Internet effect though. Flexible manufacturing technology allows rapid setup of production lines and multi-item production, thus reducing the assets specificity of some components. Therefore the vertical line in the figure moves right, indicating that some items considered highly asset-specific before, are now less specific.

The shifts of these two dimensions through the Internet adoption determine the overall reduction of transaction costs (see Chapter 1): products are easier to describe, specificity of assets has been reduced, and information transfer on the markets is far more efficient. These conditions lead to the so called frictionless commerce paradigm (Brynjolfsson and Smith, 2000). The overall effect is the increase of market situations to the detriment of hierarchies.

Such a trend has been supported by the emergence of web based tools aiming at increasing markets efficiency. The following paragraphs provide a brief description of main market tools: electronic catalogs, electronic exchanges, and electronic auctions.

Electronic catalogs
The simplest tool to conduct a transaction is the catalog, a traditional way of collecting items with relatively low complexity characteristics. Electronic catalogs have been analysed as supporting procurement efficiency; however, when they are open to the public domain, they become also a tool supporting market efficiency.

Catalog purchases are based on a *fixed-pricing logic*, where items' pricing is predetermined as result of diversification and discounting policies. However, for particular items, negotiations one-to-one are also possible.

These tools generally provide the customer with a wide range of MRO products (Maintenance, Repair, and Operating materials), but they might also include some standard direct materials. To facilitate selection among different items and different suppliers, research engines are available to the 'shopper'. Different catalogs residing in different web-sites could also be linked through communication standards enlarging the supply base.

The term *one-stop-shopping* is used to describe the purchase process through an electronic catalog. The customer literally browses and searches in the catalog choosing different items from different suppliers through product descriptions, images and technical specifications. Once selected, any product (i.e. item, supplier, quantity, and delivery mode) is dropped into a *shopping-basket*. At the end of the process the customer confirms the overall purchase with a unique order; the catalog manager then splits the order into different orders to different correspondent suppliers.

Catalog information can be updated in real time by suppliers, either the databases reside in catalog manager's servers or they reside in suppliers' own machines.

Electronic exchanges

Electronic exchanges are based on a *dynamic-pricing logic*, and work exactly like traditional stock exchanges. Buyers and sellers bid and ask for the same products and services in real time. The requests are made through the Internet and they should be filled quickly. The listed items must be sufficiently standardized in order to allow direct comparison and matching between demand and supply. For these reasons, electronic exchanges are most used for commodities characterized by high liquidity and large transactions volume.

As far as liquid exchanges are the market mechanism *par excellence*, they guarantee efficient transactions where both buy and supply markets are highly fragmented. In such conditions, all prices are transparent and purchases are guaranteed by the constant supply that generates the market's liquidity.

Electronic auctions

Another *dynamic-pricing* tool is the auction. Auctions are a very ancient market mechanism which allow automated and real time bidding for procurement or liquidation of products or services, first evidence appeared in 500 B.C. with Erodoto in Asia Minor.

There are two main classes of auctions: *direct auctions* and *reverse auctions*. Direct auctions occur where there is one seller and many offering buyers, for this reason the price goes up. Reverse auctions, on the contrary, occur where there is one buyer and many bidding sellers, for this reason the price goes down.

The requisitioning process asking potential bidders to participate in reverse auctions could assume different modalities. The acronym RFx is used to describe those different modes. *Request for Quote* (RFQ) consists of a document to be compiled by each bidder. In this document, detailed information about product specifications is already given; the bidders must agree on these specifications and provide their own bid (quote) for such product or service. *Request for Proposal* (RFP) consists of a document describing the specific needs of the auctioneer. Each potential bidder must provide its best solution (proposal), both in terms of specific product specifications and in terms of quote, to match those needs. *Request for Information* (RFI) is a simpler process in which the potential auctioneer screens the supply market by asking general information and estimates from each potential supplier. However, these requisitioning methods can also occur without necessarily resulting in an auctioning process.

Besides direct and reverse auctions, it is possible to distinguish further between *open auctions* and *sealed auctions*. Open auctions are conducted in real-time; bidders can see the bidding process and instantly raise the bid. Sealed auctions (or tenders), on the contrary, are generally conducted through a one-shot sealed bid; the best bid wins the auction. However, this sealed process could also occur twice or three times.

Finally, there are four methods to conduct the auctioning process and to determine the winner: *English auction*, *Dutch auction*, *Japanese auction*, and *Yankee auction*. In the cases, the auctioneer sets a *reserve price* that represents the threshold determining the success of the auction. In direct auctions reserve price is the minimum price at which the seller is willing to sell, while in reverse auctions it is the maximum price at which the buyer is willing to buy.

Table 2.4 Advantages and disadvantages of electronic transaction tools

		Customers		Suppliers	
		Advantages	Disadvantages	Advantages	Disadvantages
Electronic catalogs		- procurement costs reduction - supply base extension - information transparency	- the internal approval workflow might be not integrated - not very useful for complex products	- selling costs reduction - new customers opportunities - customer satisfaction	- physical and digital channel coherence - transparent comparison with competitors
Electronic exchanges		- goods are available at market prices, although volatile - save time by direct demand-supply matching	- difficulties in evaluating the suppliers - need for liquidity, therefore useful only for commodities - emphasis on single transactions	- inventory turns increase - save time by direct demand-supply matching	- direct intense competition - emphasis on prices - emphasis on single transactions
Electronic auctions	Direct	- complex products purchase - quick purchase	- possible high prices - difficulties in evaluating the suppliers - emphasis on single transactions	- price increase - inventory turns increase - selling costs reduction	- possible lower prices than desired - emphasis on single transactions
	Reverse	- complex products purchase - price reduction - quick decision	- costly process for requirements specifications - difficulties in evaluating the suppliers - emphasis on single transactions	- new customers opportunities	- direct intense competition - emphasis on single transactions - reduction of the role of negotiation capability

English auctions are the most known; the bidding process goes on until the last bidder sets the best bid (the highest in direct auctions and the lowest in reverse auctions) and nobody is willing to raise that bid.

In Dutch auctions the auctioneer progressively reduces (or increases, in reverse auctions) the price at prearranged time intervals until one bidder is willing to conclude the transaction.

In Japanese auctions the auctioneer starts from a base price and then increases it (or reduces it, in reverse auctions) step by step. At each step each bidder must decide whether to continue or to give up. Finally, the last bidder still in the game wins the auction.

Yankee auctions are a particular kind of auction aiming at selling (or buying) more identical items to more buyers (or from more sellers) with the same bidding process. The final resulting price can be the same for every participant (*uniform auction*) or diversified participant by participant (*discriminate auction*).

All these kinds of auctions can be open either to the entire market or to pre-selected potential bidders. Moreover, the parameter determining the winner could not be simply the price, but multi-parameter auctions are available in the market. E-cement, for example, is an e-auction web site in the construction industry that offers the possibility to build customized algorithms to weight different features of each bid (e.g. quality of material, service level, bidder reputation).

General Considerations about Virtual Marketplaces

Numerous B2B initiatives based their business on the described tools, leading to a proliferation of the so called *virtual marketplaces*. A first distinction among these, is between *Vertical MarketPlaces (VMP)* and *Horizontal MarketPlaces (HMP)* (Sportoletti, 2000). Vertical portals deal with problems, products and services within a specific industry (e.g. e-steel.com, plasticsnet.com, chemdex.com), while horizontal portals deal with problems, products and services across different industries (e.g. mro.com, mondus.com, fastbuyer.com). Recently, also *Meta-markets* emerged focusing across multiple industries, though offering specific services within each of them. An example is BravoBuild.com that was born as a portal supporting e-auctions and specific services in the construction industry, then enlarging its competencies in industries like food and beverage, processes, and public administration.

Kaplan and Sawhney (2000) describe virtual marketplaces, or *e-hubs*, providing an interesting classification on what companies buy and on how companies buy. The first dimension distinguishes between *manufacturing inputs* and *operating inputs*. Manufacturing inputs are items that go directly into a product or a process; they are usually bought from industry-specific or vertical suppliers. Operating inputs are not parts of the finished products, but they consist of MRO (Maintenance, Repair, and Operating materials). Such operating inputs do not tend to be industry specific and are usually bought from horizontal suppliers.

The second dimension distinguishes between *systematic sourcing* and *spot sourcing*. Systematic sourcing involves long term contracts with qualified suppliers; in that situation buyers and sellers often develop a close relationship. In spot sourcing, the buyer aims at fulfilling an immediate need at the lowest cost; in this kind of situation the two parties do not build close relationships and the object of the transaction is often a commodity.

By applying this classification scheme, the authors identify four categories of B2B hubs (Figure 2.4): MRO Hubs, Yield Managers, Catalog Hubs, and Exchanges.

MRO Hubs are horizontal markets that deal with operating inputs which tend to have low value and relatively high transaction costs, therefore these portals provide value by streamlining the procurement process. Many of the players in this field started up by licensing buy-side software for e-procurement for large companies. The natural evolution was hosting e-procurement software on their own servers to provide open markets through catalogs from a wide range of suppliers.

Yield Managers are horizontal markets for spot transactions referring to operating resources like manufacturing capacity, labor, and advertising. In situations characterized by high price and demand volatility or huge fixed-cost assets that cannot be liquidated or acquired quickly, yield managers allow companies to expand or contract their operations on short notice.

Catalog Hubs are vertical markets similar to MRO Hubs, but they are focused on industry specific products. They gather together customers and suppliers and automate the sourcing of critical non-standard manufacturing inputs, reducing transaction costs. Because the items are often specialized, catalog hubs work closely with distributors to ensure safe and reliable deliveries.

Finally, *Exchanges* are vertical markets specializing in commodities or standard products. They reduce the peaks and valleys in demand and supply by rapidly exchanging the materials needed for production through spot transactions.

What companies buy

	Operating inputs	Manufacturing inputs
Systematic sourcing	**MRO Hubs** Ariba WW Grainger MRO.com	**Catalog Hubs** Chemdex SciQuest Plasticsnet
Spot sourcing	**Yield Managers** Employease Adauction CapacityWeb	**Exchanges** e-Steel PaperExchange Altra Energy

(How companies buy)

Figure 2.4   B2B hubs classification (adapted from Kaplan and Sawhney, 2000)

The authors argue that e-hubs increase market efficiency and create value through aggregation and matching mechanisms: the former consists in bringing together a large number of buyers and sellers, the latter consists in letting members assume both the buyer and seller roles depending on their current needs.

Kaplan and Sawhney also highlight the difference between neutral hub and biased hub. Neutral hubs do not favor buyers over sellers and vice versa; while biased hubs either favor sellers by aggregating their supplies, in that case they are called *forward aggregators*, or favor buyers by aggregating their demands, in that case they are called *reverse aggregators*. Such distinction leads also to analyse the proprietary nature of the marketplace (Whitaker et al., 2001). The B2B hub could be run by a private company that decides which services activate and which customers or suppliers invite to participate to the initiative. Alternatively, the hub could be run by an independent company that plays essentially the role of a neutral market maker. Finally, a consortium of companies within a specific industry could lead the initiative, with the aim of facilitating transactions within their own industrial sector. Most of B2B initiatives can be defined as reverse aggregators, especially private and consortium hubs (e.g. General Electric, FastBuyer, Covisint, RubberNetwork).

As previously discussed, virtual marketplaces based their first businesses on transactions, thus building revenues were almost exclusively through transaction fees. Unfortunately volumes are not as high as foreseen, an excessive fragmentation exists, and pure market mechanisms are not always the solution searched by companies to conduct transactions; therefore B2B hubs need a transformation to create value in other more convincing ways (Wise and Morrison, 2000; Kalakota, 2000).

Of course, transaction based marketplaces will continue to exist, but because scale and liquidity are vitally important to efficient trading, today's fragmented and illiquid exchanges will consolidate into a small number of *Mega-exchanges* that will support transactions, but will strive to survive if basing only on low profit transaction fees (Figure 2.5).

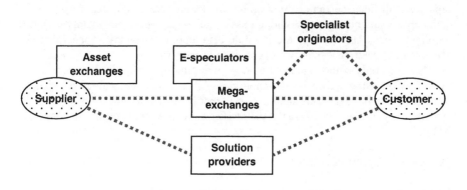

Figure 2.5 Emerging B2B hubs (adapted from Wise and Morrison, 2000)

Some e-hubs are becoming what might be called *Specialist originators*, companies that help buyers gather and analyse all information necessary to purchase more and more complex products and services electronically; they can also rely on other marketplaces to conduct the transaction. FreeMarkets, for example, does not create value through the transaction itself (carried out through an electronic auction), but the real added value is built by identifying and qualifying bidders and by standardizing RFPs that enable such bidders to provide comparable quotes even on highly complex and specialized products.

Also *E-speculators* are emerging. This kind of marketplace does not take advantage from transaction fees, but from a superior view into the dynamics of the market. Valuable information about the market allows these companies speculating by buying and selling. Enron, for example, was originally a gas pipeline operator. It has recently exploited its position to establish an on-line exchange in which it makes money not from trading commissions, but from buying and selling a variety of energy products on the market for its own account (e.g. natural gas and electric power).

A further e-hub emerging model is the *Solution provider*. This kind of company uses the Internet to bundle products, information and services in order to offer to the customer a complete solution that can improve the efficiency and the effectiveness of its processes. Milpro, for example, is a web-site selling machine tools as coolants, cutting wheels, and drills. It helps customers handle a broad number of related business challenges such as dealing with used equipment, solving technical problems, and identifying new appropriate products in any situation.

Finally, also *Asset exchanges* are emerging. These are companies supporting asset swaps among suppliers, thus allowing them to better utilize their key assets whether factories, trucks, warehouses, or containers for shipping; at the same time they enable buyers to rely on a more efficient supply base. Freightwise and Transportal Network, for example, uses the Internet to allow carriers to trade capacity with other carriers, filling empty trucks and creating a better system for both carriers and customers. Although asset exchanges were born mainly to fulfill suppliers' needs, asset swaps are possible also among customers, concerning for example raw materials excessive inventory (e.g. Steeltrading).

These are only some examples of new emerging opportunities companies can exploit by adopting web-based technologies. All the illustrated initiatives share a common goal: increase information transparency and communication in order to increase competitiveness and make the market more efficient (Phillips and Meeker, 2000).

The Internet Supporting Collaboration: e-Collaboration

In the previous two sections, it has been highlighted how web-based technologies might support procurement process efficiency and market efficiency. As a matter of fact, in the already mentioned Malone's contribution (Malone et al., 1987), the authors also envisage the existence of many cases of high asset specificity and complex product descriptions for which new technologies will be adopted to increase collaboration among companies. In such situations, companies work closely together leading to either dyadic collaboration or to network collaboration, thus building a sort of *virtual* or *extended enterprise* (Ross, 1999; Borders et al., 2001).

The roots of e-integration are in the traditional EDI (Electronic Data Interchange) point-to-point specific connections; these are dedicated systems that allow a synchronous batch communication from one company's computer system to a trading partner's computer system. In a typical EDI relationship, information is extracted by a separate system and put into a 'standard' message format (established by the American National Standard Institute, ANSI) understood by partner's applications. Such message is typically sent by telephone through a shared channel (VAN, Value Added Network) either directly to the trading partner or to an intermediary who guarantees later delivery. Generally, the most relevant barriers to this kind of tool are the high specific investments and operating costs related to per-transaction fees, and the translation of paper data into electronic format.

EDI systems provider started developing web EDI architectures accessible through common web browsers rather than specific applications, thus substituting VAN with the Internet. This solution reduces specific investments into the technological infrastructure and the exercise costs through the Internet's ubiquity and pervasiveness, but does not change the principles of communication.

	EDI	Web EDI	XML
Communication Media	Value Added Network	Internet	Internet
Specific Investments	High	Low	Low
Operating Costs	High per-transaction fees	Low	Low
Information Transfer	Batch	Batch	Both real time and asynchronous
Connection Base	Point-to-point	Point-to-point	Many-to-many
Communication Data	Determined by rigid format standards	Determined by rigid format standards	Higher variety through flexible standards

Figure 2.6 EDI, Web EDI, and XML

The use of XML standard seems to overcome all of these problems, even though the notion of a single standard language remains quite distant. Firstly, this solution allows both real-time simultaneous interaction and asynchronous communication 24times7, rather than simply batch communication once or twice a day through standard documents exchange. Secondly, Internet applications are reusable, based on Java and other portable technologies that enable virtually unlimited scalability and provide multiple points interaction, thus significantly improving inter-enterprise collaboration. Finally, new self-describing communication standards support much richer information exchange and variety of data structure, rather than mere textual data (e.g. pictures, sounds, drawings). A real diffused adoption of the Internet into collaboration activities, however, still needs to face some huge problems; some examples are the well-known data security concerns and the definition of really viable common standards (see also Section 7.1).

Such evolution of the technology can surely facilitate collaboration among organizations by using two possible architectures (Porter, 1998): *Extranets* and *Internet Hubs*. Extranets (see also Section 2.1) are software extensions of a company's enterprise system that can be delivered through the Internet to another company; the main limitations to this approach are the training complexity and the low scalability. Internet hubs establish a central hub (or portal) where all the interconnection and interfaces information are maintained; users can access using a standard web browser and view information coming from different enterprise systems. In addition, also systems integration with the Internet Hub is possible.

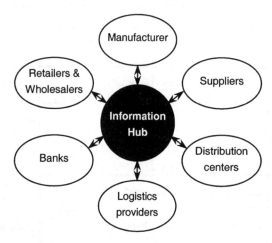

Figure 2.7 The Information Hub (Adapted from Lee and Whang, 2001)

Lee and Whang (Lee and Whang, 2001) call such Internet Hub the *Information Hub* (Figure 2.7). An Information Hub is the corporate portal that supports collaboration activities and information sharing among the partners of the supply chain. The authors highlight the concept of *e-collaboration* by defining three core integration activities, which essentially refer to the scheme describing alliances explained in Section 1.2:

- *Information sharing*: this is a first level of integration among trading partners, it consists of transferring and sharing any kind of documents and information (e.g. orders, invoices, inventory levels, technical drawings).

- *Collaborative planning*: this level involves collaboration on planning, forecasting and inventory management activities. Also DSS (Decision Support Systems) might be used in order to optimize planning decisions across the whole chain.
- *New product development*: In this case, trading partners collaborate on product development and engineering activities by exchanging and working, for example, on CAD files.

On a more operational perspective (*Information sharing* and *collaborative planning*), the Internet adoption has opened a wide range of opportunities, some of them already in process before the mature development of the technology itself.

Firstly, information sharing and collaboration might easily reduce inventories in the different tiers of the supply chain; many acronyms and models have arisen, all basing their roots on the fact that the company decides to include someone else in the management of its own inventories. Some examples are VMI (Vendor Managed Inventory), JMI (Jointly Managed Inventory), BMI (Buyer Managed Inventory), and consignment stock. Smith (Smith, 1999) classifies three VMI models made possible by electronic integration: the traditional *One on One*, in which the supplier manages the customer's inventory of its particular component; the *Captain of Industry*, in which the supplier manages all the items within a component classification (e.g. electronic device parts); the *Information Wholesaler*, in which the supplier manages all the items within a product family.

Secondly, full visibility on partners' production plans support a more efficient and effective planning process along the whole supply chain. Orders tracking (real time visibility of the order status) and tracing (visibility of the whole path and history covered by the order so far) allow companies to plan effectively all their activities. Such visibility in the production processes provides also the possibility to perform ATP (Available To Promise) and CTP (Capable To Promise) activities. In the former case, the company binds the proper available product quantity and sets directly the delivery date to the customer. In the latter case, the company does not have the items available yet, but it binds production capacity and sets the delivery date as well.

Finally, also forecasting activities can be shared. The availability of POS (Point OF Sale) data are a powerful tool to synchronize the whole supply chain and create common demand forecasts. Such forecasting activities could be either supported by whole collaboration, or managed by exceptions. A rather new methodology developed to create common forecasts between the customer and the supplier is the CPFR (Continuous Planning, Forecasting, and Replenishment). CPFR is a standard process, in the CPG industry, developed by VICS (Voluntary Inter-Industry Commerce Standards) allowing customer and supplier collaborating on final consumer demand forecasts and on distributor orders forecasts. Once agreed on these two kinds of forecasts, producer can plan production together with the distributor. The overall objective of the process is reducing inventory levels and increasing service level to the final consumer (Ireland and Bruce, 2000).

From a more technological perspective (*Information sharing* and *new product development*), the state-of-the art in collaboration activities is far less developed. It is easier exchanging information and collaborating about inventories and production plans than leveraging the Internet to support co-design activities. However, technology fully supports documents exchange such as CAD files and technical specifications. Agile Software, for example, supports collaboration among partners in new products or new versions management by coordinating the flows of activities. Moreover, workflow and project management tools are used over the Internet to coordinate inter-organization activities. In addition, peer-to-peer and net-meeting technologies will soon provide the possibility to enable effective distant and mobile working, thus supporting inter-company teams collaborating and designing together through a distributed environment.

All these practices, both operational and technological, help and support some trends in the evolution of supply chains (Fisher, 1997; Kalakota and Robinson, 1999).

A first managerial trend is called Integrated Make-To-Stock or Postponement. It consists of designing products and components in order to make it as standard as possible up to the final tier of the supply chain, the differentiation of the product is then applied at the end of the supply chain. An example is provided by Hewlett Packard, which designs standard printers together with suppliers. Such printers are standard all over the world along the supply chain; once they reach different local markets warehouses and distribution centers, they are differentiated according to the specific market characteristics (e.g. electrical power, user's guide, packaging).

A second trend is the Continuous Replenishment model with methods like Quick Response (QR) in the textile and apparel industry, and Efficient Consumer Response (ECR) in the CPG industry. In these cases, previous described collaborative planning and forecasting activities are performed in order to reduce the bullwhip effect (Section 1.3), thus reducing inventories and increasing service level to the final consumer. An example is provided by Sainsbury's, which is integrated with its biggest suppliers (e.g. Nestlè and Procter & Gamble) in order to make them see POS data, thus improving their ability to supply the right items at the right time, especially during promotional periods.

Finally, a third trend is the Build-to-Order, where information substitute inventories leading from mass-production to mass-customization. In this case, products differentiation and personalization is not applied at the end of the supply chain (as is the case in postponement), but it is done at earlier stages. An example is provided by Dell, which assembles and personalizes its products once received customer's order.

Summarizing, the described practices and trends lead to some relevant benefits along the whole supply chain (Ross, 1999):

- inventory levels reduction;
- lead times reduction;
- service level improvement;
- higher innovation and quality through collaborative development;

- Time-To-Market reduction.

In order to gain these benefits, a strong supply chain infrastructure needs to be in place before the B2B technologies can be applied, therefore organizations must identify and correct any flaws in their existing supply chains (Handfield, 2001). As a consequence, before pursuing external integration with suppliers and customers, companies first must integrate their internal purchasing, engineering, operations, marketing, and sales activities.

Once improved internal coordination, the firm can create the proper alignment firstly with first-tier suppliers and customers and then extending it to the whole supply network. Every relationship must be clearly mapped and defined, and the impact on the supply chain value proposition fully understood.

Moreover, in order to monitor and keep trace of supply chain activities, managers involved must have clear in mind the definition of performance metrics for each participant (e.g. quality, delivery lead-time, forecasts accuracy).

Finally, also the information requirements are crucial. It is extremely important defining which information should be used in which situation and by which participant. Every actor in the supply chain must have the right information at the right time in order to pursue its activities; however, there is the risk to provide too much information, which would cause only higher operating costs and more confusion.

From a more technological perspective, the B2B infrastructure should be able to integrate different ERP systems, database structures, and processes. It should be easily scalable in order to include or exclude different participants and it should support different formats and codification of information. Moreover, it should be extremely secure in order to avoid external undesired accesses (Ross, 1999; Kalakota and Robinson, 1999).

If all such conditions are in place, then the supply chain integration and related performances can be improved. Still, there will be the huge problem related to the way benefits (and risks) are shared. This aspect leads directly to trust issues among actors involved (Section 1.2) and the definition of clear and reliable decision makers.

Chapter 3

Research Aims and Methodology

3.1 Basic Assumptions

The previous chapter provides a summary of contributions regarding the use of web-based technologies for business purposes. The initial illusion and enthusiasm related to e-business have given way to the rational attention on basic economic indicators and real and viable opportunities offered by the technology. The same attitude can be found in the field of supply chain management, where, however, different and sometimes contrasting ideas have been formulated: disintermediation vs. reintermediation, markets transparency and efficiency vs. deeper collaboration, transaction tools vs. collaborative tools. Contributions made both in literature and in conferences or seminars still reveal the lack of a common view concerning basic concepts underlying the use of the Internet in supply chain management. Such a gap is very broad as it covers all the main areas included in supply chain management: dyadic customer-supplier relationships, external supply chains, and networks of companies (see Chapter 1).

The main reason of this is related to the newness of the phenomenon, which has appeared in the first nineties and has been deeply studied by scholars only in the last few years. Every innovation requires time to be clearly understood, adopted, and finally diffused; in the case of the Internet, this cycle seems to be inverted. At the beginning the technology had been opened to everyone, who had used it for all kinds of purposes; only after the first experiences of disillusionment people have tried to comprehend the underlying opportunities. Every diffusion process requires time, learning efforts, and overcoming barriers before reaching a mature state of awareness; and this often leads to periods of confusion and contrasting ideas. Internet is a typical example of critical innovation diffusion.

Within this context, this study tries to fix some basic concepts focusing its attention on customer-supplier relationships; this systematization starts from the definition of some basic assumptions.

Based on literature reviewed in Chapter 1, the overall research has been based on the following definition of Supply Chain Management:

> Supply Chain Management is a process-oriented approach to managing product, information and funds flows across the overall supply network, from the initial suppliers to the final end consumers.

The *Supply Network* is a network of firms linked by customer-supplier relationships aimed at interchanging products or services from the original supplier to the end consumer. The term 'network' is preferred to 'chain' because it emphasizes the web structure of companies' relationships as opposed to a simple linear one (Figure 1.1, Chapter 1). The overall network consists of two parts: the *upstream network*, made by suppliers, and the *downstream network*, made by customers and distributors (adapted from Handfield, 2001). Adapting the theoretical framework provided by Lambert and Cooper, three dimensions defining a supply chain can be identified:

- *Vertical structure:*   it refers to the number of tiers along the supply chain.
- *Horizontal structure:* it refers to the number of suppliers/customers represented within each tier.
- *Focal position:*   it refers to the focal company tier within the supply chain; the focal company is the one for which the supply chain is mapped.

Both graphical and analytical supply chain representation could be provided (Figure 3.1). The analytical representation consists of an array with as many positions as the numbers of tiers; in each position the number of suppliers/customers within that level is indicated assigning zero value to the focal company's tier.

Graphical representation:

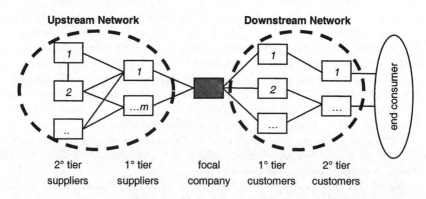

Analytical representation:

$$[n \qquad m, \qquad 0, \qquad i, \qquad j]$$

Figure 3.1 Graphical and analytical representations of the supply chain

Supply Chain Management suggests a *process-oriented approach* in managing the multiple relationships within the overall supply chain: the objective is to create the greatest value not simply for the company, but for the whole supply network across all the processes involving the supply chain firms.

Finally, such an approach has to deal with *product, information and funds flows*, as discussed in Chapter 1.

Referring to this definition of supply chain it is clear that each node of the network is related to at least another one by a customer-supplier relationship. As a consequence, the analysis of customer-supplier interactions is the first step a company should set out in order to correctly manage its supply network; the customer-supplier relationship is the kernel of supply chain management. The current competitive paradigm is not exactly supply chain versus supply chain, as stated by some authors, but supply network versus supply network (Rice and Hoppe, 2001), and the key competitive factor is the ability to manage an effective portfolio of customer-supplier relationships, from markets to vertical alliances. The choice of such a unit of analysis has been driven by the need to focus the attention on a specific problem with defined borders in order to be clearly understood. However, some drawbacks exist as far as the relationships portfolio management and the multiple interactions among companies within a network are not considered.

In Chapter 1, the different typologies of such vertical relationships have been deeply analysed. The main variables determining the convenience of one type or another have been widely discussed in literature (the presence of transaction specific investments, the frequency of the purchase, the risk and uncertainty related to the environment, the strategic relevance of the purchase, the supply market complexity, the complexity of product description). Such variables are basically referable to two main factors: the characteristics of the object of the transaction and the supply market characteristics.

As far as the differences between markets and vertical alliances are concerned, two dimensions have been adopted in order to identify the level of integration, coordination and collaboration in the relationship: depth of the alliance and scope of the alliance.

An assumption of this work is that such factors and dimensions (object of the transaction, supply market characteristics, depth of collaboration, and scope of collaboration) are still valid in explaining the kind of relationship to be created between customer and supplier. Furthermore, these variables help in explaining also the motivations and the effects of the Internet adoption within the relation and the choice of the appropriate tools according to the defined goals.

Finally, another assumption that builds the bases of the research is related to the twofold role of the Internet in such vertical relationships. As discussed in Chapter 2, on the one hand the Internet supports market efficiency, and, on the other hand, it provides opportunities for deeper collaboration. This aspect might lead to a divergence between short-term market relationships and long-term vertical alliances. Such divergence might open new opportunities for collaborative environments, even though based on short-term relationships. This last main assumption is the thread running through this work, and will be further discussed in Chapters 5 and 7.

3.2   Aims of the Research

Basing on main assumptions and definitions formulated in the previous section, the overall objective of the research is to analyse the consequences of the Internet adoption in vertical relationships between companies along the supply chain. In particular, the specific objectives of the research are described as follows.

1. *The first main objective of the research is to clarify what are the motivations that should stimulate companies to adopt web-based technologies within their relationships with suppliers.*
    As seen before, a lot of contributions have been written on benefits deriving from the adoption of the Internet. Some examples are: electronic auctions used to lower purchase prices, electronic catalogs used to streamline administrative procurement processes, electronic exchanges used to increase markets liquidity, and collaborative software used to reduce inventories and increase service levels. This research aims at collecting previous contributions and field evidence in order to provide a schematic and synthetic framework of what are the real motivations that would lead to adopt the Internet into customer-supplier relationships, and therefore what are the benefits a company could get.

2. *The second objective is to identify what are the appropriate Internet tools companies should adopt according to their specific goals.*
    Once understood what are the main motivations pushing towards the Internet adoption in customer-supplier relationships, it is important to understand two other factors. Firstly, motivations will be related to the object of the transaction between supplier and customer: companies are supposed to have different motivations according to the nature of the considered material (e.g. direct vs. indirect material). Secondly, different web-based tools would be appropriate according to both the kind of material and the motivations. This research aims at answering these two points, both creating a link between motivations and kind of materials which are object of the transactions, and identifying the appropriate tools according to specific materials and goals.

3. *Finally, the most relevant objective is to explain what are the implications on customer-supplier relationships related to the Internet adoption.*
    In Chapter 1, different typologies of vertical relationships between customers and suppliers have been described; from markets to vertical alliances, from equity partnerships to hierarchies. In particular, the scope of the research and the literature analysis have focused on the 'market/vertical alliance dilemma'. In literature it is possible to find different contributions, some of them

stressing market efficiency aspects, and others focusing on opportunities of closer collaboration between companies (Chapter 2). This research question is aimed at exploring and explaining what are main consequences of the opportunities offered by web-based technologies into both arm's length relationships and vertical alliances.

3.3 Research Methodology

Given the specific objectives of the research and the basic assumptions illustrated before, the unit of analysis of the whole study is the customer-supplier relationship. Such relationship might be either market alike or vertical alliance alike. In studying such topic, the overall research methodology has been divided into three main stages: an explorative stage, an explanatory stage, and a descriptive one (Figure 3.2).

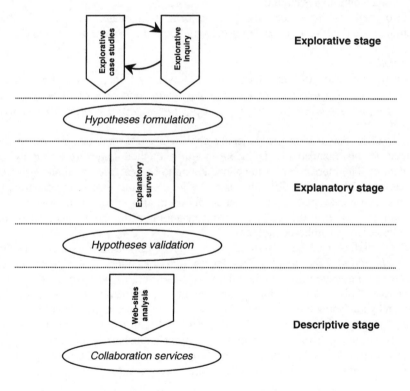

Figure 3.2 Research methodology

The aim of the first stage was to develop knowledge about new technologies, about motivations and tools of the Internet adoption in the procurement process and into customer-supplier relationship, and to refine the research hypotheses to be tested and validated in the second explanatory stage. Finally, a descriptive stage has been performed in order to describe the main features of collaboration services exploitable through the Internet.

Throughout the overall research process, state of the art in literature has been analysed following the main streams highlighted in Chapters 1 and 2.

Stage 1: Exploratory Analysis

The objective of this stage is to understand what are the variables characterizing the role of the internet in customer-supplier relationships: what are the drivers leading to the use of new technologies in the different typologies of relationships, what are the main technologies and tools, and what are the emergent effects of web-based technologies adoption.

Two methods have been used to perform, triangulate, and cross-fertilize (Patton, 1987) the investigation: some case studies and an exploratory inquiry.

Case studies[1]
A general definition of case study can be drawn by Yin: '*A case study is an empirical investigation that analyses a particular phenomenon within a real context, especially when borders between phenomenon and context are not well defined*'.

It is clear that a case study deeply considers contextual factors, which are difficult to be exhaustively included in other methodologies (e.g. survey or simulation). The more complex the phenomenon to be analysed, the more variables are relevant, and the more difficult it is to design a rigorous research methodology. For this reason case studies have been deeply used, also in conjunction with other techniques, in order to provide a better understanding of the numerous factors and variables existing within the problem.

Case studies can be classified along three dimensions (Ronchi, 1999): *approach*, *timing*, and *number*. As far as the objectives of the research are concerned, the supporting methodology is based on explorative case studies (approach). This allows exploring and identifying the different aspects of the problem by analysing the real use of the new technologies and the difficulties faced in implementing them (Platt, 1992, Yin, 1994). Cases are mainly retrospective (timing), although there is an attempt to study relationships before and after the Internet adoption. Finally, multiple cases design (number) aims at providing a quite wide perception of different possible situations in order to draw research hypotheses.

---

[1] Case studies are based on real situations; however they are described as anonymous within the whole book for confidentiality concerns. As a consequence, any reference to real names and facts are casual.

The multiple cases have been chosen through a *theoretical replication process*, as opposed to a *literal replication process* (Eisenhardt, 1989; Yin, 1994). Whereas literal replication selects cases with similar expected results, theoretical replication performs the selection with the aim of studying different foreseen results. As the aim of this first stage was to explore different kinds of effects related to the Internet adoption into the relationship, 2 cases in which arm's length relationship was emphasized and 2 cases in which coordination was emphasized were selected. In particular, the first two cases analyse the adoption of electronic auctions, the third one analyses the creation of a supplier portal enhancing coordination with suppliers, and the fourth one analyses the adoption of an electronic catalog built to increase internal processes efficiency, but resulting also in a deeper coordination with the supplier.

Moreover, as the objectives of the research are not specific to a particular industrial sector, 4 different industries have been considered: food and beverage, chemical, telecommunication, and automotive. Companies were selected from multiple sources (trade and business journals, web pages, and experts' advice). The choice of industries and companies, however, was also influenced by the difficulty of finding firms with established Internet adoption and willing to share their experiences. For this reason, quite big companies present almost worldwide were contacted in order to obtain a high probability of finding interesting practices on the Internet.

Table 3.1 Case studies sample

CASE STUDIES	**Grapes**	**Chemics - Feragri**	**Smart Technologies**	**Gias - Fiumelli**
Industry	Food & Beverage	Chemical	Telecom	Automotive
Native country	U.S.A.	Europe	U.S.A.	Europe
Revenues	$450 M	$7 B	$21 B	€3.5 B
Employees	900	6,000	110,000	19,000
Final products	Fruit based products	Fertilizers	Network systems	Spare parts
Object of transaction	Grape juice concentrate	Film spools	Components	Polyethylene envelopes
Internet tool	Electronic auction	Electronic auction	Private portal	Electronic catalog
Effects on relationship	Arm's length emphasis	Arm's length emphasis	Much higher coordination	Higher coordination and process efficiency

As far as the object of the transaction is concerned, the sampling process tried to select companies in order to study both direct and indirect materials. As a result, in the Grapes and Smart cases the acquired objects are direct to the final products, and in the Gias case it is an indirect material. As far as the Feragri case is concerned, the object of the transaction is an indirect material (flexible packaging), but its characteristics make it similar to a direct one (see the case for further details).

The initial contacts with companies took place through a phone call or an e-mail to one of expected interviewees or to a human resources representative who took care of arranging and scheduling interviews. It was difficult to find the right persons within each organization, and especially, to find some people from the suppliers of the selected companies. Suppliers' opinions are important to avoid the risk of analysing a biased case. Target informants were sent a brief description of the research that made clear the objective of the study, its expected outcome, and the contribution participants were expected to give or receive. In addition, a brief outline of the interview was included. Confidentiality of sensitive data was ensured.

The outline of the interview was based on the developed interview protocol. Such protocol aimed at analysing four specific areas of interest. The first one concerned general information about the company, those pieces of information not found through other sources. The second area investigated the scope within which Internet was adopted; in particular the object of the transaction, its characteristics, and selected suppliers. The third area aimed at discovering what motivations drove the company towards web-based tools adoption. Finally, the last section of the interview aimed at analysing major results and main effects on the relationship with suppliers.

Table 3.2 Informants profile

CASE STUDIES	Grapes	Chemics - Feragri	Smart Technologies	Gias - Fiumelli
Purchasing manager	X	X	X	X
Materials planning manager	X		X	
IT manager			X	X
Supplier account manager	X	X	X	X
Other	X	X		X

Different sources of information were selected. Of course, multiple interviews were the major sources of relevant data and information; the possibility of interviewing more people allowed to triangulate their ideas, therefore building rather objective cases (Patton, 1987). Furthermore, the research has been based on field notes, company reports or other public documentation found from the public relations offices or from companies' web sites.

Exploratory inquiry
Cases analysis has been integrated by an explorative inquiry (Kerlinger, 1986, Lee, 1991) in order to have a more superficial, but wider perception of what is happening in the different industries. Such inquiry has consisted in specialized journals analysis, Internet browsing, and over 10 open interviews with experts in the field: academics, consultants, and practitioners. Interviews have been focused on description of new web-based tools, trends in their adoption, and variations in vertical relationships.

The aim of the integration between these two methods was to create a process of cross-fertilization of ideas and propositions from one side to the other. The inquiry provided a wide perspective of the state of the art and the variables relevant to the problem within companies and industries, while case studies allowed generating cause-and-effect hypotheses through a deeper analysis.

In this first stage the study has been mainly qualitative in cross-case analysis (Trochim, 1989, Cook and Campbell, 1979, Wholey, 1979). The output has consisted of the formulation of first hypotheses answering the research questions. In particular, issues concerning the relations among motivations, the use of the Internet, and objects of the transaction emerged. Moreover, hypotheses about effects related to the use of the Internet into customer-supplier relationships have been formulated (Chapter 5).

Stage 2: Explanatory Analysis

Once research propositions have been stated in the first stage, empirical evidence coming from survey methodology may provide the basis for hypotheses testing.

It has been stated in literature that survey research is suitable for both explorative and explanatory research (Kerlinger, 1986, Lee, 1991). In fact, the observation of the real world allows building statements about the rules and norms that govern the system under study. Empirical evidence coming from survey research might also provide the basis for hypotheses testing, thus leading to build new theories or to generate new ideas or assumptions to further investigate. This second typology of survey research is the most diffused in the Operations Management discipline.

As far as the explanatory intent of this second stage is concerned, an explanatory survey has been performed.

Basing on propositions resulting from the explorative stage, a specific survey analysis was designed. The details of survey design are explained in Chapter 6 (Section 6.1), after presenting hypotheses to be validated (see Chapter 5).

Therefore, within this chapter only general considerations on the selected survey methodology are given.

There are two main typology of survey design: on the one hand, *cross-section* survey aims at collecting and analysing information in one precise instant of time; on the other hand, *longitudinal* survey aims at collecting and analysing information coming from the same subjects, but in different instants of time. Although this is not a proper longitudinal study, as data are not physically gathered in different points of time, the collection provides longitudinal evidence, as questions in the questionnaire refer to both before and after the Internet adoption (see Chapter 6). This kind of survey design is named *impure panel design* (Bailey, 1995) or *time-ordered cross-sectional design* (Menard, 1991).

In designing a rigorous survey, five main steps need to be followed: questionnaire definition, sample extraction, data gathering, data analysis, and reliability and validation.

Questionnaire definition

The first step in the survey tool definition is the choice of which variables to measure and how to measure them. Such choice depends on what are the hypotheses to be tested. In this work, variables have been derived from hypotheses formulated in Chapter 5. In particular, relevant variables are: the acquired material and the supply market characteristics, the description of the relationship with suppliers before and after the Internet adoption, the motivations driving to the adoption of the Internet, the adopted Internet tool, and, finally, the obtained performances.

Variables might be measured through either a structured or semi-structured questionnaire, and data might be collected through either nominal scales, or ordinal scales, or interval scales, or relative scales, or continuous scales (Flynn et al., 1990). Within this research a structured questionnaire has been designed, and both continuous scales (e.g. revenues), and interval scales have been adopted. In this latter case, 5-point Likert scales have been used.

The second step is to test the tool. The test might be performed by discussing with other researchers or experts in the field, and by building a pilot test with some respondents. In this research, both of these testing methods have been adopted.

Sample extraction

It is necessary to define the population, and then to extract the sample from such population according to the scope of the research. The selected sample must present some characteristics: firstly, it must be sufficiently large to allow statistical analyses, secondly it must provide equal selection probability among all cases included within the population without introducing biases, thirdly, it must be efficient, that is the researcher does not select not desired subjects.

In order to select a balanced sample, random selection is the most adopted mode. However, when the population presents some non-homogeneous subgroups (e.g. different industries) the stratification procedure allows the sample to be as most representative as possible of the whole population. The detailed selection and stratification process of this research is described in Section 6.1.

Data gathering
Once defined the survey tool, and extracted the sample, the data gathering process starts. There are different methods: direct interviews, telephone interviews, mail (including electronic mail and fax), existing databases or historical data. Of course, each method presents advantages and disadvantages. Within this research, the questionnaire was sent by snail mail, electronic mail, and also uploaded on a web site.

Data analysis
Within survey research many statistical methods might be adopted. Such methods can be either more explorative and descriptive in nature (e.g. cluster analysis, association analysis), or more explanatory (e.g. ANOVA, linear regressions).

As far as the explanatory intent of this survey, different explanatory techniques have been used to study collected data. Hypothesis testing techniques such as analysis of variance, chi-square test, logit and linear regression models have been adopted to prove correlation among variables. The detailed data analysis is reported in Chapter 6 together with results. Moreover, factor analysis reduced the number of dimensions for subsequent analyses, helped interpreting the characteristics of the sample, and provided constructs validity analysis (see below).

Reliability and validation
Constructs reliability is frequently defined as the degree of consistency of a measure. The internal consistency of a set of measurement items, therefore, refers to the degree to which items in the set are homogeneous. As a consequence, reliability also measures the ability to replicate the study (Flynn et al., 1990). Reliability can be tested through a *test-retest procedure, parallel forms,* or the proper *internal consistency.* All these procedures essentially are correlation-based methods. The first procedure implies the repetition of the experiment, the second one implies the construction of two measures for the same variable, while the third one, which is also the most adopted, implies an intercorrelation analysis among items that comprises the measured variable.

The most widely accepted measure of a measure's internal consistency is Cronbach's Alpha (Cronbach and Meehl, 1955). Alpha is the average of the correlation coefficient of each item with each other item. Measures presenting Alphas higher than 0.6 or 0.7 are considered reliable (Nunnally, 1978). Within this work, constructs reliability has been tested through the internal consistency procedure by calculating the Alpha.

Reliability is a prerequisite to establishing validity, but it is not sufficient (Schwab, 1980).

As far as validity is concerned, three main typologies are widely recognized: *content validity, construct validity,* and *criterion validity* (Hair et al., 1992).

A variable is considered to have content validity if there is general agreement from the literature or from experts that the considered items cover all the aspects of the variable itself.

A measure has construct validity if it measures the theoretical variable that it was designed to measure. The most adopted method to test construct validity is the Principal Components Factor Analysis (Hair et al., 1992).

Finally, criterion or predictive or external validity investigates the empirical relationship between the scores on a test instrument (predictor) and an objective outcome (the criterion). Usually, it is tested through a multiple correlation coefficient between the instrument score and performance.

Within the study, content validity is provided by literature review and discussions with academics and experts in the field. Moreover, constructs validity, which will be the most discussed in Chapter 6, has been tested through Principal Components Factor Analyses.

The specific design and the analyses of this second explanatory stage are discussed in Chapter 6.

Stage 3: Descriptive analysis

The second stage of the research has proved some of the research propositions formulated in Chapter 5. In particular, the last hypothesis (*H4*) refers to a *collaborative market* model, which is mentioned at the end of the quoted research assumptions (Section 3.1) and is fully described in Chapter 7.

This last stage of the research aims at investigating the existence of web initiatives that could be used to generate the main characteristics of the mentioned emergent relationship model. In particular, the services offered by those web sites have been analysed. Such analysis supports the description of main collaboration services exploitable through the Internet.

Although the web-site analysis has focused on a specific typology of portals (mainly consortia vertical portals), it provides a quite comprehensive view of available collaboration services. The choice of such portals is mainly due to the fact that private exchanges are difficult to analyse, as companies are not often willing to share their distinctive competencies.

Chapter 4

Case Studies[1]

4.1   Grapes

Firm History and Profile

The company originated in the second half of the nineteenth century when Dr. John B. Grapes, a physician and dentist by profession, successfully pasteurizes Concord grape juice to produce an 'unfermented sacramental wine' for fellow parishioners at the church where he was communion steward. His achievement marks the beginning of the processed fruit juice industry in the United States.

In 1896 grape juice becomes a national favorite as thousands of people sample it at the Chicago World's Fair. Dr. Thomas E. Grapes, son of Grapes founder, discontinues his practice of dentistry to give full attention to the marketing of grape juice. A new label is adopted, omitting the 'Dr.' before the name Grapes.

In the 20s Grapes develops its first jam product called 'Grapelade' and also its first non-grape product is introduced: Grapes Homogenized Tomato Juice. In 1949 Grapes becomes a pioneer in the frozen juice concentrate industry with the introduction of Grapes Frozen Grape Juice Concentrate.

In 1958 Grapes is acquired by the Nage Cooperative Association, Inc; a grower-owned, agricultural cooperative with 1,461 members. Nage is a family tradition sharing strong generational and cultural ties to its past and present while keeping its eye on the future. The members of the Nage produce Concord and Niagara varieties of grapes. The Concord grape variety is purple in color and is grown in the cooler regions of the United States. The Niagara grape variety is light in color and also is grown in cooler climates. Major growing areas for Concord and Niagara variety grapes include western New York, northern Ohio, northern Pennsylvania, western Michigan, and south-central Washington. Nage requires all members to sign a perpetual contract committing fixed amounts of Concord and Niagara acreage to Grapes.

Climate and cultural practices influence the yield per acre for grapes. As a result, Grapes must deal with wide swings in the total size of the crop each year.

---

[1] Case studies are based on real situations; however they are described as anonymous with fictitious names within the whole book for confidentiality concerns. As a consequence, any reference to real names, figures and facts are casual.

The security of a consistent market for grapes in times of surplus and shortage provides strong incentives for growers to join Nage.

National's growers share a commitment to standards, which are reflected in the quality and goodness of the Concord and Niagara grapes produced for Grapes products sold throughout the US and in more than 30 countries around the world.

Grapes International has developed market-specific products to meet local and regional tastes. Its management team consists of sales and business professionals with a vast working knowledge of foreign markets. Partnered with several companies in successful global business ventures, many of the same products available in the USA can be found abroad.

In 1976 Grapes introduced two new grape juice products: Red Grape Juice and White Grape Juice.

Nowadays, Grapes is one of the biggest producers in the world of fruit based products such as jelly, jam, preserves, spreads, fruit juice drinks and cocktails. It sells products mainly to trade customers and retailers all over the world through a brokers network. The main products sold in the juice industry are orange juice, apple juice, grape juice and prune juice. This sector is characterized by a fierce competition among companies, private labels and cooperatives.

Grapes' total revenues have increased from $400 million to $450 million in the last three years with a net income variable between -$7 million and +$3 million. The company employs over 900 people at its facilities around the US.

The organizational structure of the company is characterized by six market divisions that deal primarily with the distribution channel: food store, discount store, drug store, food service, warehouse clubs, international. Those divisions share four common centralized functions: research and development, plants direction (technical activities), supply chain, manufacturing and logistics (planning activities).

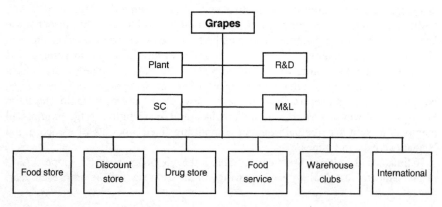

Figure 4.1 Grapes organizational structure

Processing Grapes

Every September, growers under contract to Nage begin delivering grapes to Grapes processing plants located in their region. The plants take approximately 40 days to transform raw grapes into juice. Grapes pasteurizes the fresh juice and stores it in refrigerated tank farms. Packaging operations at each plant run at a steady pace all year long and draw juice from the tank farms as needed to support production. The value of the grape juice stored in the tank farms often exceeds 50 M$ per year based on cash market value.

Raw grape juice contains insolubles that slowly settle to the bottom of the tank; after this settling process, both unsettled and settled juices can be used as ingredients in the production of finished products.

Some of Grapes' products require concentrated juice. Concentration adds another step beyond the settling process. From the time of harvest, it takes several months to obtain concentrated juice. The reduction ratio from juice to concentrated is 5:1.

Concord and Niagara grapes have a very strong and particular flavour, for this reason Grapes needs to blend it with sweeter and smoother kinds of grapes. For this purpose, it purchases white and red grape juice concentrates from Californian producers.

Finally, the final concentrated juice is used as an ingredient or is shipped as a finished product to bulk customers.

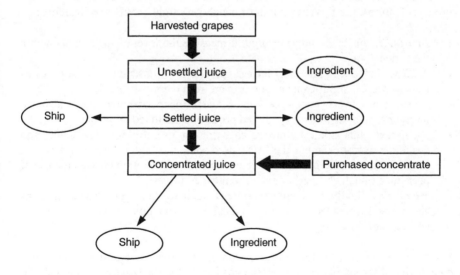

Figure 4.2   Simplified process for the production of grape juice based products

The annual grape harvest varies a great deal in size depending on the spring and summer weather. For this reason, the exact size of the grape harvest is never known until the end of the harvest itself, when all the grapes are picked. Although each grower is subject to rigid quality standards, differences in sweetness, color, and acidity do exist among growing areas. Weather also plays an important role in year-to-year crop differences. Grapes takes pride in making products with consistent recipe and taste despite crop variability across growing areas and year to year; in order to maintain a national consistency, it often transfers juice for blending among plants.

The White Grape Juice Concentrate

The unit of analysis of the case is the procurement process and the established relationships for the white grape juice concentrate procurement from California. This product, as seen in the previous paragraph, is the second base material for liquid concentrates, frozen juice concentrates, fruit juice drinks and cocktails; it represents the 15% of the total cost of the product on average and a total annual purchase volume of around $30 million on average (between 4% and 5% of the total revenues). Its purchase is based on yearly contracts, which determine the overall quantities and related prices, and it is shipped on regular basis through all over the year from suppliers to customers (see the next paragraph for a detailed description of the procurement process).

This is a standard and non-complex material, but with a strong impact on final products features. For this reason it must match very tight quality specifications:

- *Brix level:* this is an indicator used to measure the level of sugar contained in the concentrate.
- *Acidity:* the concentrate must have a specific level of acidity; in the past this used to present significant variations even from the same supplier.
- *Color:* this is very important from a marketing perspective; color is much more important in white grape based products than in red grape ones.
- *Spray tests:* this is a test aimed at checking the use of illegal insecticides and pesticides as, for example, the 'Alar' used some time ago for the apples.
- *Fructoline:* this is to prevent possible economic adulteration through the use of peer juice (much cheaper) or even chemical additives.
- *Metal tests:* finally, there are government standards that set tight specifications about the percentage of copper, nickel and iron due to the pipes of the concentrator machine.

For all these reasons, the relationships with suppliers become critical. Due to the complexity of the supply chain from the growers to the final factory, tracing all the materials is very difficult. That is why the need of trustful suppliers to be sure all those specifications are matched.

The Relationship with Suppliers

Before 1998, Grapes established close relationships with most of the direct materials suppliers. Most of these relationships were between 15 and 25 years long. In the late seventies and the early eighties, due to the strict requirements for the white grape juice concentrate and its relevance to the final products, Grapes decided to set closer relations with three suppliers from California on the basis of their production capacity and capabilities (Rousty, Berinel and Formenua).

Three companies were chosen because of the characteristics of the food industry, and in particular the grape fruit industry. The choice of suppliers is mainly based on two factors:

- quality specifications;
- price.

Once you find the supplier matching those factors, the problem is very much related to the stability of its production capacity all over the year; with a *parallel sourcing* strategy Grapes could overcome the problem by relying on more than just one producer.

Those three companies used to produce, and they still do, concentrate for wine fermentation, which requires different and less tight specifications than for juices. Grapes required them better quality both in the process and in the product in exchange for support in their improvement and a long term and exclusive relationship. As a matter of fact, the three companies had to develop a new product for Grapes. This alliance was not based on a formal contract, but on mutual trust. The contracts were stipulated year by year concerning the annual supply.

In Figure 4.3 the procurement process in this industry is briefly shown. Although the supply lasts through all over the year, the contracts determining quantities and prices are stipulated in May and June for the following twelve months. The critical aspect is related to the fact that the results of the harvest are available only in September; therefore the contract is a sort of gamble both for the customer and the suppliers. The price rates per gallon were established during the two months long negotiation process between the buyer and the suppliers, these sellers did not know each other prices.

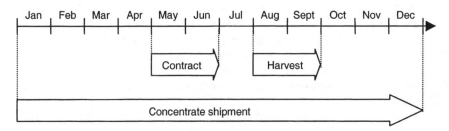

Figure 4.3 The procurement process of grape juice concentrate

Despite the tough negotiation process at the beginning of each summer, the relationships were pretty close and collaborative. Grapes and the three suppliers shared information about their own inventory levels and production plans to overcome possible spoilage and overstock and to synchronize their planning systems (due to obvious competition issues, the suppliers did not have access to each other's data). The logistics functions collaborated in the shipment scheduling, especially in winter and spring in order to anticipate transportation to Grapes sites as much as possible, due to problems related to the shipment during the hot summer. Grapes R&D people often visited the suppliers to discuss and collaborate on the development of new products; nevertheless the responsibility and decisions for what concerned new products were entirely dependent on Grapes people.

These calm and collegial relationships could be effectively described by one of the participants' statement: 'we used to solve problems together'.

Also contractual terms were flexible and allowed cooperation. After the August and September harvests, if one of these suppliers did not have enough grapes to produce the amount of concentrate stipulated in the contract, the buyer could easily speak with the other two firms to change slightly their contractual terms and ask for higher volumes.

The Internet Adoption: Electronic Auction

Starting from 1998 Grapes decided to adopt internet reverse auctions in the procurement process of some products that the company used to buy through that calm, long term and consolidated kind of relationships described in the previous paragraph. Some examples of those products are grape juice concentrate, labels, caps and plastic and glass bottles.

The decision was driven by the increasing pressure of the industry to reduce the price of the final products. The main objective in using electronic auctions was to drive the purchase prices down; in the case of labels, Grapes managed to lower the price by 30% compared to the previous one.

The intermediary chosen for the auctions was E-Marfy, one of the biggest e-auction providers present in the market. This was the first experience of E-Marfy in the food and beverage industry; previously it focused its attention on the mechanical and electronic industry.

The selection process followed the usual steps of the E-Marfy methodology.

Initially, Grapes buyers and E-Marfy consultants identified together the viable saving opportunities and found the materials whose prices could be reduced significantly; grape juice concentrated was among these. At the beginning of May 1998, the company decided to start a bidding process for 5 millions gallons of white grape juice concentrate. Considering an average price for the grape concentrate of $4.50 per gallon, the auction process regarded a total amount of $22.5 million.

From this decision till the end of the overall bidding process, E-Marfy worked as a strong intermediary: suppliers had contacts with Grapes only through the consultants and all the information flows were transferred through the market makers.

At this point, a detailed preparation of the RFP (Request For Proposal) was needed as a deep understanding of all requirements including logistics and quality levels was required by all potential competing suppliers. Grapes experts and E-Marfy people were involved together to create a comprehensive RFP which defined all elements of total cost.

E-Marfy supply market team took then the lead in identifying and contacting potential suppliers. Throughout this process, consultants, together with buyers they serviced, screened potential suppliers, narrowing the field to those whose capabilities best matched the Grapes needs. E-Marfy also provided extensive RFP support to suppliers, answering questions and gathering feedback on RFP formulation.

Ten suppliers were submitted the RFP and Grapes wanted the three consolidated previous ones (Rousty, Berinel and Formenua) among these. These ten potential suppliers prepared their proposals with the support of E-Marfy's team. By the beginning of June, Grapes selected 5 among those 10 suppliers to participate in the real-time bidding event, which took place in the middle of June.

The five selected suppliers participated in training sessions to learn every aspect of the software used to submit real-time bids. On the bidding day, suppliers dialed into a secure global network and Grapes watched the on-line bidding event from the headquarters. The actual auction lasted less than two hours.

Finally, E-Marfy and Grapes collected all the information from suppliers to validate their quotes and performed the final supplier analysis and qualification to achieve an optimal award decision.

As a matter of fact, the former supplier Rousty won the auction and the price reduction was not as significant as Grapes expected, while in other cases it was. As a consequence of the selection process, Rousty did win the contract, but the relationship became much cooler than before and the spirit of collaboration less motivated. People felt exploited by the process, and when the event was over, they were less trusting of the buyer. As one seller said: 'They talk about the relationship being a partnership and this [the auction] really takes it away. There is not a partnership there at all. What they do is throw away your existing business that you have worked very hard to achieve and maintain. You work with them to give them cost reductions over the years and they send it out across the board for a competitive bid. I just do not think that is fair'.

At the end of that summer, the demand for grape juice concentrate based products increased and Rousty did not have enough capacity to face the additional volumes. As a consequence, Grapes contacted the other bidders who lost the auction, Berinel and Formenua among the others. They managed to cover the increased demand with their capacities and the company's sales increased in the fall, but the price Grapes had to pay for each gallon was much higher than the one suppliers used to set in normal contracts.

After the negative 1998 experience, Grapes decided to change procurement strategy. The company adopted a type of edging strategy in the following years

(1999, 2000, and 2001). As a matter of fact, half of the yearly requirements are now purchased through an auction process similar to 1998's with the aim of lowering prices as most as possible, while for the other half Grapes rely again on a close relationship with Rousty.

4.2   Chemics - Feragri

Firm History and Profile

Chemics is a European company whose business is natural resources transformation. Its major businesses are oil and energy, light metals, and chemicals and fertilizers. It is one of the greatest companies in Europe and it keeps growing with numerous divisions and business units worldwide. Total revenues equal to $5 billions in 1999 and $7 billions in 2000. Net profit increased from $350 millions in 1999 to $1.1 billions in 2000.

The Chemics Group spends about 1% of its total revenues in research and development activities. It engages in R&D, both to maintain its competitive position and to develop new products and processes. The Group has reinforced its efforts to utilize its ecological knowledge as a competitive advantage. Several segments have carried out life cycle analyses for their products and are working with customers on possible reuse, recycling, waste reduction, and lower energy consumption both in production and over the life of the product.

Within Chemics, a major division is Feragri, which produces fertilizers and other chemical products and constitutes 35% of total Chemics' revenues. Feragri is the first producer of fertilizers in the world with over 6,000 employees, it sells 19 millions tons of fertilizers yearly, 6 of which are produced by subcontractors through strategic outsourcing.

Feragri has 12 operational business units (with related manufacturing plants) in Europe and it is enlarging its activities also to South Africa and Brazil.

Its distribution channel is present worldwide, and there are numerous administrative units globally. In Italy there are two administrative sites which perform both sales and purchasing activities.

Feragri distinguished competence is on fertilizers based either on nitrogenous or on phosphates. In this last case, there are often some dangers related to the transformation process and transportation activities, both for raw materials and final products.

Polyethylene Film Spools

The materials studied in this case are polyethylene film spools (polyethylene is a chemical derivative from oil) purchased by Feragri and used as flexible packaging. These spools might be made of either single sheets or double sheets forming a tubular film. The flexible plastic material is obtained through a concurrent co-extrusion process of five layers. The film is 160 micron thick and must be printed on both sides (front and back).

Co-extrusion process is obtainable through specific capital intensive plants, therefore there is the need to produce high volumes in order to cover high initial investments. Moreover, the double side printing process with more colors is very costly and complex. The printing process might be either integrated directly after the co-extrusion process or decoupled. As far as the co-extrusion process is much faster than the printing process (making the ink gets dry), the second solution allows to co-extrude with higher speed.

Different Feragri plants use such spools to package different chemical materials, especially fertilizers. The packaging process occurs through automatic machines downward the chemical transformation and production line. As a matter of fact, the production of fertilizers is a highly integrated process. Raw chemical materials are automatically picked up from the silos and then introduced into the transformation plant. Polyethylene films automatically enter at the end of the transformation process to package the fertilizer and then be sealed and cut to provide the final product, which is then put on a conveyer belt to be transferred to the warehouse (Figure 4.4).

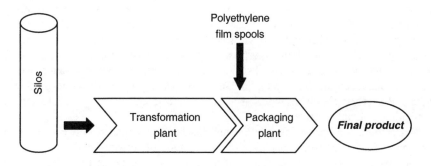

Figure 4.4 Fertilizers production process

Due to the process itself, there is a high dependence between the film and the plant used to package the final product: the film supplied by the supplier enters directly into customer's production plants. As a consequence, the packaging material must have strict characteristics:

- mechanical resistance to traction;
- heat resistance to be effectively sealed by the customer's plant;
- right dimensions to be introduced into the automatic packaging plant.

In order to test the material, the supplier produces several samplings. These samplings are then directly tested on customer's plants.

Moreover, the film must be sufficiently resistant to guarantee easy transportation and, most of all, its chemical features influence the quality of the final product. Different products require different typologies of film to be packaged correctly, and those films must be completely water and gas proof.

For all these reasons, although the package is not a direct material, in this case the polyethylene film can be considered as such.

From all these considerations, although the polyethylene film does not constitute a high percentage of total Feragri purchases, it is quite clear that the specific typology of material to be packaged, the specific graphics on the front and on the back, and the specific production plants that would use the film make the spools a complex and customized material. Moreover, although spools constitute only 4% of total Feragri's purchase volume, the frequency of the shipments is very high.

The Relationship with Suppliers

In 1985, Feragri bought a new plant, more complex then the previous ones. Such complexity also involved the automatic packaging process, thus making necessary the search for a better supplier than current ones in order to develop an appropriate packaging film. The firm contacted more potential suppliers making them develop sampling lots of film spools to be tested on the new plant. The fastest company providing the required sample, which was also very good in quality, was Malpi, an Italian SME (Small Medium Enterprise) with about €10 million of revenues. It performs internally both the co-extrusion and the printing processes mentioned in the previous section. Such supplier sells its packaging products to different industrial sectors: chemical and pharmaceutical, food and beverage, construction, publishing, and automotive.

Since then, a long lasting relationship has been established between the two companies. At the beginning, Malpi spent lots of effort in designing and developing new polyethylene films that matched specific Feragri's needs. It also modified part of its production process to reach the desired quality. The Italian SME proved also to be a valid collaborator in co-design activities as designers from both companies often worked together to develop the packaging material, thus reducing time to market.

After the first phase of technological integration, also some operational coordination activities was put in place.[2] Feragri provided to Malpi full visibility in its own inventories, and also demand signals directly coming from final customers were provided to the supplier. In addition, monthly forecasts were constantly shared and discussed.

The high level of coordination between the two companies led to inventories and stock-out reduction, by speeding up and streamlining the overall procurement process.

---

[2] For a definition of technological and operational integration, see Chapter 1, Section 1.2.

By the year 2000, the relationship was well established and could be considered as a success. Malpi has always sold its materials to three Italian production facilities realizing about 5% of its total revenues, with 320,000 kg of film each year. The other Feragri Italian facilities acquired their packaging materials from two other Italian SMEs that replicated Malpi's films through a reverse engineering process. This is due to their physical proximity to Feragri's plants. As far as the packaging process is concerned, it is important to have the supplier near the production facilities in order to solve as quickly as possible any production problems.

The three Italian companies constituted about 80% of total packaging requirement of Feragri. Malpi was surely the most important one, supplying over the 50% of it. Of course, also Feragri was a strategic customer for Malpi; for this reason Malpi's top management has always directly communicated with Feragri's central and local purchasing offices.

Prices were negotiated monthly. In particular, the film price is made of two components; the first one is related to transformation costs, and the second one is related to raw materials costs. Raw materials costs, being related to oil, are extremely volatile and about twice the transformation costs.

The Internet Adoption: Electronic Auction

At the end of year 2000, Feragri central purchasing department management decided to change the traditional procurement process. It decided to perform electronic reverse auctions on some purchased items categories in order to reduce procurement costs, thus facing increased price competition at worldwide level. E-Goods platform was chosen to manage the bidding process. Each category would have been auctioned through the so-called CBE (Competitive Bidding Event). In more detail, the specific objectives of Feragri for each category were as follows:

- collect a number of bids from different European suppliers to be easily compared;
- select few appealing bids;
- select one qualified supplier to create a collaborative relationship, even though based on one year contract.

As far as flexible packaging supply is concerned, one of the auctioned categories, Feragri searched for a supply relationship from the beginning of October 2001 to the end of December 2002. The related CBE was named 'Plastic and Paper Bags for Fertilizers and Chemicals'. In particular, 13 lots of products within this category were auctioned.

Due to the complexity and the customized nature of the supply (as previously described), Feragri and E-Goods set specific attributes suppliers should have had to participate the auction:

- the presence of a quality management system documented with results;

- process control qualification and materials track and trace tools (bar coding, shipping, and receiving);
- lab control qualification;
- testing procedures on sampling before customer's plants test.

Initial selected suppliers contained all historical ones, Malpi included, and some others extracted from E-Goods database. These latter potential suppliers were evaluated on the basis of previous E-Goods experiences. All contacted companies had to deal exclusively with E-Goods consultants and were not allowed to communicate with the Feragri central purchasing department, neither with the local ones.

As a consequence, from January 2001 Malpi has had to interact with Feragri through two different channels. On the one hand, there was the traditional interaction with local facilities in order to supply the spools till the end of the former contract; on the other hand, there was the interaction with E-Goods for the stipulation of the new contract.

E-Goods firstly acquired all necessary knowledge from the customer in order to describe clearly the auctioned products. A clear definition of materials features is essential in defining specifications to be sent to potential bidders. In particular, the joint work between Feragri and E-Goods identified some major characteristics in terms of:

- adopted raw chemical materials;
- final product chemical features and dimensions;
- testing procedures;
- labeling system;
- packaging requirements for shipment;
- quality certificates;
- delivery specifications;
- others.

All this information was included in the RFQ (Request For Quotation), which was sent to all selected potential bidders at the beginning of February 2001. In such a document, specifications for all the 13 lots were provided. For each lot also the *reserve price*[3] (it represents a reasonable threshold determining the success of the auction) was indicated. If the bids at the end of the auction were not below this reserve price plus 4%, Feragri would have maintained the current suppliers, because it would not have been worthwhile changing them.

In the RFQ, It was clearly stated that Feragri would have selected the few suppliers, amongst which award the winner, on the basis of products specifications and, of course, prices. In addition, the ability and flexibility of suppliers to bid for more than one lot would also have been evaluated. This last criteria was stimulated by the fact that one strategic objective for Feragri was to reduce and rationalize the

---

[3] For a definition of *reserve price*, see Chapter 2, Section 2.3.

supply base. However, Malpi was interested in bidding only for lot number 4, which was the film spools it had always supplied to Feragri.

By 23rd February, all potential suppliers should have installed the Bidware software provided by E-Goods and should have sent to E-Goods two signed documents: E-Goods Bidder Agreement,[4] and Lot Interest Form.[5] At the same time, on-line training courses were given to participants to familiarize with the auctioning software.

On 7th March the real auction (CBE) took place. It started at 8.00 a.m. (EST) and should have finished at 8.30 a.m. (EST). However, as specified in the bidders agreement rules, the last bid had always to wait 10 minutes more for other possible bids before closing the auction. As a result, the auction was closed at 9.07 a.m. (EST) with the lowest bid (4,85% lower than the reserve price) offered by a *new comer* contacted through E-Goods database. Malpi scored the eighth competitive bid.

In the following days, Feragri management carefully analysed all the suppliers and relative bids, and by 30th March it communicated the names of the few selected suppliers for each lot. Such companies included all historical ones and the best *new comers*. As far as lot number 4 is concerned, eight companies were contacted, amongst which, of course, Malpi.

The contacted companies were asked to send another document by 15th April. Such document is called *Cost Breakdowns* and collects all detailed information about cost structures that related to the single bids. In particular, each participant had to indicate raw materials costs, transformation costs, packaging costs, transportation costs, overheads, and expected profit. The aim of the document was to test the feasibility and reliability of the single bids.

By the end of July, Feragri published the final classification of suppliers for lot number 4, and asked the first one to start with sampling procedures (Malpi was classified in the sixth position). The first supplier was a Norwegian company with about €50 millions of revenues; it was a *newcomer* and it had not any contact with Feragri before. There were many problems during the sampling process; finally, after over three weeks, the supplier recognized not to be appropriate for those specific polyethylene spools, due to the difficulties in matching the right customer's plant requirements.

The second classified supplier was a French multinational company that had some transactions with Feragri in the past. Unfortunately, sampling spools tested on Feragri's plants did not pass the traction test.

Finally, the third classified supplier managed to sample the right spools matching all the requirements. It was a *newcomer* Italian SME with €5 millions of revenues. Feragri decided to sign the contract with this company. The contract price was set equal the reserve price.

---

[4] It is a document containing the auction rules for both customers and suppliers. It contains also a confidentiality agreement with which suppliers commit themselves to not disclosing any information acquired during the bidding process.

[5] With this document, the supplier indicates which lots it is interested auctioning for.

The whole final selection process took much more time then expected, therefore the new contract started only in November. During the month of October, Feragri had to buy spools by extending the old contracts with Malpi and traditional suppliers. This led to further negotiation with such suppliers, which were not very benevolent in responding to such need.

Some people working in one of the Italian local purchasing departments stated that some mistakes were made during the whole auction process by their colleagues in the central purchasing department.

Firstly, too much emphasis was given to prices and quantities, without consideration of other key factors such as service levels and the suppliers' inclination to collaborate on production optimization activities.

Secondly, as stated by one person: '...product specifications were not correctly defined in the RFQ document, and this caused the tedious *elimination process* we saw last summer...'. An example is provided by the ADR validation, which is a sort of certification a company must have to produce flexible packaging for certain chemical products. In the RFQ such certification was not asked from potential bidders, and this problem arose only in the final sampling process.

At the end of year 2001, Feragri was finally buying flexible packaging films from the selected supplier at the reserve price and the contract with Malpi was definitely terminated, but this solution was reached through a long and difficult process which lasted over 10 months. Moreover, the customer is now trying to build with the supplier, the same collaborative relationship it had with traditional suppliers, amongst which was Malpi.

4.3   Smart Technologies

Firm History and Profile

In the second half of the nineteenth century Anne Green and Tim Scott formed 'Green and Scott' a small manufacturing company producing electrical equipment in Ohio. Three years later they moved their activity to Michigan, changing the name into 'Electric Manufacturing Company'. In 1876, Anne Green filed a patent application for the telephone; the same year James Taker put in a similar patent application and founded the 'Telephone Taker', a telephone network company.

By 1880, the Electric Manufacturing Company was one of the largest electrical manufacturing company in the United States, noted for its production of a variety of electrical equipment, including the world's first commercial typewriters, telegraph equipment, and Edison's electric pen. In 1881, when the growth of telephone network was outstripping the capacity of smaller suppliers, the Telephone Taker purchased a controlling interest in Electric and made it the exclusive developer and manufacturer equipment for the Taker telephone companies.

A few years later, John Moore combined the Taker and Electric engineering departments into a single organization that, in 1928, would become 'Taker Innovations'. Since then a series of breakthrough innovations has occurred within

Taker's laboratories, amongst others: the first commercially viable system for adding sound to motion pictures, and the experimental confirmation of the wave nature of electrons, the transistor.

During the three decades from 1950 to 1980, the giant Taker encountered several restrictions due to antitrust regulation by the U.S. Department of Justice. As a result, many business units were sold to the public and many spin-offs took place. During the 1980s Taker pursued a globalization strategy by investing in projects in Spain, Korea, Saudi Arabia, and Iran.

Complexities in the marketplace and within Taker itself led to a decision to totally restructure the corporation in the early 1990s. As a result, in 1994, 'Smart Technologies' spin-off occurred including many divisions of Taker.

Since its launch, Smart has become a major player in optical, data, and wireless networking; web-based enterprise solutions that link public and private networks; communications software; professional network design and consulting services; and communications semiconductors and optoelectronics. It employs over 110,000 employees all over the world with total revenues equal to $19 billion in 1999 and $21 billion in 2000. Smart's net profit was $2.8 billion in 1999 and $2.3 billion in 2000. Its research and development arm is one of the most prolific invention factories in the world; R&D annual spending is about $3 billion, 14% of total revenues.

Since its foundation, Smart's mission is 'to provide customers with the world's best and most innovative communications systems, products, technologies and customer support, and to deliver superior, sustained shareowner value'. Such a mission in pursued through 5 main business units within Smart, in addition to R&D:

- *Networking Systems (NS):* it develops, manufactures, services, and markets data networking products and solutions for service providers.
- *Optical Solutions:* it delivers reliable, secure, and scalable end-to-end optical transport network solutions for band-with hungry services.
- *Switching Solutions:* it delivers the distributed next-generation communication networks that enables telecommunications services supporting high quality voice, data, video and the latest multimedia applications.
- *Wireless Solutions:* it provides innovative solutions to network operators supporting mobile and wireless voice and data services.
- *Worldwide Services:* it is the largest networking services and consulting organization in the world.
- *Taker Labs:* it is the R&D center operating 24times7 in different offices all over the world.

Since the second half of 2000, Smart has been suffering a downturn, partially due to the disillusion related to e-business. However, during this period the company, led by its Chairman and CEO's conviction that Internet will be the future, focused its core business on the broadband and mobile Internet, also by spinning off some activities. One of the results of this new vision was also the redefinition of Smart's supply chain (see below).

Within this context, the case provides the analysis of a supply chain initiative based on the Internet adoption rather than describing one specific relationship. Such choice is justified by the interesting topics arising from a more complete perspective (e.g. strategic and 2nd tier suppliers relationship), which, however, includes customer-supplier relationships by default.

Smart's Supply Chain

In the past, sourcing strategy was not a high competitive priority and a modest part of production was run into Smart's own facilities. Moreover, suppliers were simply considered as production capacity providers, without any other value added capability. In the late 1990s Smart started a process of deep redefinition of its supply chain. Top management recognized supply management as central to success in this business and invested a huge commitment in creating a world class supply chain management organization. Such recognition led to the conviction that suppliers should have played a greater role in the business and that Smart's dictatorial behavior should have been transformed into a more collaborating one by building relationships respecting mutual interests.

This change in culture resulted in the definition of a *Supply Chain Networks* division managing four key areas: suppliers' relationships, supply chain planning and execution, logistics, and customer service. The activities performed by top management and this division led to many changes.

Firstly, a process of rationalization of the supply base reduced the number of suppliers to less in number and more reliable companies. Direct materials suppliers are now classified into three categories. *Strategic suppliers* are those with strategic goals and objectives aligned with Smart's, they demonstrate the ability to meet all of the supplier evaluation characteristics, and the relationship with them requires an extensive time commitment and executive level engagement. Sharing strategic goals and objectives means sharing risks and rewards, supply continuity, openness and trust, pursuing together technology leadership, continuous improvement programs, and reducing together time to market and costs. *Preferred suppliers* supply materials critical to Smart's success, but they are not strategically aligned on all business goals. Finally, *select suppliers* support specific needs and are not involved in long-term relationships. The supplier relationship management group decides the attribution of suppliers to such categories.

Secondly, a large part of manufacturing activities was outsourced also by selling many plants to those strategic suppliers. This process radically transformed Smart, which has decidedly moved towards the model of a virtual company.

Moreover, a strategic program was started with the aim of building long-lasting collaboration with key suppliers; this program led to the constitution of supplier partnership councils (SPCs), one for each key product. Such councils are now held periodically with the aim of establishing a collaborative environment which influences product design and the supply chain, ideally at the earliest possible stage to maximize the use of strategic suppliers' capabilities to achieve target costs and time-to-market requirements. One of the interviewed suppliers stated: 'The last SPC meeting went extremely well, the information I received is more than I have had in seven years in dealing with Smart. Many pieces of the puzzle were brought together, and now that a target has been expressed it is known what needs to be achieved'.

Another main initiative consisted in creating a learning center called SCS University (Supply Chain Solutions). This center accomplishes the task to gather Smart's buyers and suppliers transferring to them supply chain concepts specific to their reality.

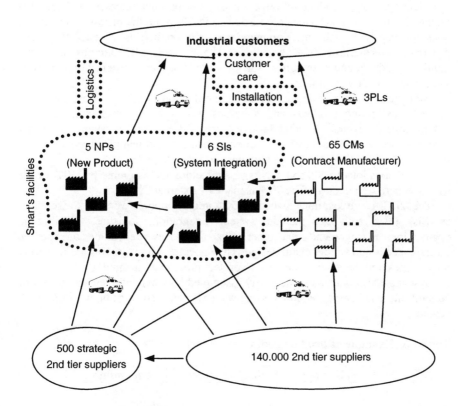

Figure 4.5 Smart's supply chain

Although all these initiatives brought some benefits, actors belonging to the supply chain still had inefficient coordination processes. Demand forecasts and production planning were exchanged via e-mail, it was very complex to obtain inventory visibility across the whole global chain, technical and administrative documents were managed off-line using multiple databases. For this reason a supply chain portal was developed with the aim of improving coordination between Smart and the supply base. The characteristics of such portal are described in the next section.

As described, Smart is becoming more and more a virtual enterprise, consolidating relationships with main suppliers. The structure of the current supply chain is shown in Figure 4.5. Only 11 plants, all over the world, are owned by Smart itself. These plants have been transformed into two different typologies: System Integration (SI) and New Products (NP).

SIs are key supply chain nodes that do 'system and solution integration' for a selected group of Smart's most complex systems and solutions. These operations include complex final assembly and test, solution integration, configuration, and test, selective new product introduction of new product releases, and supplier facing logistics. Such activities are insourced in SIs when the necessary capability does not readily exist from a commercial source, or there is the need to protect proprietary technology (e.g. complex customer network solutions including multiple products and assemblies, software download and system configuration, system test / quality assurance).

NP centers are key nodes dedicated to introduction of Smart's most advanced, major breakthrough products and solutions. Focus is on accelerating time to volume/time to revenues to breakthrough levels. Once product is 'stable' (typically 1 year or even less), it is moved to either external contract manufacturers locations (CM) or SI, depending on supply chain design.

The 11 locations (6 SIs and 5 NPs) manufacture and assemble the 10% of the overall Smart's production. The 90% is made by external CM.

The 65 CMs are locations owned by 5 strategic suppliers who work essentially as SIs; their activities include system integration, logistics, distribution, engineering, management, and other related services, depending on specific business needs and supply chain design. They operate where systems are relatively not complex and there is not the need to protect proprietary technology.

Systems and products can be partly assembled by CMs and then sent to SIs or NPs for ultimate operations; in the same way, SIs can send work in progress to NP centers.

Table 4.1 Example of product coding for Smart

Technology	Sub-technology	Part number
Circuit module	Logic	406986646
		406986699
		...
	Optic receiver	406054322
		406054576
		...
	Power module	406116565
		...
	...	...

All these production facilities are fed by over 140,000 suppliers who supply all necessary components. These are called second tier suppliers, in opposition to CMs who are first tier suppliers. 500 of second tier suppliers are classified as strategic suppliers. These strategic suppliers, which provide altogether the 95% of direct materials, either manage a not yet mature technology, or supply huge volumes, or provide a large number of items.

Components' coding follows a three-level identification. Each component has its own part number, which differs supplier by supplier; components are then grouped into sub-technologies (e.g. optical connector, wire termination); and finally sub technologies are grouped into about 150 technologies (e.g. adapter, amplifier, circuit module, diode switching, fuse).

All materials flows are managed by Third Party Logistics (3PLs), with the support of Smart's logistics function, of Smart's installations and customer care in the case of shipment to customers.

The Internet Adoption: the Supply Chain Portal

As mentioned in the previous section, Smart developed a supply chain portal. The project started in the middle of 2000, all the activities were performed by internal IT staff, and the first version was delivered in January 2001.

The mission accomplished by that portal has been stated by one of Smart's IT people: 'Enable the most flexible and efficient supply chain by leveraging strategy, processes and technology that integrate Smart organizations, trading partners, and eMarketplaces to create real-time, global visibility and decision making control over the virtual supply chain'. According to Smart, the portal performs as a gateway into information, applications, and global data, and defines common processes across its virtual community; as a result, the all chain would benefit from:

- increased speed to market of new products;
- lower design and operational costs;
- higher customer fulfillment rates.

Up to date, integration with eMarketplaces has not been done yet, but a collaboration initiative with a vertical marketplace in the high-tech industry started during the summer 2001.

The supply chain portal supports a number of coordination and collaboration services between Smart and its suppliers. All these services are exploitable through the web simply using a web browser. Currently, the access to the portal has been given to the five CMs and about 200 second tier strategic suppliers; it is foreseen to extend the access to all the 500 suppliers.

In controlling the accesses there are three layers of security. The entry to the system is controlled through the usual *user-ID* mechanism; only selected suppliers can obtain user names to enter the portal. Through the user-ID the user is univocally identified, and all web pages are customized with appropriate information. The second level of security (*tab-level security*) allows the specific user seeing and using only specific services. Finally, the *raw level security* allows the specific user seeing and using only specific applications and information within each service.

Smart's users can see and use every service, every application, and every information. Suppliers can use a large number of services, depending on their importance in the supply chain, but are not allowed to see information regarding direct competitors.

Services are exploitable through different tabs (or screens): communication content, escalation management, price management, engineering/technical management, performance dashboard, demand management, and inventory management.

Communication content
The general communication content found on the main tab within the portal is rolled-out to all subscribed users. This main tab exists as a single area for supply chain partners to visit and be provided with general supply chain information. Currently, this information consists of an overview of the portal, training manuals for each service, links to Smart's web pages, supplier related announcements, supplier related news, industry related news, programs and events, and frequently asked questions. The user notifications represent an area within the portal where exceptions, alerts and relevant information are collected for individual users. It allows them to effectively manage tasks and exceptions while utilizing the applications contained within the portal.

Escalation management
During an order lifecycle it may be necessary for supply chain partners to communicate the problems related to specific stock-out issues. These issues can be entered, tracked and managed to resolution effectively in the portal utilizing the escalation tool and workflow. The escalation application is designed to provide CMs the ability to effectively communicate the risk of components shortages and order cancellation issues; as the business changes and the needs arise, the tool can evolve to handle new urgent requirements. All interested suppliers are notified of shortages, and they can solve the problem by using the escalation tool and, where possible, communicating the shipment of components.

Price management
The price management tab can provide Smart's users and supply chain partners with the ability to collaborate on pricing new businesses, repricing existing ones and in the tracking of price and supplier performance history to ensure that the best sourcing decision are made based on price and quality. Workflow supporting RFP and RFQ services are available to involve interested suppliers in proposing new pricing; moreover suppliers can change pricing policy through this tool, and buyers are immediately notified. These tools also enable supply chain partners to generate

aggregated income statements, balance sheets and metrics reports in order to compare pricing policies more easily.

Engineering/technical management
The engineering/technical data management section of the portal was developed to provide suppliers and external manufacturers with a gateway into the most recent revision of manufacturing, design, and other engineering specifications needed to complete their jobs. This capability reduces e-mail and paper mail provisioning of documents and resolves document revision control issues. Depending on users security level of access, they will find information on different topics: documents on design and manufacturing specifications, general product specifications, bar coding standards and instructions for Warranty Eligibility Standards, PDM search for design packages and drawings granted on a user to user basis, and engineering change process information. Furthermore, Smart is now developing a direct link to a software tool supporting collaborative design activities.

Performance dashboard
The dashboard metrics section of the portal is designed to share information on financial performance, quality, service level, and partner development with suppliers. Users, on a user to user basis, will have the ability to quickly review and compare supplier performance metrics and perform analyses on these measures to generate the information necessary to improve and build optimal supply chains.

Demand management
Demand management section is divided into two main functionalities: *demand aggregation* and *demand collaboration*.

The *demand aggregation* capability provides components demand forecasts over a 52-week rolling cycle. This demand can be seen in monthly and weekly buckets, and users can drill down from aggregated view to item level or a combination of technology, sub-technology, part number, vendor name, demand source location, or demand source organization. Basing on this tool, Smart's supplier managers can obtain secure allocation of materials and competitive pricing, manufacturing and assembly facilities can optimize distribution of allocated components, and component suppliers are helped in capacity planning and strategic capacity acquisition.

The *demand collaboration* capability leverages the previous enterprise wide demand aggregation to support a demand collaboration process to pro-actively avoid parts shortage occurrences, which may result in lost revenues. The collaboration community includes the supplier manager, the supplier account manager, and the material manager for each relationship. Collaboration occurs whenever demand or forecasts changes significantly or suppliers are not able to meet required components. Suppliers are able to insert real-time new commitments and shortages of components, Smart's user is immediately notified and searches for alternative suppliers re-allocating demand. Currently, this collaboration functionality is accessible only by all CMs and 25 2nd tier component suppliers, but its use will be enlarged to some others.

Moreover, in the demand management section daily reports are available highlighting dropped demand, new demand, significantly changes in demand, variances in demand allocation on different suppliers, and a progress report that summarize collaboration activities.

Inventory management
The inventory management section essentially provides three capabilities. Firstly, it gives visibility into global inventory present in SIs, NPs and CMs at different levels of aggregation (technology, sub-technology and part number) in units, days of stock, and dollar value. Secondly, it automatically allows matching excess inventory with existing demand at any internal manufacturing or contract manufacturing location. Finally, it provides the ability to identify obsolete inventory with no demand anywhere in the supply chain. All these functionalities are very useful in effectively reallocating excess and identifying obsolete inventory.

In addition to these main services, also other applications are available (e.g. documents management, administrative reports, invoices and purchase orders visibility).

The described services are all viable through the web, and users upload most of information real-time. The system is integrated with Smart's ERP and MRP systems, but it is not integrated with suppliers' though, as the investment would have been huge while the IT strategy of Smart consists of proceeding step by step. Currently, CMs and suppliers' data concerning demand and inventory positions are sent daily through a flat file which standard format has been defined. This file automatically updates portal information.

As explained before, the number of actors involved in Smart's supply chain is huge and every company adopts its own part numbers, for this reason it was necessary to include a 'translator' into the portal components. Such translator is a database containing all items with different part numbers associated for each partner of the supply chain. Thank to this database, every company can exploit portal services by using either their item codes or Smart's. The translator is updated weekly.

Using the supply chain portal brought a number of benefits. The relationship with suppliers has been improved; as one of the suppliers said: 'The full view that was given through the portal helps us with our forecasting and planning... we can see a major change'. Portal adoption lead to 100 M$ stockout less than previous year in the same period and an inventory reduction from 6.5 B$ to 3.2 B$ across the whole supply chain. Estimates state that time and resources spent in coordination have been reduced by 50% for both Smart and suppliers.

4.4   Gias - Fiumelli

Firm History and Profile

Gias was founded in Europe at the end of the nineteenth century. Gias cars won instant popularity, both in Europe and overseas, as a luxury item designed for a consumer elite. The brand also enjoyed recognition in car racing.

By 1909, Gias had a factory in the US and was quickly expanding into the manufacture of trucks, tractors, trains, marine engines and aircraft.

In 1922, Gias transformed itself from an exclusive brand to one that was available to the growing mass of ordinary consumers, and was challenged to produce a car currently lacking in the bigger US market: one with a small engine that was affordable for everyone.

Along all Gias history, manufacturing diversification was accentuated by its growing commitment to the sectors of metallurgy and components, later followed by production systems, insurance and services. Throughout Gias history, this diversification has certainly contributed to the success of the globalization that the company has always pursued. Its presence on the global markets, which is an essential part of Gias Group policy, is now directed towards emerging countries such as India and China, in Asia, and Brazil and Argentina, in South America.

Nowadays, Gias Group is a big multinational holding company with total revenues of €37 billions. It operates all over the world in 51 countries. The Group employs 153,000 employees. There are 127 production facilities around the world; also research centers are present worldwide.

The companies belonging to the Group are organized into ten categories of activities: automotive, agriculture and construction machinery, industrial vehicles, metallurgy, components, production machinery, aviation, publishing and communication, insurance and services. In particular, in the 'components' category it is possible to find Fiumelli.

Gias and Gustavo Fiumelli founded Fiumelli at the beginning of the twentieth century. It soon became a global enterprise in the automotive components and spare parts industry. It designs, develops, and produces high technological components, systems and modules for the automotive industry.

Fiumelli is one of the biggest companies worldwide in the automotive lighting sector, in dashboards and in fuel ignition systems. Its production facilities are located in Europe, North and South America, and Asia. Its global sales amount is about €3.5 billions, 5.2% of which are invested in R&D. It employs 19,000 employees globally, with 49 production facilities and 16 research centers.

The two major markets for Fiumelli are the first equipment and the after-market. In the former case, customers are the biggest car manufacturers worldwide; whereas in the latter case, components are sold directly to final consumer through repair shops worldwide.

Polyethylene Envelopes

The analysed objects of transaction are plastic envelopes made of polyethylene film (a molecule deriving from oil) and purchased by Fiumelli in order to wrap its components.

The production process of this material follows three steps. Firstly, through an extrusion process, the polyethylene film is obtained from raw granulate, which is made of oil, ldpe, and other chemical additives. Afterwards, through the printing process, graphics are printed on the film; it is possible to use from a minimum of one color to a maximum of six colors. Finally, through the welding process, the film is sealed (usually on three sides) and cut to obtain the final envelopes.

Fiumelli uses them as flexible packaging for two typologies of materials:

- automotive spare parts produced within manufacturing plants and then sent to single repair shops through distribution centers;
- small mechanical parts like nuts, screws, and bolts sent together the spare part by default.

Such a package is an indirect material with low strategic relevance and low purchase volume for Fiumelli. Precisely, employees manually insert components into the envelopes, which, therefore, do not enter the production process either.

However, the considered material is highly customized to Fiumelli both in terms of measures (height, length, and thickness) and graphics. As far as the graphics are concerned, each envelope is printed with one or more colors in order to represent different brand logos. Due to the rigidity of printing and welding plants in this specific industrial sector (packaging industries), the customized definition of measures and graphics increases the asset specificity, thus leading to a sort of dependence between customer and supplier.

However, such technical specifications (measures and graphics) are easy to communicate through a technical description of the format, an AutoCAD drawing, chemical specifications of the film, and a paper print representing the upper drawing in order to develop the appropriate cliché for the printing process.

The Relationship with Suppliers

The supplier providing the described envelopes to Fiumelli is Alexy, a European SME (Small-Medium Enterprise) with about €10 million of revenues. It performs internally all the three stages of the production process described in the previous paragraph. Such supplier sells its packaging products to different industrial sectors: chemical and pharmaceutical, food and beverage, construction, publishing, and, of course, automotive. Fiumelli represents about 2% of Alexy's total revenues.

Fiumelli has purchased envelopes from Alexy for decades, building an historical and reliable relationship. Due to the relevance of the customer, Alexy's top management has always directly communicated with:

- Fiumelli's production managers, in order to provide and receive necessary technical information;
- Fiumelli's central purchasing department, in order to establish contractual terms (e.g. frame contracts, annual prices, possible monthly changes);
- Fiumelli's local purchasing departments, in order to manage orders, confirmations, and reminders with single business units.

The interactions with these three typologies of actors are due to the overall procurement process itself. That process consisted of two main phases.

The first stage was finalized at stipulating a long-term frame contract, usually lasting for 4 to 5 years. The central purchasing department has always conducted this negotiation in order to establish two fundamental figures: total purchased volumes for each year, and average prices. However, prices are only approximate estimates, due to the volatility of the basic raw material (oil) and its incidence over the final cost of the envelope (almost 40%). After the stipulation of the contract, all Fiumelli business units and production facilities would have directly ordered sealed envelops from Alexy, the official supplier, according to their specific needs.

The second stage was the more operative one. Single local purchasing departments sent orders by fax to the supplier, within the frame contract, on the basis of production facilities needs. Each order contained specific items codes and quantities required for the following month. Every time there was a required change in a single order line, the whole order was sent again to the supplier. In this way, Alexy received four to five communications each month by fax from each customer's production facility. This, of course, led to high confusion in the supplier's production planning process.

The Internet Adoption: Electronic Catalog

Different companies belonging to Gias Group have always managed purchasing activities separately through local purchasing departments, Fiumelli's was one of these. Such configuration was extremely inefficient, especially for indirect and MRO (Maintenance, Repair, and Operations) materials; fragmentation does not allow to reach most efficient economies of scale and, moreover, it replicates activities and resources department by department. On average, purchasing costs constitute the 60% of total Gias costs; with these huge volumes there is the opportunity to aggregate demands and save high inefficiencies.

For these reasons, at the beginning of year 2000, Gias decided to launch its own e-procurement platform: *E-Buyer*. The objective of this initiative was threefold. Firstly, Gias decided to aggregate all purchasing activities performed within the group in one unique purchasing department; this would have led to the desired economies of scale and to a more efficient demand and requirements management. At the same time, through a web-based catalog, all procurement activities in the different production facilities would have been streamlined and automated, from items search on the catalog to the final shipment to the facilities. Thirdly, the ambitious project had also the aim of becoming a European marketplace addressed to external customers and suppliers, and not only captive ones. For this last reason, E-Buyer platform has started providing also auction services. As far as the scope of the study is concerned, the attention will be focused on the first two objectives of the initiative and the relationship between Gias and Alexy.

In more detail, specific goals pursued by Gias were the following:

- internal administrative procurement costs reduction (e.g. invoicing, authorizations, telephone calls);
- data gathering and reporting in order to monitor and control overall expenses;
- reduction of order cycle lead time;
- integration of purchasing with other functions (e.g. production, engineering);
- negotiation power increase with suppliers;
- Giving to purchasing professionals the possibility to spend time in more value added activities than orders processing.

The platform collects electronic catalogs from more suppliers, which reliability is guaranteed by the selection Gias has performed among the supply base. These catalogs are integrated with the legacy systems (including ERPs and MRPs) of all companies belonging to the Gias Group.

Customers order materials directly to suppliers through the platform and might also contact suppliers for non-catalog products through E-Buyer experts. E-Buyer is responsible for the management of relationships with suppliers and for the maintenance of the overall system. Suppliers might directly extend and update their offer on the platform (Figure 4.6). The chosen technology provider was Catalogs Technology, a European company supplier of e-content services all over the world.

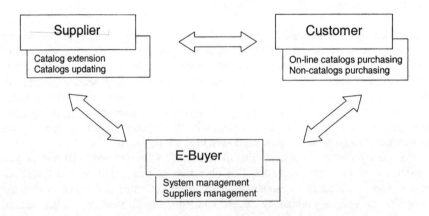

Figure 4.6 New procurement organization (adapted from Gias, 2001)

E-Buyer decided to start the experimentation with indirect materials, with the aim of extending the platform and the transaction services in the future to include also direct materials. Therefore, the initial offer consisted of about 400.000 items classified through the international standard UN/SPSC^{TM} and divided in 14 categories belonging to two groups:

- *industrial materials:*
  - tools, ball bearings, anti-accidents, chemicals and lubricants, packaging, electrical materials, pneumatic tools, shop furniture, manual tools.
- *office materials:*
  - stationery, paper and forms, office furniture, personal computing, telephony.

The catalog is configured in a dynamic way in terms of products and prices; that is products can continuously change and improve over time and prices can be continuously re-negotiated. The customers can see and compare all the items, both in terms of product features and price, but suppliers cannot see each other's offers.

As result, E-Buyer is a database standardizing items data and contracts, it provides technical, logistics and economics (prices) information, it supports search and comparison among different items, and it streamlines the order process.

Gias new central purchasing department started a process of comparison and selection amongst its over 20,000 indirect material suppliers; such comparison was based on past performances in terms of quality and reliability. At the beginning of December 2000, 260 suppliers were contacted to participate the initiative; Alexy was amongst these.

Initially, Alexy's management was not enthusiastic of the 'opportunity' offered by its customer, as it did not see any big advantage in joining the initiative and dealing with a much bigger purchase department than previous single local offices. However, some factors pushed the company to accept the invitation. Firstly, Gias had always been a strategic customer with a high contractual power, therefore, if Alexy wanted to keep selling its products to it, it should have surely joined the platform. Secondly, there was the real opportunity to extend the customer base from the only Fiumelli to other Group's companies. Finally, there was also the strategic aim for E-Buyer to become a European marketplace, thus offering even more appealing market opportunities to Alexy.

Of course, there were some costs to be face by Alexy in joining the platform. The smallest ones were those finalized at the creation of the catalog itself: $3.5 for each item uploaded by Catalogs Technology on the platform times a total of 57 items equals a very low cost of about $200. The biggest effort was spent in terms of time and human resources spent into the physical realization of the catalog and into participating the numerous meetings organized by Gias and Catalogs Technology.

Alexy's products fall within the category Industrial / Packaging (see previous categories), together with another similar supplier of flexible plastic packaging, 2 suppliers of pallets, and 3 suppliers of cardboard boxes.

In January 2001, a series of meetings were organized in order to explain to suppliers how to build the catalogs. Catalogs Technology provided two options:

- 'Self-Authoring Tools' (SATs): in this case the supplier might have directly designed the content after following a specific training on the needed software tool.
- 'Content Creation Service': in this case the supplier would have sent to Catalogs Technology the necessary information through an Excel spreadsheet, and then Catalogs Technology would have created the catalog content.

Alexy decided to adopt the first option. This was due to the opportunity to really personally customize and design the content. Moreover, as a strategic objective for Alexy was extending its market share, a directly controlled content would have allowed higher control over the clear and well-defined description of its products. In February, the Alexy's designated person start following a specific on-line training on the software tool. The effort spent by this person led also to the development of specific drawings that could have been easily understood also by people not directly involved in the packaging industry. Such choice was extremely good, as other suppliers having chosen the 'Content Creation Service' option had numerous problems in uploading their items with the desired clear descriptions and specifications.

During the same period, the terms of long-term frame contract between Gias and Alexy were defined. In particular, they defined, besides the technical specifications, the size of minimum lots, the minimum invoice amount, the return conditions, the delivery lead times, the payment conditions, the packaging size, and, of course, the current prices. Those prices are monthly updated, and Alexy can continuously maintain and improve the catalog offer.

In October 2001 the pilot system was activated, and Alexy obtained its user ID and password to enter the platform. Through this access, the supplier can see in real time all the orders coming from all Gias Group's companies.

With the new structure, direct communication between Alexy and the local production facilities does not exist any more. The supplier deals only with E-Buyer in phase of contract negotiation, and then receives orders from different facilities through the web site. For this reason, it is even more important to have well-described products on the catalog, in order to enable the customer to understand their specific features from the catalog itself.

In such a way, besides the frame contract negotiation, the new tool supports a more automatic procurement process than before, made of two main stages: *order approval* and *order fulfillment*.

Order approval
Selected people within each organization belonging to the Gias Group, have their own user ID and password to enter the catalog system. These are typically production managers or plant directors. Whenever they perceive any need for an indirect material, they access and browse the catalogs searching for the desired

material. They compare descriptions, specifications, and prices, and then select their choice in terms of item, supplier, and quantities according to contractual terms.

As already mentioned all the catalogs are integrated with the enterprise systems. Each user has its own profile and its own budget of expenses within specific product categories, therefore a first system control works as filter according to the user rights. After passing this filter, the request for order is automatically sent to the correspondent authorizer through an internal workflow (this depends on the single enterprise's organizational structure). The authorizer can then approve or reject the request. If the order is approved, it is then directly published on the web and a notification message via e-mail is sent to the related supplier. The approval process is highly customizable to all the companies within the Group, from the most simple to the biggest and most complex ones.

The integration between the catalog and the workflow speeds up the process, thus reducing both lead times and costs of the procurement activities. In addition, the user might continuously monitor the order approval status on the system.

Order fulfillment

The supplier acknowledges the presence of the new order through the electronic message. The detailed order can then be seen by accessing the web and entering E-Buyer system. On the system, the supplier sees its own screen with all the open orders and their last possible variations.

The fulfillment process then begins according to contractual terms agreed with the customer's central purchasing department (e.g. in terms of delivery time). According to the contract, the supplier updates each order status on the web on a predetermined frequency (e.g. every three days). In this way the customer can continuously monitor all its orders status. Finally, the supplier ships the items, still according to all contractual terms.

The adoption of this e-procurement platform has led to higher efficiency in the overall procurement process, by reducing costs and lead times. Gias has managed to increase its procurement efficiency mostly aggregating demands coming from all captive enterprises and eliminating replicated and fragmented activities. Moreover, the automation of internal processes has surely reduced procurement times and costs within every organization.

As far as Alexy is concerned, it might seem that such initiative has not provided many improvements, also considering the initial efforts in designing the catalog and the increased contractual power of the customer. In reality, some improvements can be noted also on the supply side. Firstly, the fulfillment process has been speeded up, as communication with customers is managed through the web without time consuming multiple faxes and telephone calls aiming at monitoring the orders status. Secondly, Alexy has accessed to other customers within the Gias Group, thus increasing its market share. This increment might further increase once E-Buyer access the European market.

4.5   Cases Discussion

Empirical evidence shown by the four case studies provides some ideas related to research questions. In particular, the general aim of the research is to discover what are the motivations driving companies towards the use of the Internet in customer-supplier relationships, what are the possible tools, and what is the effect on the relationships themselves (see Chapter 3).

From the cases, several motivations emerged. Grapes and Feragri clearly shared similar objectives and motivations: increasing market efficiency by contacting both traditional and potential new suppliers and making them bid in order to lower purchase prices. In pursuing such a goal, they exploited the capabilities of one intermediary in order to make the search, selection, and negotiation process as efficient as possible. The whole procedure was finalized at conducting the final competitive bidding event through a reverse electronic auction. As already mentioned in Section 2.3, electronic auctions are one of the most common tools used to increase market efficiency.

In the Smart's situation, on the other hand, the use of the Internet had a far different motivation. Smart's management wanted to create a supply chain as lean, flexible, and responsive as possible by providing full visibility to first and second tier suppliers and extending collaboration activities to some key strategic ones. In developing its private portal, Smart proceeded gradually, step by step. The first stage consisted of increasing inventory and demand visibility along the supply chain, the second stage consisted of creating a more complete operational integration through collaboration activities such as demand planning, and, finally, also technological integration activities were planned (e.g. co-design software). The entire solution led to higher efficiency and effectiveness in the whole supply process in terms of, lead times, operating costs, inventory levels, time-to-market, product quality, to give only some examples.

As far as the Gias and Fiumelli case is concerned, top management had the major aim of streamlining and leaning all internal procurement procedures. Such an objective was pursued by aggregating the whole Group's demand through a central purchasing department in order to minimize the replication of activities. Moreover, the creation of electronic catalogs (see Section 2.3) automated many administrative and operating procedures allowing local production facilities to order material directly through an integrated platform exploiting open frame contracts. In this way, the overall internal procurement process was made far more efficient. In addition, the relationship with Alexy has improved due to the real time information exchange concerning orders status and fulfillment procedures. This is not, of course, the same level of coordination found within Smart's supply chain, but, considering the indirect material characteristics, such a high level of coordination would have not been useful either.

As a matter of fact, the characteristics of the object of the transaction resulted in the essential adoption of Internet tools. In the first case, the object was a direct material (grape juice concentrate) crucial in determining final product characteristics; however, its specifications, though very strict, were easy to define, and this did not lead to problems during the RFQ and auctioning process. On the contrary, in the second case, the polyethylene spools resulted to be much more complex to describe than previously foreseen by Feragri. Such spools were also crucial in preserving final product features, therefore, although they were used as flexible packaging, they could be considered as direct material. Smart applied its coordination portal on every kind of direct component used within its final products; this was done thanks to consolidated contracts and close relationships with suppliers, which allowed standardizing sufficiently required information. Finally, Gias adopted catalogs for indirect and rather simple to describe material; such use of electronic catalogs was also widely described in literature (see Section 2.3).

An interesting issue arising especially in Grapes, Feragri, and Gias cases is the contractual power between the two parties. The Internet initiative has been led by the customer, which represented a rather conspicuous part of supplier's revenues. In such a condition, on the supplier's perspective, not participating means terminating the supply. This is an important factor to be considered in exploring suppliers' motivations. Although, other incentives might exist (e.g. the opportunity for Alexy to increase its customers base).

Relevant issues emerge also on the relationship perspective. The Internet adoption had strongly effected the relationship in all the analysed cases.

The first two companies illustrate typical situations in which the Internet has been used to emphasize the market efficiency and reduce the purchase price as much as possible. The auction process resulted in destroying stable and consolidated relationships built with efforts on both parties in the past. Relationships based on vertical alliances have become market governance relationships.

The prices of a bidding process are the results of two factors: the cost structure of the vendors and what market can bear. The auction process forced bidders to analyse carefully their own cost structure, in particular they needed to know exactly their marginal costs and their wished margin (on a cost plus based accounting). In the Feragri case, for example, selected suppliers had also to fill in a precise cost breakdown form. For this reason, the lower limit of their bids should be a function of desired margin, standard costs and, most of all, marginal costs. The latter depend also on the capacity constraints and the utilization of the plants. The upper limit of the bid could be represented by what they expect the market can bear.

In such a situation, vendors are much more stressed in considering many aspects than in traditional relationship. This is a big element of complexity in managing the sale, in particular in the grapes industry in which the contract is stipulated before the harvest (Grapes case). Of course, this stressful situation represents an advantage for the buyer.

Another major effect is the loss of flexibility and reliability in procurement. In the past, Grapes had three established relationships characterized by mutual help and adjustment. Any problem was solved within those relationships and variations in planning schedules, shipments and forecasts were discussed around a table.

After the auctioning process, it was strictly linked to one vendor, which was less willing to help in case of problems (due to the auction process); and the others, who lost the auction, would have not been helpful in solving shortages issues. In the Feragri case, the traditional supplier terminated its contract with the customer, which was trying to build a similar relationship with the *newcomer*.

Furthermore, suppliers account managers were used to personal interactions with buyers, and these kind of interactions were completely interrupted during the overall auction process; they had to interact exclusively with the intermediary.

A potential risk related to auctioning every year with the same suppliers could be their possible adaptive behavior. They could become more and more expert in the mechanism and implement proper practices to damp down the price reduction during the bidding process. At an extreme, this could lead to collusion among suppliers.

These are some of the risks tied to the changed nature of the relationship. The question is whether it is worth getting into a more risky situation in the long run, jeopardizing well established relationships, in order to lower costs in the short period.

In the end, Grapes decided to balance these risks by auctioning half of the needs and building a long-term alliance for the other half. In this way, the company tries to reduce costs as much as possible, while still keeping an open behavior and flexibility through a vertical alliance. This practice is also emerging in other companies, which started by adopting a 100% auctioning strategy and then came back on their step to pursue such edging strategy.

The second two cases, especially Smart, show increasing integration and coordination between trading partners. The Internet provides the potential to increase the effectiveness of communication through its standard protocols and worldwide access. Technology might be adopted in two different levels. On the one hand, it provides full visibility and information sharing on the entire inter-enterprise supply process. On the other hand, it supports distant collaboration among people belonging to different organizations. Such levels of coordination might be applied with different suppliers, providing simply visibility to common ones and collaborating with more strategic ones (e.g. Smart).

Within coordination among companies, systems integration plays a big role. In Smart's case, the portal is integrated with Smart's and contract manufacturers' facilities, but made accessible by other suppliers through a web browser whose ERP systems are not integrated. Data communication occurs through a daily batch mode. In order to transfer data, all must agree on the same format in order to allow Smart's system to automatically update portal's information. In addition, a part numbers translator was required in order to match all different codes present in the different organizations. As far as Gias is concerned, E-Buyer is totally integrated with internal ERP and MRP, but not yet with suppliers, who can also access it through a web browser.

Although the adoption of web portals increases coordination, systems integration is the last step in high collaboration among companies; however, it is a very costly activity. Moreover, it is difficult for all supply chain members to invest in such integration. For this reason, the definition of clear and well-established communication standards is crucial in providing the full opportunity for collaboration. Through such standards, all enterprise systems could communicate with each other in real time without further investments.

Chapter 5

Research Hypotheses

5.1 Motivations to the Internet Adoption in Customer-Supplier Relationships

The first research question of this study addresses the motivations companies have in using web-based tools in customer supplier relationships. Analysing the case studies discussion (Section 4.5), a preliminary answer can be given.

Various contributions seem to lead to a quite consolidated view in defining benefits and motivations. As seen in Chapter 2, there are three main motivations driving companies in the use of the Internet. The first is the pursuit of leaner and more efficient internal procurement processes (Section 2.3). The second resides in the will to shift relationships towards markets by increasing market efficiency (Section 2.3). Finally, the third one is the improvement of collaboration activities between the two parties (Section 2.3).

All these issues were surely found in the field, however a deeper interpretation arises. Some of such motivations are considered primary objectives, but some others are more instrumental goals than real pursued objectives. Speaking with people and analysing interviews, the real motivations could be summarized as follows.

First of all, the prime need that emerged was surely the requirement for higher efficiency in internal procurement processes; this essentially means reducing order cycle time, reducing inventory, streamlining activities, and reducing pure transaction management costs.

Secondly, another need is the reduction of the overall procurement costs; this essentially means the reduction of suppliers searching and selection costs, negotiation and evaluation costs, and the proper purchasing cost of acquired materials. It can be noted that the first two mentioned components are exactly the first two components of transaction costs (Section 1.2), while the third transaction cost (transaction management) has been included in the previous motivation.

Finally, the third main motivation can be defined as the improvement of supply process effectiveness; this includes quality issues, time to market reduction, innovation requirements, and service level to final customer.

Motivations found in literature and those found in the field are not inconsistent, but they are slightly different.

The first motivation is exactly the same in the two perspectives, and the reduction of procurement costs, as stated in literature, essentially coincides with the will to increase market efficiency. The main difference resides in the collaboration objective. From the field analysis, it has not been considered as a primary goal *per se*, but it is an instrumental objective pursued by companies in order to increase both process efficiency and effectiveness (Figure 5.1).

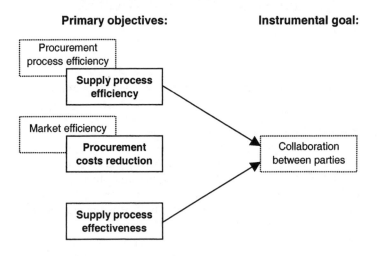

Figure 5.1 Motivations to the Internet adoption

From these considerations the first proposition of the work emerges:

H1:   The search for customer-supplier collaboration exploiting web-based technologies is explained by the need to increase process efficiency and effectiveness.

In order to prove this hypothesis a regression model among the mentioned variables will be tested (see Section 6.4). On the basis of what found in literature and in case studies analysis the operationalization and validity and reliability analyses of the described concepts have been done during the survey design phase, and it is deeply discussed in Chapter 6. In particular, motivations and the collaboration aspect are described in Section 6.2.

5.2   Internet Tools Choice

The second research question addresses the relation among motivations, acquired materials, and typology of Internet tools adopted.

The three main motivations have just been described: supply process efficiency, procurement costs reduction, and supply process effectiveness.

The dimensions characterizing materials are those described in Chapter 1 (Williamson, 1979; Kraljic, 1983; Olsen and Ellram, 1997; Malone et al., 1987; De Maio and Maggiore, 1992). In particular, in the study, considered dimensions essentially refer to the presence of transaction specific investments, the frequency of the purchase, the strategic relevance of the purchase, the supply market complexity, and the complexity of material description.

As far as web-based tools are concerned, they can be classified through different characteristics (see Chapter 2). Firstly, there are transaction tools, which are essentially electronic catalogs, electronic exchanges, and electronic auctions. Secondly, portals offering such services can be either vertical or horizontal. Thirdly, the actor managing such portals can be either the supplier, or a consortium, or an independent entity, or the company itself. Finally, especially in private portals, companies might use web-EDI services or specific team working tools enabling distant collaboration.

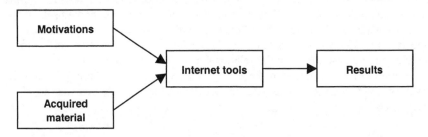

Figure 5.2 Relations among motivations, acquired material, adopted tools, and results

As far as multiple relationships among all these variables could exist, they all have been introduced in the questionnaire in order to set interdependencies and correlation among motivations, acquired materials, and web-based tools (see Chapter 6). In order to analyse such interdependencies the general model represented in Figure 5.2 will be tested. In particular, the influence of the motivations and the characteristics of the acquired material on the Internet tools choice will be analysed. Moreover, results obtained through the adoption of each tool will be also tested.

The operationalization, validity, and reliability of these constructs is discussed in Chapter 6. In particular, motivations, the dimensions characterizing the acquired material and results will be discussed in Section 6.2, while the Internet tools have already been described (see also Chapter 2). The relations among these constructs will then be tested in Section 6.5.

5.3   The Market-Vertical Alliance Divergence

The third research question addresses the key topic concerning the implications on customer-supplier relationships related to the Internet adoption. As described in Chapter 2, there are a number of contributions stressing the aspect related to market efficiency, thus hypothesizing an overall shift towards arm's length relationships. Some others focus their attention on integration and collaboration aspects.

Considerations illustrated by these previous studies, case studies evidence, and inquiries among experts delineate, in reality, a progressive divergence between markets and vertical alliances: the two typologies of relationship and the behavior of people involved are becoming more and more different.

On the one hand, it is possible to find cases where arm's length transactions are exasperated through the use of electronic auctions, or, even more, consolidated alliances have been destroyed to pursue purchasing cost reduction (e.g. Grapes). On the other hand collaborative partnerships are emphasized thanks to visibility and collaboration tools offered by the technology (e.g. Smart Technologies).

As a matter of fact, such divergence is evident and can be explained by the opportunity offered by web-based technologies to shift the trade-off efforts-integration into customer-supplier relationship as illustrated in Figure 5.3.

A trade-off exists between the efforts invested into the relationship and the level of integration obtained: the higher the efforts the higher the level of integration.

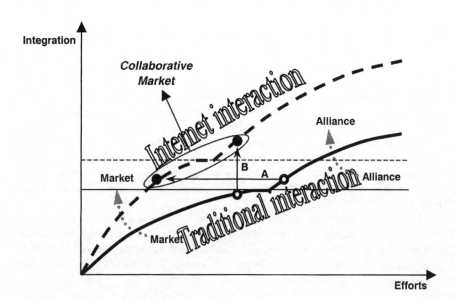

Figure 5.3 Efforts-Integration trade-off shift

The level of integration or coordination can be measured through a number of variables found in literature, essentially referring to the scheme proposed in Figure 1.11. Such scheme differentiates between scope of collaboration and depth of collaboration. In particular, variables explaining the level of integration or coordination are divided into operational ones and technological ones. On the operational perspectives, higher coordination is provided by inventory levels visibility, final customer's demand signals visibility, production plans sharing, or even collaborative inventory management practices, production planning and demand forecasting. On the technological perspective, higher coordination is provided by technical drawings visibility, prototype tests visibility, or even collaborative product and process design, and technology co-development (for more details see also Chapter 2, Section 2.3).

The efforts required to manage the relationship are not widely studied in literature (Monczka et al., 1998; Moore, 1998); however, from literature and empirical evidence some variables emerged: time and resources spent into sustaining the relationship, costs in Information and Communication Technology, costs sustained for joint team working, and investments in specific tangible assets (e.g. dedicated plants). This last dimension contributes to increase switching costs once established a vertical alliance.

The horizontal segments in the figure represent such switching costs. When companies start to establish a vertical alliance, they face initial investments that are specific to the relationship. These investments are necessary to start an effective and efficient relationship and are considered as switching costs when the customer and the supplier want to terminate the alliance.

Literature contributions in customer-supplier relationships can be read as an attempt to find ways of managing such trade-off; most of them consider the object of the transaction or the supply market characteristics as the main driving factors in choosing the position a company should assume on the trade-off curve (see for example Kraljic's contribution in Section 1.2). If the object of the transaction and the supply market complexity do not make necessary a high level of integration, it is not worthwhile to spend a lot of efforts trying to build a vertical alliance (Figure 5.4).

The Internet has shifted such trade-off allowing either higher levels of integration with the same level of efforts or lower efforts with the same level of integration. Moreover, the maximum level of collaboration can be even higher than before thanks to the new technological platforms, which allow higher information richness and integration (e.g. CPFR applications, mobile team work infrastructures).

In this situation the border between market and vertical alliance has (see the 'A' arrows in Figures 5.3 and 5.4). As a matter of fact, where companies decided to build a long-term alliance to reach the desired level of efficiency and effectiveness and because of the high transaction costs on the market, today it is possible to improve the procurement process with any other firm thanks to standard communication protocols and the lower transaction costs. This trend has already been foreseen by Malone (Malone et al., 1987, 1989) and would support an overall shift of customer-supplier relationships towards markets.

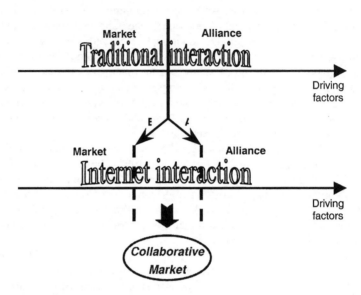

Figure 5.4 Markets and vertical alliances divergence

However, another surprising effect of the Internet can be hypothesized (see the 'B' arrows in Figures 5.3 and 5.4). Where companies adopted market mechanisms with components or sub-assemblies for which they would have liked to have a more efficient and effective integrated procurement process, but the investment-gap between market and vertical alliance did not make worthwhile further integration, today those companies can build possible alliances without higher efforts into the relationship.

The consequences of the previous considerations are clearly shown in the figures. The distinction between markets and vertical alliances has been exasperated by the twofold role of the Internet (arrows 'A' and 'B'). The effect of this divergence is the possible creation of a new kind of relationship. This typology of relationship is called in this work *'Collaborative Market'*. Such model of relationship will be fully described in Chapter 7, after testing the hypotheses supporting the emergence of the model itself.

Summarizing these considerations, three main propositions can be drawn:

H2:   A trade-off exists between the efforts invested into supporting the customer-supplier relationship and the level of integration reached within the relationship itself.

H3:   *This efforts-integration trade-off can be shifted through the Internet adoption in the relationship.*

H4:   *The shift of the curve leads to the divergence between markets and vertical alliances, opening opportunities to a new typology of relationship: the Collaborative Markets.*

This three hypotheses will be tested by operationalizing a trade-off model including the two main mentioned concepts: efforts and integration. Such dimensions will be measured before and after the Internet adoption. In particular, operationalization, validity, and reliability will be discussed in Section 6.2. The tested model will then be described in Section 6.6.

Chapter 6

Survey Analysis

6.1 Survey Design

In the previous chapter, main hypotheses underlying the answers to research questions have been formulated. Within this chapter, such hypotheses will be carefully tested. In order to proceed, a survey analysis has been performed to measure, collect, and analyse variables related to the aspects discussed in Chapter 5. In particular, as far as research hypotheses are concerned, relevant variables are: the acquired material and the supply market characteristics, the description of the relationship with suppliers before and after the Internet adoption, the motivations driving to the adoption of the Internet, the adopted Internet tool, and, finally, the obtained performances.

Questionnaire Definition

Different aspects and problems faced when formulating a questionnaire have been considered in the definition of the survey tool (see Section 3.3).

Firstly, appropriate questions were chosen to collect data in order to build reliable and valid measures (see Section 6.2 for reliability and validity tests). Of course, questions were based on propositions formulated in Chapter 5. The unit of analysis, in each case, was a specific acquired material and the relative relationship with the supplier.

Within such choice, the first proposition (*H1*) required to measure what motivations drove the company to adopt web-based tools, whereas the last three (*H2, H3, H4*) required to measure what levels of integration and efforts were in place in the selected relationship. As far as these last three propositions were concerned, the survey design was supposed to ask companies information about two different situations in time: before and after the Internet adoption. Therefore, although this is not a proper longitudinal study, as data are not physically gathered in different points of time, the collection provides longitudinal evidence. This kind of survey design is named *impure panel design* (Bailey, 1995) or *time-ordered cross-sectional design* (Menard, 1991).

The considered four propositions refer to research questions 1 and 3. As far as research question 2 is concerned, the questionnaire aimed at collecting information about the use of specific web-based tools (Section 2.3).

All the items in the questionnaire were derived, where possible, from other studies in literature, evidence, and examples; for example, variables measuring the integration with supplier are those found in literature analysing customer-supplier collaboration (Chapter 1). Where items were not available from literature, for example in the case of efforts required to manage the relationship, evidence collected from case analysis supported the choice of questions. However, as already said, all measures were tested for reliability and validity. All data have been collected across the questionnaire sections both through continuous scales (where possible) and discrete scales using Likert like five-item scales.

Questions related to the same aspect or similar aspects were gathered together in order to facilitate the compiling process; this lead to the definition of five sections (see below). Moreover, the design was as lean and simple as possible in order to make the answers even simpler.

Once defined the questions and their design, the overall questionnaire was discussed with four academic professors and experts in the field. From the interviews some problems related to content and format emerged. Such problems were solved modifying appropriately the tool.

The final draft was then sent to eight respondents in order to conduct the pilot test. Within this test respondents were asked to highlight difficulties faced in answering the questions; as a result some comprehension problems emerged. The phrasing of some questions was then further modified.

At the end of this process, after the selection of the sample (see Section 6.1), the tool was ready to be sent.

Questionnaires were sent to purchasing managers and agents from the selected sample in three different ways. Some companies received a letter of presentation of the project and the questionnaire itself through snail mail. Some others received the material through electronic mail. Finally, the questionnaire was uploaded on a web site and selected companies were sent an electronic message with invitation to participate by visiting the web site. With some of the potential respondents a follow-up was done in order to increase the number of responses. In all the cases, personalized letters had been sent.

The questionnaire consisted of five sections (see the Appendix): general information about the company, description of the material, description of the relationship before and after the Internet adoption, the Internet adoption, performances improvement.

Section A: General information about the company
This first section aims at identifying the general contingent characteristics of the company in terms of revenues, number of employees, purchases amount, and globalization of both sales and purchases. Moreover the company's industry, market and position in the supply chain have been investigated. Companies that had not adopted the Internet yet were asked to fill-in only this first section.

The general aim of this section was to provide a characterization of the sample and to analyse the influence of contingent variables on the Internet adoption.

Section B: Description of the material
Companies adopting the Internet were asked to proceed in the compilation.[1]
The second section refers to the selection of a material for which the
company introduced the Internet in the procurement process.

The questions asked for information both on product characteristics and on
supply market, on the basis of what was studied in Chapter 1. The aim of
this section was to provide an exhaustive description of the material, in
order to relate it with selected web-based tools and company's motivations
in the use of the Internet (research questions 1 and 2).

*Section C: Description of the relationship before and after the Internet
adoption*
The third section was aimed at understanding the characteristics of the
relationship with the supplier supplying the material described in the
previous section. Same questions were asked in relation to the situation
before and after the Internet adoption. Gathered information referred to the
length of the relationship, the amount of purchases, the kind of information
shared, the level of operational and technological collaboration, and the
efforts required to manage the selected relationship.

The description of the characteristics of the relationship before and after the
Internet adoption was used to study the effects and the consequences of
such change (research question 3).

Section D: The Internet adoption
The fourth section collected information about the Internet adoption. In
particular it considers the kind of tool or tools selected in the procurement
process of the described material, for how long the company has been using
such tools, and the goals set.

This section was aimed at identifying the relation among the choice of web-
based tools, the features of the material and the goals set by the company
(research question 2).

Section E: Performances improvement
Finally, the last section refers to performances improvement. According to
goals identified in the previous section, companies were asked to measure
the level of satisfaction for each objective.

The aim of this fifth section was to analyse the correlation among adopted
tools and perceived performances.

---

[1] See Section 6.1 describing the sampling process to understand the motivation driving
towards such questionnaire design.

Sample Description

Considering the general and cross-industry objectives of the research, the sample selection has considered companies across different industries. This choice has been driven also by the fact that relatively few companies really already adopt web-based tools in the procurement process; therefore pursuing a study focused on a specific industry could have led to very few available cases, thus making difficult a statistical analysis. However, any pure services industry was excluded from the sample, as materials procurement is not a primary concern.

Therefore, ISIC definitions (International Standard Industrial Classification) and the first two digits of selected industry codes are the following:

- construction (15-17);
- manufacturing (20-39);
- wholesale trade (50-51);
- retail trade (52-59).

Using these codes as filter, a broad database containing over 15.000 companies operating in the U.S. was built starting from data provided by three major North American associations: NAPM (National Associations of Purchasing Management), CLM (Council of Logistics Management), and PMAB (Purchasing Management Association of Boston). The distribution of companies across industries was approximately the same in all the three initial databases, therefore the overall sample could be considered as representative of the industrial population in the United States.

Table 6.1 Sent questionnaires and responses in July-August 2001

Initial selection	**1,500**	-
Wrong addresses	183	12.2%
Second selection	**208**	
Wrong addresses	27	13.0%
Total sample	**1,498**	-
Responses	185	**12.3%**
Good responses	**162**	10.8%

As already mentioned in the previous section, the questionnaire was designed in order to collect specific information regarding the object of the transaction and the relationship with the supplier from each company adopting the Internet. More precisely, these pieces of information were asked both before and after the Internet introduction. This sampling and questionnaire procedure was preferred to the one consisting in analysing and comparing companies adopting the Internet with companies not adopting it for a precise reason. This latter choice might have introduced bias in the sample, with the reasonable risk of comparing companies adopting the Internet, which probably are the most innovative and best performers on the market generally leading in terms of best practices, with companies not adopting the Internet, which probably are not the best in the market in any sense. The research wanted to study motivations and effects of the Internet adoption *ceteris paribus*, in order not to bias the results of the analyses; the best way to obtain *ceteris paribus* conditions is to compare the same set of companies before and after the Internet adoption.

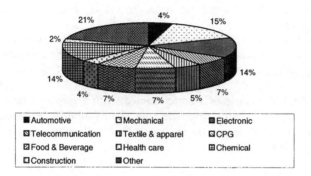

Figure 6.1 Sample industries

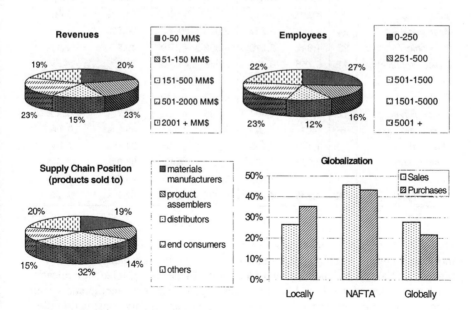

Figure 6.2 Sample description

1,500 companies were selected from the broad database; the number of companies for each industry has been selected through a stratification process on industrial sectors. Within each industry, a random selection was performed. As part of contacts had wrong addresses, a second number of cases were selected (Table 6.1).

Some of them were contacted twice in order to complete missing answers. In very few cases and only for continuous variables (e.g. revenues, employees) it was necessary to deal with missing values. In such situations missing answers were replaced with the average of the total sample, according to a standard procedure used to replace missing values (Norusis, 1993a). This is a slight approximation, but allows performing the analysis on a larger set of data, thus increasing the significance of results.

As far as non-respondents are concerned, in the big majority of cases, they replied to the letter of participation stating their interest in the research, but saying that company policies forbade them to divulge any kind of information (privacy concerns).

A total of 1,498 companies were contacted, with a response rate of 12.3 per cent (185 responses). Finally, after the data quality filtering process, 162 good responses have been received and analysed. Data collection refers to the period July and August 2001.

Table 6.2 Cross-industry perspective

Industry	N	Revenues (MM$)		Employees		Purchases / Revenues	
		Mean	St.Dev.	Mean	St.Dev.	Mean	St.Dev.
Automotive	7	10,819	9,110	77,757	97,405	61.9%	5.4%
Mechanical	24	1,507	3,287	8,073	20,477	50.5%	16.1%
Electronic	23	1,847	3,716	4,398	8,679	49.9%	18.1%
Telecommunication	11	5,755	8,362	31,990	43,419	54.5%	14.5%
Textile & Apparel	8	2,715	4,180	3,513	3,602	55.3%	4.4%
CPG	12	665	733	3,592	4,369	53.8%	17.2%
Food & Beverage	12	1,055	1,407	3,736	4,552	47.7%	19.4%
Health care	6	401	292	2,810	1,771	48.8%	6.7%
Chemical	22	1,174	2,163	3,291	6,955	54.6%	7.1%
Construction	4	2,273	2,603	18,793	22,453	57.0%	11.3%
Other	33	539	1,003	3,175	6,732	48.5%	13.4%
Total	**162**	**1,945**	**4,239**	**9,731**	**28,882**	**51.7%**	**14.2%**

The 162 North American companies are spread across different industries as shown in Figure 6.1. The largest number came from the mechanical industry (15 per cent), followed by chemical and electronic (14 per cent), telecommunication, consumer packaged goods and food and beverage (7 per cent), textile and apparel (5 per cent), health care and automotive (4 per cent), and finally construction (2 per cent). Such proportions reflect the initial population ones. A rather conspicuous

number of them (21 per cent) are classified as *other* in the classification obtained by the union of the three initial contacts sources. As a matter of fact, the initial population presented a similar proportion (24 per cent).

Other characteristics describing the sample are shown in Table 6.2. The sample distribution by size, in terms of revenues and number of employees, is quite various. There are cases of companies with less than 50 MM$ revenues (20 per cent) and cases with more than 2000 MM$ (19 per cent). Some companies hire less than 250 employees (27 per cent) and some of them hire more than 5000 people (22 per cent). From these figures, it is clear that the analysis has mainly focused on medium-large companies, typical representation of the U.S. reality.

A large number of firms sell their products to distributors (32 per cent), followed by those selling products to materials manufacturers (19 per cent), to end consumers (15 per cent), to product assemblers (14 per cent). Some of the respondents (20 per cent) had not recognized themselves into this classification.

Considering the sample level of globalization, most of companies (46 per cent) sell most of their products in the NAFTA (North American Free Trade Agreement), some of them to local markets (27 per cent), and the others (28 per cent) sell their products worldwide. The situation is similar analysing the purchase volume proportions; most of companies acquire most of their materials from the NAFTA market (43 per cent), a rather large number of them acquire materials from local markets (35 per cent), finally, some of them acquire material from the global market (22 per cent).

Figure 6.4 provides a detailed perspective of size, both in terms of revenues and number of employees, and material purchases, as percentage of revenues, in the sample across industries. The table shows that the largest companies are in the automotive and telecommunication industries. It is interesting to notice that textile & apparel industry has similar revenues to construction industry, but the number of employees is much lower. Smallest companies are in the health care industry. However, standard deviation figures show how much the data are scattered.

The sample ratio purchases over revenues is 51.7 per cent on average. Food and beverage companies are those buying the least (47.7 per cent), while in the automotive industry such ratio is the highest (61.9 per cent). In this case standard deviations are lower, meaning that mean values are quite good representatives of reality.

Constructs Validity and Reliability

Once data have been collected, it was necessary to test constructs validity and reliability (see Section 3.3). The first step of the analysis consisted in the reduction of the number of variables considered in order to simplify the description and the understanding of phenomena, by creating valid and reliable measures. This task was performed through a series of *factor analyses* followed by related *reliability analyses* (O'Leary-Kelly and Vokurka, 1998).

The idea of factor analysis is obtaining few factors/components, each of which describing a set of dimensions/variables grouped according to their mutual correlations. These few factors allow the researcher to describe the cases in a more appropriate way, and most of all, explorative and confirmatory factor analyses provide evidence for construct and content validity (see Section 3.3).

Since the goal of factor analysis is to obtain valid factors that help explain the correlations among variables, these must be related to each other for the factor model to be appropriate. *Bertlett's test of sphericity* was used to test the hypothesis that the correlation matrix in each case was an identity matrix. As illustrated in the tables in Section 6.2, this hypothesis was always rejected.

Another indicator that needs to be tested before proceeding with the proper factor analysis is the *Kaiser-Meyer-Olkin (KMO) measure*. If variables share common factors, the partial correlation coefficients between pairs of variables should be small when the linear effects of the others are eliminated. If the KMO measure is approximately equal to 1 then the partial correlations are approximately equal to 0. In all the cases values were higher than 0.6 and accepted (Norusis, 1993c).

The main factors were then extracted through the Principal Component method using a varimax rotation in order to distinguish and understand the dimensions more clearly. The number of factors was determined according to the cumulative percentage of variance explained, the change of the slope in the *scree plots* (mainly considering factors with eigenvalues higher than 1; Norusis, 1993c), the correlation among variables, and the interpretability of the resulting factors themselves. Variables presenting either factor loadings lower than 0.4 or similar factor loading values in more factors were excluded from the analysis (Fullerton and McWatters, 2001).

The resulting components were then analysed in terms of scale and construct reliability, measuring the Cronbach's Alpha coefficient among the grouped variables. The factors presenting low values of Alpha were further split until a good coefficient was obtained. The Alpha's threshold value was 0.6 (Fullerton and McWatters, 2001).

The overall results of such constructs validity and reliability analyses are shown in Section 6.2.

6.2   Constructs Analysis

As explained in Section 6.1, the questionnaire consisted of 5 sections; the reduction of dimensions and constructs validity and reliability analyses were performed for the following ones:

B.   Description of the material
C.   Description of the relationship before and after the Internet adoption
D.   The Internet adoption
E.   Performances improvement

As explained in Section 6.1, principal factors have been found within each of these questionnaire sections (see results below). The factors obtained through such validity and reliability analyses were then measured for each case using the following weighted average equation:

E1. $$F_{kj} = \sum_{i=1}^{V} \frac{FL_{ij}}{\sum_{n=1}^{V} FL_{nj}} X_{ki}$$

where:

F_{kj}	is the value of the factor j for the case k;
V	is the number of total variables constituting the factor;
FL_{ij} (FL_{nj})	is the factor loading of the variable i (n) for the factor j;
X_{ki}	is the value of the variable i for the case k.

The factor values might also be measured through a simple arithmetic average of factor loadings; equation *E1* aims at weighting differently the variables within each factor, according to their importance in describing the factor itself.

These principal factors were then used in subsequent analyses.

Section B: Variables Describing the Material

In the questionnaire the characteristics of the selected procured material were described by the following variables:

- *nature of material (indirect/direct)*
- *frequency of the purchase*
- *purchase volume*
- *percentage of the cost*
- *relevance to the product*
- *internal complexity*
- *process complexity*
- *novelty*

- *descriptive complexity*
- *customization*
- *specific investments*
- *number of potential suppliers*
- *number of usual suppliers*
- *suppliers' power*
- *competition among suppliers*

The variables *purchase volume, number of potential suppliers*, and *number of usual suppliers* were normalized on a 1-5 scale before running the factor extraction, in particular the *purchase volume* was considered as percentage of the total purchases. Furthermore, the *number of potential suppliers'* scale was inverted in order to explain the results more clearly. In Table 6.3 the results of the factor analysis are shown.

The *frequency of the purchase* was excluded´from the analysis because its factor loadings were low in every component. Looking at the data, most of the purchases were occasional or recurrent, and this does not seem to influence any factor. Also *competition among suppliers* and *number of usual suppliers* presented very low factor loadings and do not contribute to explain the variance of the sample.

As far as *internal, process,* and *descriptive complexities* are concerned, they presented significant values both for material relevance and for material criticality. For this reason, they were excluded from the analysis, obtaining factors as orthogonal as possible in order to make themselves more explainable and to avoid multicollinearity problems in subsequent analyses.

From the analysis three main factors describing the purchased material emerged: material relevance, material criticality, supply market complexity.

Table 6.3 Factor analysis for purchased material characteristics

KMO and Bartlett's Test

Kaiser-Meyer-Olkin Measure of Sampling Adequacy		.671
Bartlett's Test of Sphericity	Approx. Chi-Square	379.712
	df	45
	Sig.	.000

Purchased material variables	Factor 1 Material Relevance	Factor 2 Material Criticality	Factor 3 Supply market complexity
Percentage of the cost	.890		
Nature of material (Indirect/direct)	.802		
Relevance to the product	.787		
Purchase volume	.715		
Novelty		.888	
Descriptive complexity		.781	
Specific investments		.732	
Customization		.727	
Suppliers' power			.934
Number of potential suppliers (inv.)			.922
Eigenvalue	3.845	1.865	1.729
Variance explained	38.45%	18.65%	17.29%
Cronbach's Alpha	.73	.81	.61

Extraction Method: Principal Component Analysis. Rotation Method: Varimax with Kaiser Normalization. Total variance explained: 74.39%.

Material relevance
This factor describes the relevance of the purchase in different terms. First of all, it considers the percentage of the product cost covered by the material; the nature of the purchase influences this factor as well: the fact that the material is direct to the final product contributes to increase its relevance. Also the impact of the purchased material to the features, performances and key characteristics of the final product is included in this component. Finally, the higher the purchase volume the more the material is relevant for the company.

All these variables support and draw the concept of strategic importance of the purchase mentioned in Chapter 1 (Kraljic, 1983; Olsen and Ellram, 1997).

Material criticality
This measure describes the degree of specificity and the difficulty in finding the acquired material. The more the material is new and innovative, the more it is difficult to be found. Also the high descriptive complexity makes the material a critical purchase. The specificity of the investments needed by the supplier to supply the material and the efforts required to customize it are all variables increasing the criticality of the purchase as well.
All these dimensions gather some of the contributions analysed in Chapter 1 (Williamson, 1983; Malone et al., 1987; De Maio and Maggiore, 1992). In particular this factor supports the evidence of a sort of correlation between the specificity of the investments and the descriptive complexity as hypothesized in literature.

Supply market complexity
Finally, this last factor describes the relationship supply market. It includes the trade power of the suppliers and the concentration of the supply market: the more the market is concentrated and the higher is suppliers' power the higher is the supply market complexity.
The general concept of supply market complexity provided by Kraljic, Olsen and Ellram consisted of a sort of union of these two last factors: material criticality and supply market complexity.

In Table 6.4 the descriptive statistics of these three factors are provided for the considered sample. From the data, it is possible to see that the sample has adopted the Internet in the procurement of materials where the supply market complexity was rather high (mean equal to 3.79).

Table 6.4 Descriptive statistics of the factors describing the material

	Min.	Max.	Mean	Std. Dev.
Material relevance	1.00	4.64	2.48	1.25
Material criticality	1.00	4.53	2.19	0.98
Supply market complexity	1.00	5.00	3.79	1.33

Section C: Variables Describing the Relationship

The relationship was described both in terms of characteristics and in terms of efforts required to manage the interaction between the two companies.

Characteristics of the relationship
In the questionnaire the characteristics of the selected relationship before and after the Internet adoption were described by the following variables:

- *length of the relationship*
- *length of the contracts*
- *volume of the purchases*
- *arm's length transaction*
- *marketing activities*
- *order tracking/tracing*
- *production information*
- *inventory information*
- *product information*

- *JIT coordination*
- *collaborative planning and forecasting*
- *VMI*
- *consignment stock*
- *collaborative product design*
- *collaborative process and technology development*

The variables *length of the relationship*, *length of the contracts*, and *volume of the purchases* were normalized on a scale 1-5 before running the factor extraction, in particular the *volume of purchases* was considered as percentage of the total purchases of the selected material. Furthermore, the *arm's length* scale was inverted in order to explain the results more clearly.

Due to the structure and the purpose of the questionnaire, for each variable two values were available: before the Internet adoption and after the Internet adoption. For this reason, two factor analyses were conducted and then a summary table was worked-out (Table 6.5). In this table the KMO measure, the Bartlett's test, the eigenvalues, the variance explained, and the Cronbach's Alphas are shown for both the analyses and the resulting factor loadings are calculated through the following equation:

$$\textbf{E2.} \qquad FL_{ij} = \frac{FL_{ij}(before) + FL_{ij}(after)}{2}$$

where:

FL_{ij} is the resulting factor loading of the variable i for the factor j reported in the table;

$FL_{ij}(before)$ is the factor loading of the variable i for the factor j resulting from the factor analysis obtained from the data before the Internet adoption;

$FL_{ij}(after)$ is the factor loading of the variable i for the factor j resulting from the factor analysis obtained from the data after the Internet adoption.

Adopting equation *E2* is possible because the two analyses, before and after the Internet adoption, presented very similar results. Therefore the three obtained factors are consistent and reliable in both cases (see Table 6.5).

The *arm's length transaction* was excluded from the analysis because its factor loadings were low in every component. This variable was therefore used only to cross-check the presence of possible incompatibilities in the answers (e.g. an arm's length relationship with collaboration activities in place); for the results of this cross-checking see Section 6.6 (Table 6.18). *Length of contracts* and *volume of purchases* presented low factor loadings and appeared within different factors in the two analyses; for these reasons they were excluded from the table as well.

As far as *order tracking and tracing* is concerned, it presented significant values both for operational integration and for information sharing. That is quite reasonable, as in both cases, order tracking is a basic aspect. For this reason, it was excluded from the analysis, obtaining factors as orthogonal as possible in order to make themselves more explainable and to avoid multicollinearity problems in subsequent analyses.

From the analysis three main factors describing the relationship emerged: operational integration, technological integration, information sharing. The empirical evidence supports the classification describing the characteristics of a vertical alliance derived in Chapter 1. It partially recalls the concepts of scope and depth of the relationship.

Operational integration
This component describes the relationship in terms of operational processes and activities jointly performed by the two companies. They consist of just in time coordination in production and materials management, collaborative planning and forecasting, practices of vendor managed inventory and consignment stock. All these variables recall the same concept of operational integration mentioned in Chapter 1 (Spina in De Maio and Maggiore, 1992).

Furthermore, from the analysis, also another dimension seems to contribute in building a collaborative operational relationship: collaboration in marketing activities. Although the corresponding factor loading is the lowest, jointly performed promotions, advertisement and co-branding practices contribute in determining the level of operational collaboration.

Technological integration
This second main factor describes the relationship in terms of development processes jointly performed by the two companies. Collaborative design in product development and collaboration in new processes and technologies development are typical practices determining the level of technological collaboration. As for the previous factor, all these dimensions support evidence from the literature described in Chapter 1 (Spina in De Maio and Maggiore, 1992).

Not surprisingly this kind of relationship is characterized also by a quite long history (the Cronbach's Alpha would be 0.83 and 0.82 respectively measured before and after the Internet adoption if the variable *length of the relationship* were included). Collaborative development implies a high level of knowledge sharing and therefore a high level of trust between the two parties; this takes time and requires long-term relationships. As a matter of fact, the adoption of the Internet cannot influence the length of the relationship, as it is related only to time. For this reason, this dimension was excluded from the analysis because it would not have explained the variance of the sample before and after the Internet adoption.

Table 6.5 Factor analysis for relationship characteristics

KMO and Bartlett's Test for data before the Internet adoption

Kaiser-Meyer-Olkin Measure of Sampling Adequacy		.638
Bartlett's Test of Sphericity	Approx. Chi-Square	480.016
	df	105
	Sig.	.000

KMO and Bartlett's Test for data after the Internet adoption

Kaiser-Meyer-Olkin Measure of Sampling Adequacy		.701
Bartlett's Test of Sphericity	Approx. Chi-Square	456.028
	df	105
	Sig.	.000

Relationship variables	Factor 1 Operational integration	Factor 2 Technological integration	Factor 3 Information sharing
Consignment stock	.778		
JIT coordination	.772		
Collaborative planning and forecasting	.735		
VMI	.713		
Marketing activities	.575		
Collaborative product design		.901	
Collaborative pss and tech. develop.		.885	
(Length of the relationship)²		(.691)	
Inventory information			.764
Product information			.617
Production information			.550
Eigenvalue before the Internet	4.448	1.828	1.692
Eigenvalue after the Internet	5.120	1.762	1.293
Variance explained before the Internet	31.66%	19.19%	11.28%
Variance explained after the Internet	36.14%	16.75%	10.62%
Cronbach's Alpha before the Internet	.76	.91 (.83)	.70
Cronbach's Alpha after the Internet	.75	.89 (.82)	.78

Extraction Method: Principal Component Analysis. Rotation Method: Varimax with Kaiser Normalization. Total variance explained before the Internet: 62.13%. Total variance explained after the Internet: 63.51%.

---

[2] This variable would not explain the variance of the sample before and after the Internet adoption because the length of the relationship does not change when adopting the Internet. For this reason it was excluded from the analysis. See the paragraph titled 'Technological integration' for more details.

Information sharing
Finally, this last factor describes the amount of information shared between the two companies. This dimension does not imply collaboration as sharing the decision making process, but consists of providing visibility to the other party. Such visibility could be in terms of sharing information about inventory levels, about technical specifications of the product, and about production planning schedules.

In Table 6.6 the descriptive statistics of these three factors are provided for the considered sample. For a detailed discussion of this table and the analysis of variances, see Section 6.6.

Table 6.6 Descriptive statistics of the factors describing the relationship

	Before the Internet				After the Internet			
	Min.	Max.	Mean	Std. Dev.	Min.	Max.	Mean	Std. Dev.
Operational integration	1.00	3.98	1.82	0.68	1.00	4.33	2.25	0.91
Technological integration	1.00	4.00	1.69	0.85	1.00	4.00	1.84	1.00
Information sharing	1.00	4.00	2.26	0.74	1.00	4.81	2.95	1.11

Efforts required to manage the relationship
In the questionnaire the efforts required to manage the selected relationship before and after the Internet adoption were described by the following variables:

- *time and resources*
- *ICT costs*

- *joint team working costs*
- *investments on assets*

As in the previous case, for each variable two values were available: before the Internet adoption and after the Internet adoption. For this reason, two factor analyses were conducted and then a summary table was worked-out (Table 6.7). In this table the KMO measure, the Bartlett's test, the eigenvalues, the variance explained, and the Cronbach's Alphas are shown for both the analyses and the resulting factor loadings are calculated through the equation *E2*.

From the analysis only one main factor describing the efforts required to manage the relationship emerged.

Efforts
This unique component describes the efforts in terms of costs in information and communication technology, costs sustained for the organization of joint team work sessions, investments in tangible assets within the relationship from both the company and the supplier, and, finally, time and resources spent to sustain and coordinate the relationship.

In Table 6.8 the descriptive statistics of this factor are provided for the considered sample. For a detailed discussion of this table and the analysis of variance, see Section 6.6.

Table 6.7 Factor analysis for efforts required in the relationship

KMO and Bartlett's Test for data before the Internet adoption

Kaiser-Meyer-Olkin Measure of Sampling Adequacy		.639
	Approx. Chi-Square	58.8826
Bartlett's Test of Sphericity	df	6
	Sig.	.000

KMO and Bartlett's Test for data after the Internet adoption

Kaiser-Meyer-Olkin Measure of Sampling Adequacy		.748
	Approx. Chi-Square	115.9368
Bartlett's Test of Sphericity	df	6
	Sig.	.000

Efforts required to manage the relationship	Factor 1 Efforts
ICT costs	.844
Joint team working costs	.831
Assets	.757
Time and resources	.596
Eigenvalue before the Internet	2.382
Eigenvalue after the Internet	2.623
Variance explained before the Internet	58.05%
Variance explained after the Internet	65.58%
Cronbach's Alpha before the Internet	.67
Cronbach's Alpha after the Internet	.82

Extraction Method: Principal Component Analysis. Total variance explained before the Internet: 58.05%. Total variance explained after the Internet: 65.58%.

Table 6.8 Descriptive statistics of the efforts required by the relationship

	Before the Internet				After the Internet			
	Min.	Max.	Mean	Std. Dev.	Min.	Max.	Mean	Std. Dev.
Efforts in the relationship	1.00	3.75	2.38	0.74	1.00	4.08	2.05	0.74

Section D: Variables Describing the Internet Adoption

The Internet adoption within the relationship was described both in terms of web-based tools and in terms of objectives. As far as web-based tools are not scales, but categorical variables (in particular binary variables), they have been analysed only in terms of content validity (see Section 3.3). Moreover, as objectives items are mirrors to performances, such analysis was performed in parallel to the one on performances, in order to measure both objectives and performances with mirror items. In order to pursue such objectives, a series of exploratory and confirmatory analyses has been carried out (O'Leary-Kelly and Vokurka, 1998).

Objectives
In the questionnaire the objectives pursued through the Internet adoption were described by the following variables:

- *reduce searching costs*
- *reduce negotiation costs*
- *reduce operative costs*
- *reduce material cost*
- *improve internal efficiency*
- *reduce inventory costs*

- *improve delivery performance*
- *improve quality*
- *reduce stock-outs*
- *reduce TTM*
- *enhance innovation*

The summary table of the factor analysis is provided in Table 6.9.

From the analysis three main factors describing the objectives pursued through the Internet emerged: reduce procurement costs, improve effectiveness, and improve process efficiency.

Reduce procurement costs
This first component refers to part of the variables considered in the transaction costs theory (Coase, 1937; Williamson, 1979; Watson, 2000). It describes the total cost sustained by the company to acquire the material, in terms of suppliers' search and selection, costs of negotiation and evaluation, and the proper purchase cost of the material. It does not include the operative or proper transaction management costs (see Table 1.2 in Chapter 1), as they are considered within the process efficiency component (see below).

Improve effectiveness
The second main factor refers to the improvement of process effectiveness both in terms of quality and service. In particular, it consists of new products time to market reduction, innovation enhancement, and quality improvement; all of which are related to a general concept of quality and innovation. Furthermore, this dimension includes also the reduction of stock-outs as a priority; this aspect is directly related to the level of service to the final customer.

Improve process efficiency
Finally, this last factor considers the improvement of internal processes efficiency. This priority regards the reduction of costs related to the internal ordering process, inventories, and leaning and automating most of the activities. Also the component of transaction costs related to proper

transaction management process (e.g. control of shipment, control of quality, payments, possible compliance or breach of contract (Watson, 2000)) is included within this dimension. Finally, process efficiency refers to the improvement of supplier's delivery performance in terms of reliability, speed, and flexibility.

Table 6.9 Factor analysis for objectives

KMO and Bartlett's Test

Kaiser-Meyer-Olkin Measure of Sampling Adequacy		0.702
Bartlett's Test of Sphericity	Approx. Chi-Square	300.816
	df	45
	Sig.	.000

Objectives	Factor 1 Reduce procurement costs	Factor 2 Improve effectiveness	Factor 3 Improve process efficiency
Reduce negotiation costs	.904		
Reduce material costs	.855		
Reduce searching costs	.769		
Reduce TTM		.858	
Reduce stock-outs		.760	
Enhance innovation		.693	
Improve quality		.534	
Improve internal efficiency			.827
Reduce operative costs			.773
Reduce inventory costs			.667
Improve delivery performance			.649
Eigenvalue	3.104	2.732	1.283
Variance explained	31.05%	27.32%	12.83%
Cronbach's Alpha	.83	.73	.69

Extraction Method: Principal Component Analysis. Rotation Method: Varimax with Kaiser Normalization. Total variance explained: 71.20%.

Table 6.10 Descriptive statistics of the factors describing the objectives pursued through the Internet adoption

	Min.	Max.	Mean	Std. Dev.
Reduce procurement costs	1.00	5.00	3.33	1.09
Improve effectiveness	1.00	4.09	2.33	0.97
Improve process efficiency	1.00	5.00	3.94	0.82

In Table 6.10 the descriptive statistics of these three factors are provided for the considered sample. From the results of this analysis, it is possible to see that the main priority companies have in adopting the Internet in the procurement process is efficiency improvement, both in terms of procurement costs and in terms of process activities efficiency. The effectiveness improvement has a second role when adopting the Internet.

Section E: Variables Describing Performances

In the questionnaire the performances achieved through the Internet adoption were measured following the same variables considered as objectives:

- *searching costs reduction*
- *negotiation costs reduction*
- *operative costs reduction*
- *material cost reduction*
- *internal efficiency improvement*
- *inventory costs reduction*

- *delivery performance improvement*
- *quality improvement*
- *stock-outs reduction*
- *TTM reduction*
- *Innovation enhancement*

The summary table of the factor analysis is provided in Table 6.11.

From the analysis three main factors describing the performances achieved through the Internet adoption emerged, they recall the components resulting from the objectives analysis: effectiveness improvement, procurement costs reduction, and process efficiency improvement.

Effectiveness improvement
This first factor is the mirror image of previous process effectiveness objective on the performance side. It is related to aspects concerning the quality in general terms: reduction of time to market, innovation enhancement, and quality improvement. Moreover, this factor considers also performances related to the level of service provided to the final customer through the reduction of stock-outs.

Procurement costs reduction
As in the previous case, this second component follows the same scheme provided for the objectives. It measures performance considering the total cost sustained by the company to acquire the material, in terms of suppliers' search and selection, costs of negotiation and evaluation, and the proper purchase cost of the material. The variable *operative* or proper *transaction management costs* has been excluded from the analysis because of its factor loadings (see above).

Process efficiency improvement
Finally, this last factor measures the improvement of internal processes efficiency. Similarly to what concerns the objectives analysis, this performance regards the reduction of costs related to the internal ordering and material management process. Process efficiency also refers to the improvement of supplier's delivery performance in terms of reliability,

speed, and flexibility. Finally, also reduction of inventory costs and operative costs are included within this dimension.

Table 6.11 Factor analysis for performances

KMO and Bartlett's Test

Kaiser-Meyer-Olkin Measure of Sampling Adequacy		0.719
Bartlett's Test of Sphericity	Approx. Chi-Square	326.572
	df	45
	Sig.	.000

Performances	Factor 1 Effectiveness improvement	Factor 2 Procurement costs reduction	Factor 3 Process efficiency improvement
Time to market reduction	.861		
Innovation enhancement	.788		
Quality improvement	.761		
Stock-outs reduction	.586		
Negotiation costs reduction		.885	
Searching costs reduction		.820	
Material cost reduction		.810	
Internal efficiency improvement			.872
Delivery performance improvement			.780
Operative costs reduction			.631
Inventory costs reduction			.577
Eigenvalue	3.874	2.322	1.028
Variance explained	38.74%	23.22%	10.28%
Cronbach's Alpha	.81	.81	.75

Extraction Method: Principal Component Analysis. Rotation Method: Varimax with Kaiser Normalization. Total variance explained: 72.24%.

Table 6.12 Descriptive statistics of the factors describing the performances achieved through the Internet adoption

	Min.	Max.	Mean	Std. Dev.
Effectiveness improvement	1.00	4.20	2.07	0.97
Procurement costs reduction	1.00	5.00	3.06	1.03
Process efficiency improvement	1.00	5.00	3.35	1.00

In Table 6.12 the descriptive statistics of these three factors are provided for the considered sample. As shown in the figure, it is possible to see that the main performances the companies in the sample have improved through the Internet adoption regard mainly efficiency improvement, both in terms of procurement costs and in terms of process activities efficiency. The effectiveness improvement has not been considered as a major result while adopting web-based tools in the procurement process.

6.3 Contingent Drivers of the Internet Adoption in the Purchasing Process

Within the 162 considered cases, 72 of them (44.4 per cent) have adopted web-based tools in their procurement process (Figure 6.13). These companies have been using the Internet for 17.8 months on average, ranging from 3 months to 60 months experiences (reminding that collected data refer to the period July-August 2001).

Automotive, telecommunication and food and beverage industries are the ones presenting the highest percentage of adoption; while consumer packaged goods and textile and apparel industries presents the lowest percentages. However, the earliest adoptions have been found in the construction and mechanical industries (36 and 28.4 months respectively). Finally, on average, web-based tools have been slightly more used in the direct materials procurement.

Table 6.13 Internet adoption in the sample

	Sample	Internet adopters		Material		Time (months)	
	Cases	Cases	%	Direct	Indirect	Mean	St.Dev.
Automotive	7	6	85.7%	4	2	17.0	8
Mechanical	24	11	45.8%	8	3	28.4	18
Electronic	23	11	47.8%	9	2	19.4	13
Telecommunication	11	8	72.7%	6	2	14.1	9
Textile & Apparel	8	2	25.0%	2	0	12.0	0
CPG	12	2	16.7%	0	2	12.0	0
Food & Beverage	12	8	66.7%	5	3	15.4	7
Health care	6	3	50.0%	1	2	16.0	7
Chemical	22	8	36.4%	5	3	10.8	2
Construction	4	2	50.0%	0	2	36.0	0
Other	33	11	33.3%	2	9	15.2	10
Total	162	72	44.4%	42	30	17.8	12

The first part of the questionnaire collects data about general variables characterizing companies. In this section a first exploratory analysis is shown with the aim of identifying possible contingent variables driving towards the use of the Internet in the procurement process. In particular, the correlation among those variables and the Internet adoption was tested.

To pursue such aim, a logit multiple regression model was tested. Logistic regression models directly estimate the probability of an event occurring, starting from a set of independent variables. In this specific case, the dependent variable is the adoption of web-based technologies (binary variable indicating 0 for no use or 1 for use), while the independent variables are contingencies. Equation *E3* was tested:

E3. $\ln\left[\dfrac{P(Internet)_i}{P(no\ Internet)_i}\right] = \beta_0 + \beta_1 employees_i + \beta_2 revenues_i + \beta_3 \% purchases_i +$
$+ \beta_4 sales\_glob_i + \beta_5 purchases\_glob_i +$
$+ \beta_6 mktshare_i + \overline{\beta_7 industry_i} + \overline{\beta_8 sc\_position_i} + \varepsilon_i$

where:

$P(Internet)_i$	is the probability the company i adopts the Internet in procurement;
$P(no\ Internet)_i$	is the probability the company i does not adopt the Internet in procurement;
$employees_i$	is the number of employees working in company i;
$revenues_i$	is the total turnover of company i;
$\%purchases_i$	is the percentage representing the ratio purchases on sales for company i;
$sales\_glob_i$	is the level of sales globalization for company i;
$purchases\_glob_i$	is the level of purchases globalization for company i;
$mktshare_i$	is the market share in most representative products for company i;
$industry_i$	is the industry in which company i operates; this is a categorical variable, therefore it has been split in binary variables;
$sc\_position_i$	is company i position in the supply chain (in terms of which are the main customers); this also is a categorical variable, therefore it has been split in binary variables.
ε_i	is the residual term, which is assumed as normally distributed, mean zero and constant variance.

The results of the analysis are shown in Table 6.14. The overall model is quite robust, and the prediction capability is quite good (75.9 per cent). However, the Wald statistics referred to single parameters are difficult to interpret due to their statistic properties. When the absolute value of the regression coefficient becomes large, the estimated standard error is too large; this produces a Wald statistic too small leading to fail to reject the null hypothesis that the coefficient is 0, when in fact it should be rejected. In order to overcome this problem, a further number was calculated for non-significant parameters (ΔLL). Such number represents the decrease of Log Likelihood when the related variable is dropped from the model; for simplicity, variables presenting absolute values higher than 1 were considered relevant (Hauck and Donner, 1977).

Table 6.14 Logit regression model on the Internet adoption

Unrestricted model

	B	S.E.	Wald	df	Sig.	Exp(B)	ΔLL
Employees	.000	.000	4.013	1	.045	1.000	
Revenues	.000	.000	.034	1	.853	1.000	-0.017
%purchases	1.060	1.445	.538	1	.463	2.888	-0.184
Sales_glob	-.693	.889	.607	1	.436	.500	-0.158
Purchases_glob	-1.089	.969	1.263	1	.261	.337	-0.642
Mktshare	.889	.965	.849	1	.357	2.433	-0.557
Industry			7.707	10	.657		-4.421
Automotive	.807	1.821	.443	1	.503	2.241	
Mechanical	.482	.668	.521	1	.471	1.619	
Electronic	.427	.729	.343	1	.558	1.533	
Telecommunication	.934	.912	1.050	1	.306	2.545	
Textile & Apparel	-.239	1.122	.045	1	.831	.787	
CPG	-1.264	1.032	1.500	1	.221	.283	
Food & Beverage	1.316	.821	2.572	1	.109	3.730	
Health care	.349	.967	.130	1	.718	1.417	
Chemical	.249	.695	.129	1	.720	1.283	
Construction	-.766	2.152	.127	1	.722	.465	
Sc_position			4.146	4	.387		-3.717
Materials manufacturers	-.391	.723	.293	1	.589	.676	
Product assemblers	.978	.715	1.869	1	.172	2.659	
Distributors	.374	.600	.389	1	.533	1.454	
End consumers	.654	.726	.812	1	.367	1.924	
Constant	-1.410	.999	1.992	1	.158	.244	-1.022

Log Likelihood value: -83.98. Chi-square: 17.390 (8 df); sig. 0.026.

Classification Table

Cases	Predicted Internet adoption		Percentage Correct
	No	Yes	
Observed Internet adoption — No	77	13	85.6%
Observed Internet adoption — Yes	26	46	63.9%
Overall percentage correct			75.9%

The cut value is 0.5.

Analysing results, it can be asserted that any of the contingent variables explored are significant drivers of the use of the Internet in the procurement process among those considered. The number of employees presents a significant coefficient, but its value is 0.000 (exp(B)=1), meaning that the size of the company in terms of number of employees does not affect the probability the company adopts web-based technologies. Some other considerations can be drawn about industry and supply chain position. As these have been treated as categorical variables, their parameters can be compared among themselves, but not in absolute terms within the model.

As highlighted before, industries in which Internet adoption in procurement is more likely to occur are automotive, telecommunication and food & beverage; on the contrary, textile & apparel, CPG and construction industries present low probabilities of Internet adoption.

As far as the position in the supply chain is concerned, the presence of web-based tools in procurement is more likely diffused among companies selling products mostly to product assemblers or end consumers; which means mainly among manufacturers and distributors. Not surprisingly, companies at the very beginning of the supply chain (e.g. raw materials) do not have many chances, or reasons, to adopt the Internet in the procurement process.

After this first exploratory analysis, the remainder of the study is clearly based on companies adopting the Internet. Such study is aimed at testing the research hypotheses formulated in Chapter 5.

6.4   Motivations to the Internet Adoption

Section 6.2 already provides the first preliminary evidence supporting the first formulated hypothesis in Chapter 5 (*H1*). Construct validity and reliability analyses confirm the existence of three main motivations companies recognize in adopting the Internet into the procurement process (Figure 6.3): supply process efficiency, procurement costs reduction, supply process effectiveness.

In the figure, parameter estimates and 2-tailed significance levels of a simple linear regression model between collaboration and primary motivations are provided.[3] Collaboration between parties has been measured as the increment of the level of integration level (see Section 6.6) after the Internet adoption. The change might be either positive or negative. One simplified assumption within the model is a direct relation between the aim of increasing or decreasing the collaboration and the actual occurred change in terms of collaboration itself.

This result shows that the higher integration reached with the supplier is reasonably explained by the will to improve process efficiency and effectiveness, thus confirming the first hypothesis (*H1*). On the contrary, procurement costs reduction objective is not significantly correlated to the increase of collaboration between customer and supplier.

---

[3] To test the assumption of linearity among the exogenous and endogenous variables, scatter plots were reviewed. To ensure that residuals were not correlated, the Durbin-Watson statistic was calculated (Dillon and Goldstein, 1984; Maddala, 1992).

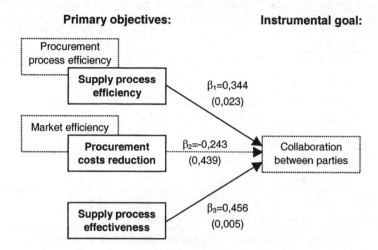

Figure 6.3 Motivations in the Internet adoption. $R^2=0.54$, F-sig.$=0.007$

6.5 Internet Tools Choice

The second research question aims at identifying which typologies of Internet tools have been adopted by companies in which situations and what are the impact on performances (Section 3.1).

The analysis considered the main web-based tools described in Chapter 2. Three main classes have been studied: the proper tool, the nature of the portal supporting the tool, and the property of the portal itself. In Figure 6.4 the percentage of adoption for each of these classifications within the sample is shown.

Evidence shows that companies use mainly transaction supportive tools, such as sell-side catalogs, liquid exchanges, and reverse auctions. However, analyses shown below suggest that many respondents stated to use liquid exchanges without knowing exactly what they are, but simply considering them as synonym of marketplaces. In fact, none of analysed variables seem to explain their adoption, which should be driven, instead, by the will of increasing market efficiency, thus reducing procurement costs.

It is important to note that sell-side catalogs are designed by suppliers, but they might be uploaded either on the supplier, or a private, or whatever kind of portal. Direct auctions and team working tools are the least diffused web tools so far.

Previous tools are mainly used through vertical portals (27.8 per cent of cases), although also horizontal marketplaces are quite diffused, especially in the case of electronic auctions (e.g. Freemarkets, 1city.biz, Bravosolution).

Finally, an interesting result is related to the property of the portal running the selected tools. Most of the companies rely on private portals, either suppliers' (36.1 per cent) or their own (37.5 per cent). Few use independent portals, or even initiatives run by industry consortia. Such evidence further supports the topic of competitive concerns highlighted in Section 5.3.

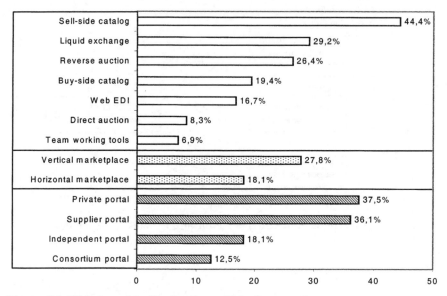

Figure 6.4 Web-based tools adoption within the sample

After considering web-based tools diffusion within the sample, a logit multiple regression model was tested in order to explore the influence of material characteristics and motivations on the tools choice. For a detailed description of logistic regression models see Section 6.3. Equation *E4* was tested:

E4. $\ln\left[\dfrac{P(tool_k)_i}{P(no\ tool_k)_i}\right] = \beta_0 + \beta_1 relevance_i + \beta_2 criticality_i +$
$+ \beta_3 sm\_complexity_i + \beta_4 pro\_cost_i +$
$+ \beta_5 efficiency_i + \beta_6 effectiveness_i + \varepsilon_i$

where:
$P(tool_k)_i$	is the probability the company *i* adopts the tool *k*;
$P(no\ tool_k)_i$	is the probability the company *i* does not adopt the tool *k*;
$relevance_i$	is the relevance of the acquired material in the case *i*;
$criticality_i$	is the criticality of the acquired material in the case *i*;
$sm\_complexity_i$	is the supply market complexity for the acquired material in the case *i*.
pro_cost_i	is the priority assigned to the goal of reducing procurement costs by company *i*;

efficiency$_i$ is the priority assigned to the goal of increasing the supply process efficiency by company i;

effectiveness$_i$ is assigned to the goal of increasing the supply process effectiveness by company i.

ε_i is the residual term, which is assumed as normally distributed, mean zero and constant variance.

The results of the logit analyses are shown in the following pages (Table 6.15). Significant results are highlighted in italics in the tables.

As far as liquid exchanges, buy-side catalogs, vertical marketplaces, and consortia portals are concerned, Chi-square statistics have significance levels higher than 0.05; therefore, in these cases the sample does not allow to reject the hypothesis that all the parameters equal zero. However, some considerations can be drawn for the other web tools.

Sell-side catalogs are mainly used for non-critical materials procurement in order to increase supply process efficiency. This is the typical case of MRO materials (see Section 2.3). In such cases, the criticality and the relevance of materials do not make necessary a high involvement of the customer in the catalog definition; the catalog is then uploaded and integrated with internal systems in order to streamline procurement processes.

Reverse auctions are preferred for the procurement of highly relevant materials in order to reduce the overall procurement costs (suppliers' search, selection, negotiation, and the price itself). Such materials are generally direct to the final product, relevant to its features and constitute a high percentage of the cost.

Web EDI is adopted for any kind of material, but their supply market complexity is usually low. This can be related to the fact that the supplier must also invest into the adoption of the EDI, and the higher the number of other potential suppliers and the competition among them, the more likely such supplier would be willing to make itself more attractive, and the more likely the customer would have the power to impose web EDI transactions. By using web-EDI, the company does not pursue the reduction of procurement costs, but it is interested into increasing the effectiveness of the supply process, especially in terms of time to market and stock-outs.

Direct auctions present for the buyers the same motivations of reverse auctions. Generally speaking, the electronic auction is seen as a tool allowing the purchase of a relevant material at the lowest cost as possible.

Team working tools are adopted mainly in situations where supply market complexity is high. In such a condition, the company is willing to create long-lasting relationship with good suppliers (see also Kraljic, 1983), eventually supported by web team working tools in order to facilitate the interaction. Not surprisingly, the primary goal is not the reduction of the procurement cost, but the increase of the process effectiveness in terms of time, quality and innovation.

Table 6.15 Logit regression model on web-based tools adoption

Sell-side Catalog (44.4% adopters): unrestricted model

	B	S.E.	Wald	Df	Sig.	Exp(B)	ΔLL
Material relevance	-.036	.239	.023	1	.880	.965	-.011
Material criticality	-.834	.375	4.961	1	.026	.434	
Supply market complexity	.068	.205	.110	1	.741	1.070	-.055
Procurement cost reduction	.331	.286	1.345	1	.246	1.393	-.702
Process efficiency	.993	.458	4.691	1	.030	2.698	
Process effectiveness	.142	.375	.142	1	.706	1.152	-.071
Constant	-3.987	2.484	2.576	1	.109	.019	-1.432

Log Likelihood value: -40.640. Chi-square: 17.642 (6 df); sig. 0.007. Percentage correct: 69.4% with cut value 0.5.

Liquid Exchange (29.2% adopters): unrestricted model

	B	S.E.	Wald	Df	Sig.	Exp(B)	ΔLL
Material relevance	.475	.252	3.551	1	.060	1.608	-1.849
Material criticality	-.796	.397	4.017	1	.045	.451	
Supply market complexity	.049	.220	.050	1	.822	1.051	-0.025
Procurement cost reduction	.353	.278	1.611	1	.204	1.424	-0.853
Process efficiency	-.164	.373	.192	1	.661	.849	-0.095
Process effectiveness	.380	.660	1.113	1	.291	1.462	-0.553
Constant	-2.047	2.140	.915	1	.339	.129	-0.467

Log Likelihood value: -41.310. Chi-square: 8.938 (6 df); sig. 0.177. Percentage correct: 75.0% with cut value 0.5.

Reverse Auction (26.4% adopters): unrestricted model

	B	S.E.	Wald	Df	Sig.	Exp(B)	ΔLL
Material relevance	.780	.420	3.454	1	.063	2.181	-1.954
Material criticality	.150	.460	.107	1	.744	1.162	-.053
Supply market complexity	-.100	.243	.169	1	.681	.905	-.084
Procurement cost reduction	2.893	.856	11.423	1	.001	18.047	
Process efficiency	-.801	.754	1.127	1	.288	.449	-.062
Process effectiveness	-.192	.632	.092	1	.761	.825	-.042
Constant	-10.187	4.615	4.872	1	.027	.000	

Log Likelihood value: -22.257. Chi-square: 37.962 (6 df); sig. 0.000. Percentage correct: 86.1% with cut value 0.5.

Table 6.15 Logit regression model on web-based tools adoption (cont.)

Buy-side Catalog (19.4% adopters): unrestricted model

	B	S.E.	Wald	Df	Sig.	Exp(B)	ΔLL
Material relevance	129	.289	.200	1	.654	1.138	-.089
Material criticality	.137	.411	.111	1	.739	1.146	-.055
Supply market complexity	.001	.270	.000	1	.996	1.001	-.000
Procurement cost reduction	-.671	.311	4.636	1	.031	.511	
Process efficiency	.291	.452	.414	1	.520	1.337	-.219
Process effectiveness	-.040	.416	.009	1	.923	.960	-.005
Constant	-1.067	2.507	.181	1	.670	.344	-.081

Log Likelihood value: -31.765. Chi-square: 7.406 (6 df); sig. 0.285. Percentage correct: 79.2% with cut value 0.5.

Web EDI (16.7% adopters): unrestricted model

	B	S.E.	Wald	Df	Sig.	Exp(B)	ΔLL
Material relevance	-.174	.396	.193	1	.660	.840	-.100
Material criticality	.295	.454	.421	1	.517	1.342	-.211
Supply market complexity	-.444	.295	2.261	1	.133	.642	-1.130
Procurement cost reduction	-.976	.417	5.477	1	.019	.377	
Process efficiency	-.206	.558	.137	1	.712	.814	-.068
Process effectiveness	.939	.483	3.779	1	.052	2.558	-1.995
Constant	1.115	2.655	.176	1	.675	3.050	-0.85

Log Likelihood value: -24.209. Chi-square: 16.463 (6 df); sig. 0.011. Percentage correct: 86.1% with cut value 0.5.

Direct Auction (8.3% adopters): unrestricted model

	B	S.E.	Wald	Df	Sig.	Exp(B)	ΔLL
Material relevance	1.148	.572	4.025	1	.045	3.152	
Material criticality	.298	.570	.273	1	.601	1.347	-.132
Supply market complexity	-.499	.383	1.693	1	.193	.607	-.905
Procurement cost reduction	2.307	1.019	5.126	1	.024	10.047	
Process efficiency	.930	1.183	.618	1	.432	2.535	-.331
Process effectiveness	-.142	.889	.026	1	.873	.867	-.013
Constant	-16.941	7.659	4.893	1	.027	.000	

Log Likelihood value: -13.564. Chi-square: 14.176 (6 df); sig. 0.028. Percentage correct: 90.3% with cut value 0.5.

The Internet and the Customer-Supplier Relationship

Table 6.15 Logit regression model on web-based tools adoption (cont.)

Team working tools (6.9% adopters): unrestricted model

	B	S.E.	Wald	Df	Sig.	Exp(B)	ΔLL
Material relevance	.203	1.051	.037	1	.847	1.225	-.019
Material criticality	-.688	1.354	.259	1	.611	.502	-.151
Supply market complexity	3.248	2.513	1.671	1	.196	25.747	-2.338
Procurement cost reduction	-1.748	1.023	2.920	1	.087	.174	-2.342
Process efficiency	-.600	1.175	.261	1	.609	.549	-.140
Process effectiveness	2.890	1.672	2.988	1	.084	17.997	-3.562
Constant	-16.885	11.385	2.200	1	.138	.000	-1.104

Log Likelihood value: -10.87. Chi-square: 16.139 (6 df); sig. 0.013. Percentage correct: 91.7% with cut value 0.5.

Vertical Marketplace (27.8% adopters): unrestricted model

	B	S.E.	Wald	Df	Sig.	Exp(B)	ΔLL
Material relevance	.253	.241	1.098	1	.295	1.288	-.547
Material criticality	.017	.336	.003	1	.960	1.017	-.002
Supply market complexity	.057	.220	.066	1	.797	1.058	-.033
Procurement cost reduction	-.012	.257	.002	1	.964	.988	-.001
Process efficiency	.000	.388	.000	1	1.000	1.000	-.000
Process effectiveness	.215	.353	.370	1	.543	1.240	-.184
Constant	-2.336	2.170	1.159	1	.282	.097	-.742

Log Likelihood value: -41.281. Chi-square: 2.500 (6 df); sig. 0.868. Percentage correct: 72.2% with cut value 0.5.

Horizontal Marketplace (18.1% adopters): unrestricted model

	B	S.E.	Wald	Df	Sig.	Exp(B)	ΔLL
Material relevance	.345	.420	.676	1	.411	1.413	-.336
Material criticality	-.026	.567	.002	1	.964	.975	-.001
Supply market complexity	.652	.502	1.689	1	.194	1.920	-1.267
Procurement cost reduction	2.135	.698	9.342	1	.002	8.454	
Process efficiency	-1.986	.877	5.124	1	.024	.137	
Process effectiveness	.209	.725	.083	1	.774	1.232	-.041
Constant	-5.962	3.703	2.592	1	.002	8.493	

Log Likelihood value: -17.309. Chi-square: 33.384 (6 df); sig. 0.000. Percentage correct: 91.7% with cut value 0.5.

Table 6.15 Logit regression model on web-based tools adoption (cont.)

Private Portal (37.5% adopters): unrestricted model

	B	S.E.	Wald	Df	Sig.	Exp(B)	ΔLL
Material relevance	-.052	.265	.038	1	.845	.949	-.020
Material criticality	.774	.365	4.497	1	.034	2.168	
Supply market complexity	-.401	.219	3.361	1	.067	.670	-1.722
Procurement cost reduction	-.750	.294	6.493	1	.011	.472	
Process efficiency	.166	.406	.168	1	.682	1.181	-.085
Process effectiveness	.139	.367	.143	1	.705	1.149	-.072
Constant	.821	2.115	.151	1	.698	2.273	-.079

Log Likelihood value: -37.754. Chi-square: 19.757 (6 df); sig. 0.003. Percentage correct: 72.2% with cut value 0.5.

Supplier Portal (36.1% adopters): unrestricted model

	B	S.E.	Wald	Df	Sig.	Exp(B)	ΔLL
Material relevance	-.195	.262	.553	1	.457	.823	-.280
Material criticality	-.957	.411	5.405	1	.020	.384	
Supply market complexity	-.018	.210	.008	1	.930	.982	-.004
Procurement cost reduction	.039	.311	.016	1	.901	1.040	-.008
Process efficiency	.965	.509	3.601	1	.058	2.625	-2.273
Process effectiveness	.856	.418	4.191	1	.041	2.353	
Constant	-4.057	2.626	2.387	1	.122	.017	-1.330

Log Likelihood value: -36.489. Chi-square: 21.205 (6 df); sig. 0.002. Percentage correct: 76.4% with cut value 0.5.

Independent Portal (18.1% adopters): unrestricted model

	B	S.E.	Wald	Df	Sig.	Exp(B)	ΔLL
Material relevance	.167	.332	.253	1	.615	1.182	-.175
Material criticality	.014	.440	.001	1	.974	1.014	-.000
Supply market complexity	.763	.516	2.186	1	.139	2.144	-1.817
Procurement cost reduction	1.171	.462	6.434	1	.011	3.225	
Process efficiency	-1.548	.679	5.196	1	.023	.213	
Process effectiveness	.830	.621	1.787	1	.181	2.293	-.973
Constant	-5.477	3.011	3.309	1	.069	.004	-1.829

Log Likelihood value: -24.028. Chi-square: 19.946 (6 df); sig. 0.003. Percentage correct: 87.5% with cut value 0.5.

Table 6.15 Logit regression model on web-based tools adoption (cont.)

Consortium Portal (12.5% adopters): unrestricted model

	B	S.E.	Wald	Df	Sig.	Exp(B)	ΔLL
Material relevance	-.025	.361	.005	1	.945	.976	-.002
Material criticality	-.432	.733	.348	1	.555	.649	-.183
Supply market complexity	-.323	.290	1.240	1	.265	.724	-.630
Procurement cost reduction	-.031	.398	.006	1	.937	.969	-.003
Process efficiency	.013	.477	.001	1	.979	1.013	-.001
Process effectiveness	-1.457	.833	3.059	1	.080	.233	-2.393
Constant	2.861	3.291	.756	1	.385	17.478	-.412

Log Likelihood value: -21.311. Chi-square: 11.633 (6 df); sig. 0.071. Percentage correct: 84.7% with cut value 0.5.

The adoption of horizontal portals is less clearly explainable than previous tools. Companies seem recurring to horizontal marketplaces when supply market complexity is high in order to reduce the overall procurement cost. Supply process efficiency does not seem to be a priority.

As far as the property of the hub supporting the selected tools is concerned, companies prefer leveraging their own portals when acquiring highly critical and customized materials within relatively low complexity supply markets. This is explainable through the privacy and competitive concerns related to critical components and the need for contractual power over suppliers, which must be willing to adopt the customer's initiative. In such a situation, buyers do not seem caring about reducing the overall procurement cost.

Companies in the sample adopt suppliers' portals mainly for standard and low criticality materials procurement. In such situations, buyers consider the supplier's initiative as a way of increasing supply process efficiency and effectiveness, thus reducing lead times, operative costs and increasing quality and service level.

Finally, independent or public marketplaces are used in order to smooth the supply market complexity and the contractual power of suppliers. As a matter of fact, in such situations the buyer pursues the reduction of supplier search, selection, and negotiation costs and the material price as well. This goal is pursued also to the detriment of process efficiency.

The adoption of vertical rather than horizontal portals and of private rather than supplier, independent, or consortium, is surely related to the typology of transaction tools they offer. In the analysed sample, horizontal portals offer mainly liquid exchanges and reverse auctions, which are typically tools adopted to increase market efficiency. On the contrary, vertical portals appeared to offer a wider range of tools, including catalogs and team working tools. Private initiatives within the sample, either customer's or supplier's, offer a wider range of tools than independent or even consortium initiatives. These last portals are mainly focused on increasing market efficiency; therefore it is logical that companies adopt them in order to reduce their procurement costs.

In order to understand the effectiveness of such web-based tools, analyses of variances were performed. Performance indicators were compared between companies adopting a particular tool and those not adopting it. The results of the analysis for each tool are shown in Table 6.16.

Table 6.16   Analysis of difference in means and variances of performance indicators according to the different web-based tools

ANOVA & Test of Homogeneity of Variances[4]

	Non-adopters		Adopters		Mean test		Variance test	
	Mean	St.Dv	Mean	St.Dv	F[5]	Sig.	Lev. Stat.[6]	Sig.
Sell-side catalog								
Procurement costs	2.861	1.202	3.300	.704	3.352	.071	*14.118*	*.000*
Process efficiency	3.204	1.199	3.538	.665	1.995	.162	*11.680*	*.001*
Process effectiveness	2.081	.965	2.061	.986	.007	.933	.464	.498
Liquid exchange								
Procurement costs	2.999	1.102	3.194	.834	.531	.469	2.715	.104
Process efficiency	3.379	1.039	3.288	.938	.120	.730	.635	.428
Process effectiveness	2.097	1.014	2.011	.862	.115	.735	.990	.323
Reverse auction								
Procurement costs	2.823	1.060	3.705	.569	*11.841*	*.001*	*7.934*	*.006*
Process efficiency	3.483	.988	2.988	.986	3.503	.065	.168	.683
Process effectiveness	2.136	.994	1.894	.889	.871	.354	.349	.556
Buy-side catalog								
Procurement costs	3.139	.993	2.712	1.139	1.969	.165	1.436	.235
Process efficiency	3.265	1.005	3.714	.954	2.294	.134	.248	.620
Process effectiveness	1.983	.929	2.440	1.067	2.570	.113	.292	.591
Web EDI								
Procurement costs	3.173	1.041	2.472	.752	*4.886*	*.030*	.882	.351
Process efficiency	3.210	1.000	4.063	.699	*7.885*	*.006*	.978	.326
Process effectiveness	1.953	.864	2.665	1.255	*5.774*	*.019*	*5.670*	*.020*
Direct auction								
Procurement costs	3.026	1.033	3.388	1.002	.679	.413	.001	.973
Process efficiency	3.357	.990	3.305	1.261	.014	.905	.394	.532
Process effectiveness	2.033	.966	2.500	.958	1.286	.261	.009	.924

[4] Tests with 2-tailed significance level lower than 0.05 are in italic numbers.
[5] F statistic total degrees of freedom: 71.
[6] Levene statistic degrees of freedom: (1; 70).

ANOVA & Test of Homogeneity of Variances[4] (cont.)

	Non-adopters		Adopters		Mean test		Variance test	
	Mean	St.Dv	Mean	St.Dv	F[5]	Sig.	Lev. Stat.[6]	Sig.
Team working								
Procurement costs	3.086	1.056	2.656	.408	.810	.371	*4.187*	*.044*
Process efficiency	3.296	1.004	4.112	.705	3.162	.080	.496	.483
Process effectiveness	1.997	.933	3.070	.941	*6.131*	*.016*	.048	.827
Vertical marketplace								
Procurement costs	3.007	1.066	3.183	.937	.421	.519	.337	.564
Process efficiency	3.285	1.040	3.526	.908	.824	.367	1.389	.243
Process effectiveness	1.980	.947	2.310	1.001	1.691	.198	.000	.990
Horizontal marketplace								
Procurement costs	2.899	1.043	3.768	.577	*8.395*	*.005*	*4.922*	*.030*
Process efficiency	3.529	.914	2.547	1.040	*11.699*	*.001*	2.220	.141
Process effectiveness	2.161	.992	1.667	.749	2.845	.096	1.680	.199
Private portal								
Procurement costs	3.415	.821	2.456	1.073	*18.216*	*.000*	*6.632*	*.012*
Process efficiency	3.239	1.015	3.541	.977	1.535	.220	.149	.701
Process effectiveness	1.975	.915	2.232	1.046	1.193	.279	1.331	.253
Supplier portal								
Procurement costs	2.861	1.065	3.400	.877	*4.788*	*.032*	.906	.344
Process efficiency	3.130	1.057	3.744	.779	*6.680*	*.012*	3.182	.079
Process effectiveness	1.872	.889	2.425	1.015	*5.781*	*.019*	.702	.405
Independent portal								
Procurement costs	2.894	1.024	3.793	.692	*9.062*	*.004*	2.805	.098
Process efficiency	3.447	.930	2.922	1.245	2.985	.088	1.634	.205
Process effectiveness	2.097	.978	1.959	.942	.214	.645	.273	.603
Consortium portal								
Procurement costs	3.027	1.020	3.262	1.127	.409	.524	.734	.395
Process efficiency	3.365	.988	3.260	1.173	.086	.771	.086	.770
Process effectiveness	2.153	.983	1.507	.636	3.645	.060	2.008	.161

In a similar way to what was found before, nothing interesting can be said about the performances through the adoption of liquid exchanges, buy-side catalogs, vertical marketplaces, and consortia portals.[7] Also analyses on direct auctions do not provide interesting evidence.

Analysing the other results, it is possible to note that sell-side catalogs, contrarily to what is expected by companies, have not led to higher efficiency in

---

[7] In those cases, the sample did not allow properly testing the differences in means and variances.

the procurement process; neither they have led to increased effectiveness or to reduced procurement costs.

On the contrary, reverse auctions seem satisfying the expectation of companies. Within the sample, the reverse auction adopters managed to significantly reduce the overall procurement costs more than non adopters (significance=$0,001$).

The use of web EDI has procured to companies high efficiency and effectiveness within the supply process. Since EDI is an integrating tool, this result further supports the hypothesis that the integration with the supplier is an instrumental objective for the primary goal to improve the supply process (*H1*). However, those advantages occur to the detriment of procurement costs. Probably, imposing web EDI to the supplier, negotiation costs and the material fixed costs increase.

Not surprisingly, team working tools increase the effectiveness of the supply process, both in terms of quality, innovation and service level to the final customer.

Analysing Table 6.15, it has been noted how companies adopted horizontal portals in order to intermediate a complex supply market. Results shown in Table 6.16 actually confirm the fact that horizontal portals help reducing the overall procurement costs, but this happens to the detriment of process efficiency. Probably this is due to the still high coordination costs occurring between the company and the portal itself. However, as seen before, in such cases process efficiency is not a primary concern.

The analyses support the fact that private portals are adopted mainly in dealing with critical and customized materials, thus stressing the privacy concerns issue. Results show that companies adopting private portals see their procurement costs increasing. Probably this is related to the request for adaptation from suppliers.

On the contrary, suppliers' portals seem fully satisfying companies needs. The overall procurement costs decrease, probably due to discount and incentives policies by the supplier; at the same time both the supply process efficiency and effectiveness increase.

Finally, as expected by companies, independent portals help aggregating demand and reducing the overall procurement cost.

6.6   The Market-Vertical Alliance Divergence

In Chapter 2 the effect of the Internet adoption on both markets and vertical alliances has been analysed; the aim of this section is to test the hypotheses formulated in Chapter 5 underlying the emergence of a *collaborative market* model. In particular, the use of Internet based tools is supposed to shift the trade-off between the degree of collaboration characterizing the relationship and the efforts required to manage the relationship itself (see Figure 5.3). Such shift would emphasize the dichotomy between market and vertical alliance.

Such hypothesis was tested through two subsequent steps. Firstly, a one-way ANOVA was performed in order to test differences in means and variances of integration levels and efforts before and after the Internet adoption, secondly, a multivariate regression model was tested to verify the correlation among integration levels, efforts, and the Internet adoption.

One-way ANOVA

In Tables 6.6 and 6.8, descriptive statistics for integration levels and efforts required by the relationship are provided for the two different situations: before and after the introduction of the Internet. Values of mean and standard deviation are different for most of the variables in the two cases. Are those differences significant?

Before answering the question, a further step has been done in the research. As the overall objective of the analysis was to test the trade-off between level of integration and efforts, another component was built to summarize the overall level of coordination and collaboration either in terms of operational integration or technological integration or simply information sharing.

To pursue that objective, an overall measure of total integration between customer and supplier was worked out. This measure, called *Integration level* is a weighted average of information sharing and operational and technological integration; it describes in general terms the overall level of collaboration between the company and the supplier (Table 6.17).

Table 6.17 Descriptive statistics of the integration level

	Before the Internet				After the Internet			
	Min.	Max.	Mean	Std. Dev.	Min.	Max.	Mean	Std. Dev.
Integration level	1.00	3.17	1.93	0.57	1.00	4.11	2.37	0.82

In order to cross-check the results obtained in variables describing the level of collaboration with the perceived level of competitive market relationship with supplier (*arm's length relationship*) Pearson correlation was tested (Table 6.18). The results show that the level of competitiveness within the relationship is significantly negatively correlated to the levels of integration. The lowest absolute value is the one representing the correlation with *information sharing*, thus indicating that simple information sharing is the lowest level of integration.

Table 6.18 Correlation between arm's length measure and collaboration measures

	Information sharing	Operational integration	Technological integration	Total Integration
Arm's length	-0.374	-0.552	-0.506	-0.536
	(.000)	(.001)	(.007)	(.000)

Pearson correlation. 2-tailed significance levels into brackets.

At this stage it was possible to run the analysis of variances; the results are shown in Table 6.19. Similar results are obtainable through samples T-test.

The hypothesis of equal means was rejected for every variable excluded *technological integration*, which presents a significance level of 0.306. Similarly, the hypothesis of equal variances was rejected for every variable excluded *technological integration* and *efforts*, which present respectively significance levels of 0.120 and 0.523.

These results can be better understood by observing Figure 6.5, in which the distributions of the analysed variables are shown before and after the Internet introduction.

Table 6.19   Analysis of difference in means and variances before and after the Internet adoption

ANOVA

		Sum of Squares	df	Mean Square	F	Sig.
	Between Groups	6.80	1	6.80		
Operational Integration	Within Groups	91.13	142	.64	10.601	.001
	Total	97.93	143			
	Between Groups	.90	1	.90		
Technological integration	Within Groups	121.43	142	.86	1.053	.306
	Total	122.36	143			
	Between Groups	17.17	1	17.17		
Information sharing	Within Groups	126.15	142	.89	19.332	.000
	Total	143.32	143			
	Between Groups	7.02	1	7.02		
Integration level	Within Groups	70.31	142	.50	14.174	.000
	Total	77.33	143			
	Between Groups	4.05	1	4.05		
Efforts	Within Groups	78.20	142	.55	7.348	.008
	Total	82.25	143			

Test of Homogeneity of Variances

	Levene Statistic	df1	Df2	Sig.
Operational Integration	7.410	1	142	.007
Technological integration	2.442	1	142	.120
Information sharing	12.070	1	142	.001
Integration level	12.387	1	142	.001
Efforts	.409	1	142	.523

The mean value characterizing the operational integration distribution has become greater after the Internet adoption in the procurement process. This shows how companies, on average, reach a higher level of collaboration on issues concerning production coordination, inventory management, production planning and scheduling, demand forecasting, and so on. At the same time, also standard deviation, both in absolute value and percentage, increases. This fact indicates that the range of levels of integration in such activities has become wider, and includes both very low and very high degrees of coordination and collaboration.

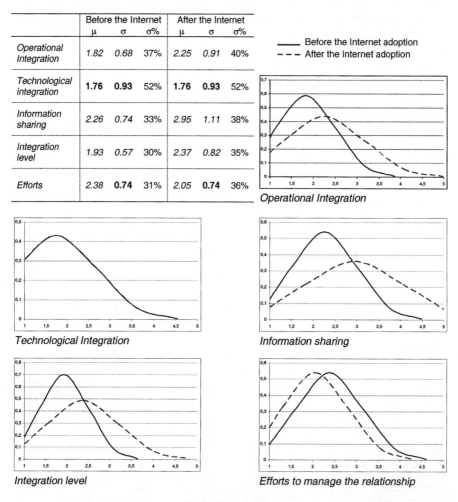

	Before the Internet			After the Internet		
	μ	σ	σ%	μ	σ	σ%
Operational Integration	1.82	0.68	37%	2.25	0.91	40%
Technological integration	**1.76**	**0.93**	52%	**1.76**	**0.93**	52%
Information sharing	2.26	0.74	33%	2.95	1.11	38%
Integration level	1.93	0.57	30%	2.37	0.82	35%
Efforts	2.38	**0.74**	31%	2.05	**0.74**	36%

Before the Internet adoption
After the Internet adoption

Operational Integration

Technological Integration

Information sharing

Integration level

Efforts to manage the relationship

Figure 6.5 Distributions of variables characterizing the relationship[8]

The cases concerning information sharing and total level of integration have analogous distributions before and after the Internet introduction. The average

[8] The bold values in the table are those for which tests of differences are not significant; for this reason, they are the average of the original values (before and after the Internet from Tables 6.6, 6.8, and 6.18). On the contrary, significant differences are in italic numbers.

level of collaboration has increased widening the spectrum of solutions adopted by companies.

A different and very interesting result has emerged for technological Integration. As shown in Table 6.19 and Figure 6.5, that variable does not present significant changes both in mean and standard deviation. This indicates that the Internet adoption has not provided any further collaboration in activities concerning product, process and technology co-development between customer and supplier. Furthermore, the range of solutions has kept unaltered. Such results provides evidence for two possible conclusions: on the one hand, at this stage the Internet could not support appropriately the co-development process; on the other hand, companies could have not used the technology with the objective to increase collaboration in such activities.

Finally, efforts invested into the relationship have significantly decreased on average with the Internet adoption, but they have not changed on standard deviation. That means that companies need a smaller amount of time and resources, ICT costs, team working costs and investments in assets in order to coordinate the relationship. The spectrum wideness of efforts does not change; as a matter of fact there were no hypotheses indicating that would have been altered.

Summarizing the results of this analysis concerning the situation before and after the Internet adoption in the procurement process, the level of integration has increased on average. The spectrum of such level has also increased, indicating a higher presence and emphasis of both very low and very high level of integration situations. All these considerations are valid, excluded the case of technological integration, which seems not significantly affected by the use of the Internet. As far as the efforts required to manage the relationship are concerned, they have shown to be lower on average.

Such evidence is a first proof of the hypotheses *H3* and *H4* formulated in Chapter 5.

Multivariate Regression Model

The second step of this analysis was aimed at proving the existence of the trade-off between level of integration and efforts required by the relationship and the hypothesized shift of such trade-off through the adoption of the Internet technologies. In order to pursue that goal, a multivariate regression model was tested; the main results of which are reported in Table 6.20. The model considers operational integration, technological integration, information sharing, and integration level as dependent variables. A Multivariate model was chosen because of the interrelations existing among these variables. To test the normal distribution of the dependent variables, their stem&leaf diagrams have been analysed (Norusis, 1993b).

The model was built as follows for each of the integration variables:

E5. $y_i = \beta_0 + \beta_1 d_i + \beta_2 \ln(efforts_i) + \beta_3 d_i \ln(efforts_i) + \beta_4 relevance_i +$
$+ \beta_5 criticality_i + \beta_6 sm\_complexity_i + \varepsilon_i$

which can be read also as follows:

E6. $y_i = (\beta_0 + \beta_1 d_i) + (\beta_2 + \beta_3 d_i)\ln(efforts_i) + \beta_4 relevance_i + \beta_5 criticality_i + \beta_6 sm\_complexity_i + \varepsilon_i$

where:

y_i is the value of one of the four dependent variables (i.e. type of integration) considered for the case i;

d_i is the dummy variable indicating '0' if the data refers to the situation before the Internet and '1' if the data refers to the situation after the Internet;

$efforts_i$ indicates the level of efforts measured for the case i;

$relevance_i$ is the relevance of the acquired material in the case i;

$criticality_i$ is the criticality of the acquired material in the case i;

$sm\_complexity_i$ is the supply market complexity for the acquired material in the case i.

ε_i is the residual term, which is assumed as normally distributed, mean zero and constant variance.

Relevance, criticality, and supply market complexity are the variables described in Section 6.2; they have been introduced as control variables in the model, as they are supposed to explain part of the coordination and collaboration pursued by the customer and the supplier.

The dummy variable has been introduced for two reasons: firstly, it allows testing the significance of the difference of the intercept before and after the Internet adoption; secondly, it allows testing the difference in the slope of the relation between efforts and integration before and after the Internet adoption.

Finally, a logarithmic relation between efforts and level of integration has been introduced for two reasons. On the one hand, modeling the hypothesized function (see Chapter 5) would have needed too many parameters to be estimated considering the sample size, therefore a simple decreasing derivative of the integration level has been hypothesized. On the second hand, a function of the dependent variable with a saturation limit could cause heteroschedasticity problems, as the variance of the dependent variable could not be constant in proximity of the limit. Statistical analyses have proved that a logarithmic relationship fits the variables better than a simple linear one.[9]

---

[9] The R^2 values of ',639', ',546', ',605', and ',702' measured through the logarithmic relationship decrease to ',598', ',492', ',591', and ',644' if measured through a linear relationship.

Table 6.20a Multivariate regression model between Integration and Efforts[10]

Multivariate Tests (based on Pillai's Trace test)

Effect	Value	F	Sig.
Intercept	.182	7.466	.000
D	.031	1.060	.379
ln(efforts)	.118	4.499	.002
d* ln(efforts)	.095	3.512	.009
Relevance	.100	3.734	.006
Criticality	.187	7.715	.000
Sm_complexity	.018	.602	.662

Table 6.20b Multivariate regression model between Integration and Efforts[11]

Univariate Parameter Estimates

Model	Parameter	B	Std. Error	T	Sig.[12]	F	Sig.[5]	R^2	Durbin-Watson[13]
Operational Integration	*Intercept*	*1.052*	*.250*	*4.208*	*.000*				
	D	-.123	.247	-.496	.621				
	ln(efforts)	*.401*	*.182*	*2.215*	*.025*				*2.173*
	d* ln(efforts)	*.949*	*.303*	*3.135*	*.002*	19.198	.000	.639	*(1.827)*
	Relevance	.003	.048	.072	.943				(1.80)
	Criticality	*.247*	*.067*	*3.698*	*.000*				
	sm_complexity	-.029	.040	-.727	.468				
Technological Integration	*Intercept*	*.355*	*.313*	*1.136*	*.006*				
	D	.201	.309	.650	.517				
	ln(efforts)	*.762*	*.305*	*2.499*	*.014*				*1.965*
	d* ln(efforts)	.120	.379	.316	.752	10.743	.000	.546	(1.80)
	Relevance	.005	.060	.078	.938				
	Criticality	*.302*	*.083*	*3.620*	*.000*				
	sm_complexity	.010	.050	.201	.841				
Information Sharing	*Intercept*	*1.345*	*.303*	*4.442*	*.000*				
	D	.201	.300	.671	.503				
	ln(efforts)	*.673*	*.295*	*2.279*	*.024*				*1.992*
	d* ln(efforts)	*.912*	*.367*	*2.486*	*.014*	19.090	.000	.605	*(1.80)*
	Relevance	*.204*	*.058*	*3.545*	*.001*				
	Criticality	.017	.081	.212	.833				
	sm_complexity	.048	.048	-.993	.322				
Integration level	*Intercept*	*.947*	*.194*	*4.895*	*.000*				
	D	.086	.192	.451	.653				
	ln(efforts)	*.602*	*.189*	*3.190*	*.002*				*2.185*
	d* ln(efforts)	*.689*	*.234*	*2.940*	*.004*	32.518	.000	.702	*(1.815)*
	Relevance	*.074*	*.037*	*2.013*	*.046*				*(1.80)*
	Criticality	*.183*	*.052*	*3.548*	*.001*				
	sm_complexity	-.024	.031	-.781	.436				

---

[10] Significant parameters are shown by italic numbers.
[11] Significant parameters are shown by italic numbers.
[12] Two-tailed significance.
[13] The Durbin-Watson measure (DW) tests the residuals auto-correlation. With 144 cases and 7 parameters, the upper bound to be exceeded in order to reject the auto-correlation is *1.80*. If the DW measure is higher than 2, the test has been done on 4-DW (Dillon and Goldstein, 1984; Maddala, 1992).

As far as the multivariate model is concerned, results show that all the independent variables considered are significantly correlated to the dependent ones, excluded the dummy (before and after the Internet) and the supply market complexity. In order to interpret deeply such results, the univariate parameter estimates are useful.

The operational integration model explains 63.9 per cent of its variance. Intercept, efforts, the product dummy by efforts, and material criticality are all correlated with the level of operational integration. The intercept value is 1.025, which means that there is low integration when the independent variables are at the lowest level in the scale. The model proves the trade-off existing between operational integration and efforts invested into the relationship through a logarithmic expression, which also means that a saturation effect exists. The most interesting evidence is that also $d* ln(efforts)$ has a significant and relevant coefficient (0.949); this result shows how the slope of the relation between efforts and operational integration increases after the Internet adoption (see equation *E6*). That proves the shift of such trade-off. Finally, criticality of the material is also significant in explaining the level of integration: the more the material is specific, customized, new and complex, the more companies pursue operational integration.

The simple dummy variable does not present a significant parameter (two-tailed significance 0.621). This result proves that the simple introduction of the Internet does not provide a higher level of integration if it is not supported by greater efforts. In a similar way, material relevance and supply market complexity seem not explaining the level of integration. This is quite surprising for what concerns the relevance aspect in terms of percentage of purchases and total costs, nature of the material, and relevance to final product characteristics. These variables seem explaining operational integration less than material criticality.

The technological integration model is the less explained (54.6 per cent). In that model, analogous considerations to the operational integration model can be drawn about the intercept, the dummy, the efforts, and the product characteristics. Exception is made in the $d* ln(efforts)$ parameter. Such parameter is not significant (two-tailed significance 0.752); it means that the Internet introduction in the relationship has not shifted, on average, the trade-off between technological integration and efforts. This result implies two possible conclusions (calling back those formulated in the previous section): on the one hand, at this stage the Internet could not support appropriately the co-development process; on the other hand, companies could have not used the technology with the objective to increase collaboration in such activities.

The information sharing model is explained by the independent variables with a percentage of 60.5 per cent. The effect of the first four parameters is similar to operational integration: the trade-off between information sharing and efforts exists, and such trade-off has been shifted through the use of the Internet; the dummy contribution is not significant in shifting the interception. The Intercept is higher than in the other cases, illustrating that reaching information sharing is less demanding than other kinds of integration (operational and technological). As far as material characteristics are concerned, only relevance seem explaining the higher level of information sharing.

Finally, not surprisingly the interpretation of the integration level model is similar to the multivariate model one. The variance explained is 70.2 per cent. All the variables significantly explain the level of integration, excluded the usual dummy and supply market complexity. This result means that the overall level of integration is in trade-off with the efforts required by the relationship, such trade-off has been changed in slope through the Internet; although it is not moved up (the dummy presents a two-tailed significance of 0.653). Material relevance and criticality all contribute in the explanation of higher levels of integration, while supply market complexity is not a driver in increasing coordination and collaboration.

Figure 6.6 clearly shows the underlying concept of the model; only the integration level model is provided, but analogous considerations could be drawn for the others, excluded technological integration that does not show to be influenced by the Internet adoption (as seen before). The Interpretation of the graph is significant in the middle range of dependent variable values, as it is supposed to be normally distributed and 1 and 5 are accumulation points cutting off the distribution itself. However, general conclusions can be drawn.

Integration level

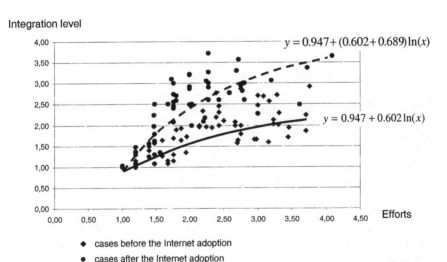

$$y = 0.947 + (0.602 + 0.689)\ln(x)$$

$$y = 0.947 + 0.602\ln(x)$$

Efforts

♦ cases before the Internet adoption

● cases after the Internet adoption

Figure 6.6 Trade-off between Integration level and Efforts before and after the Internet adoption

The Internet introduction into the relationship has doubled the slope of the curve describing the trade-off efforts-integration in the analysed sample while keeping unaltered the minimum level of integration (intercept 0.947); though, as this is in the proximity of the accumulation point, the variance could vary. In general terms, it means that the adoption of the Internet *per se* is not useful if not supported by efforts in terms of time and resources, joint team working, and appropriate investments in ICT and assets. The two curves show that web based technologies make possible either higher level of coordination and collaboration with equal efforts than before or lower efforts with equal level of coordination and collaboration.

Integration level

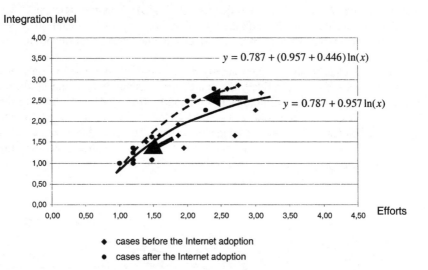

$$y = 0.787 + (0.957 + 0.446)\ln(x)$$

$$y = 0.787 + 0.957\ln(x)$$

♦   cases before the Internet adoption

●   cases after the Internet adoption

Figure 6.7   15 companies decreased their integration level with suppliers. Total model R^2=0.81

Analysing data in more detail and dividing the sample into companies that decreased the level of integration on one side, and those that increased the level of integration on the other side, the results are analogous. In particular, the 15 companies that emphasized the arm's length nature of the relationship or simply kept the same level of integration lowering the efforts invested into the relationship are shown in Figure 6.7. The other 57 cases in the sample, which increased the level of collaboration, are shown in Figure 6.8.

   The biased proportion between companies emphasizing arm's length transactions (15) and companies emphasizing collaboration (57) do not confute the overall result. The multiple regression does not aim at proving markets or alliances preferences by companies, but proving the existence of the trade-off efforts-integration and its shift through the Internet adoption.

Integration level

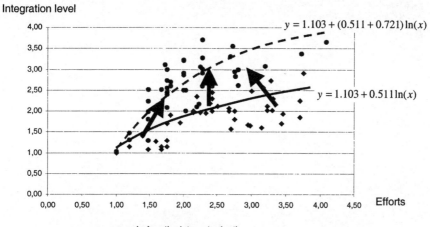

$$y = 1.103 + (0.511 + 0.721)\ln(x)$$

$$y = 1.103 + 0.511\ln(x)$$

◆ cases before the Internet adoption
● cases after the Internet adoption

**Figure 6.8 57 companies increased their integration level with suppliers.
Total model R^2=0.65**

The overall results shown in this section prove the theoretical hypotheses underlying the model of *collaborative markets* as illustrated in Chapter 5 (*H2, H3, H4*). On the one hand, the Internet emphasizes the difference between markets and vertical alliances providing a wider spectrum of levels of integration and shifting the trade-off efforts-integration. On the other hand, such shift opens new opportunities for intermediate relationships of collaboration in the short term, which are referred to as *collaborative markets* in this work.

In the next chapter, a descriptive model for such *collaborative market* relationships is provided by analysing some web sites offering collaboration services on the web.

Chapter 7

The Emergence of
Collaborative Markets

7.1 The Collaborative Markets

Research Hypotheses stated in Chapter 5 and tested in Chapter 6 underlie the emergence of collaborative markets. In particular, such hypotheses state the shift of the efforts-integration trade-off in customer-supplier relationships through the adoption of the Internet (see Figure 5.3).

The hypothesized shift occurs especially for materials placed in proximity of the border between markets and vertical alliances. Keeping in mind Kraljic's, Olsen and Ellram contributions (Section 1.2), there are four typologies of acquired materials: non-critical, critical, bottleneck, and leverage. As far as non-critical and critical components are concerned, the choice in the relationship is still oriented towards respectively markets and vertical alliances. However, there are certain components that position themselves across the border between markets and alliances: bottleneck and leverage. Nowadays, the Internet technology opens the opportunity to manage those components through neither markets nor vertical alliances. Such materials might be managed through collaborative market relationships (Figure 7.1). Within a collaborative market, companies choose trading parties through a market-oriented approach, but new technologies allow them to reach a high level of integration without great investments. These are short-term relationships with low initial investments and therefore low switching costs: if the relation is not worthwhile any more trading companies can give it up and find someone else on the market.

Some research companies delineate the future of B2B speaking of collaborate commerce (Gartner, 2000), dynamic collaboration (Forrester, 2001), or private collaboration (AMR, 2000). Within this trend, collaborative markets should allow companies reaching higher flexibility in the supply market by leveraging a dynamic collaborating network and using either private or public portals.

In the previous chapter, analyses showed how companies prefer adopting private exchanges or extranets to support the relationships with suppliers. In the last months, *web services* applications, which might support *collaborative market* relationships among companies, have been emerging (e.g. developed by companies like IBM, Microsoft, and Oracle). A *Web service* is a network-based, distributed, modular component that performs specific tasks, and conforms to a specific set of technical specifications that make it interoperable with other compatible components. Different private networks might communicate with each other by recognizing and adopting such standard services. Web services integration among different systems could, therefore, provide to companies the possibility to share information and collaborate on specific processes.

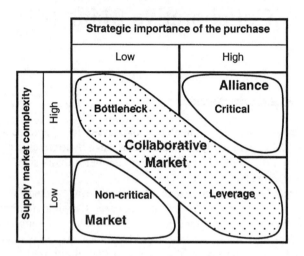

Figure 7.1 Classification of purchases and collaborative markets

Due to the difficulty of properly analysing private extranets and the newness of *web services* applications, in the following section, the main characteristics of collaborative markets are illustrated through the analyses of 12 public portals which seem or are willing supporting collaborative market relationships.

Collaborative Markets Features

In Chapter 2, it has been highlighted how marketplaces cannot rely only on transaction services anymore, but they need some other initiatives (Section 2.3). In the last year, within this scenario, a discrete number of portals or marketplaces have started offering supply chain services supporting collaborative market interactions. In order to find some examples and derive the main characteristics, a wide web inquiry has been done. In Section 7.2 the results of the inquiry are shown, and twelve marketplaces that can be considered as emergent collaborative markets supporting portals are briefly described.

     In the presented tables (Tables 7.1 and 7.2) a summary of the inquiry is provided highlighting main characteristics of analysed portals and what value added services and supply chain or collaboration services are offered by each of them. Value Added Services (VAS) are those supporting the proper transaction, through payments and financing systems, marketing intelligence tools, and information and content facilities. Supply chain services are those supporting coordination and collaboration between customer and supplier; these are discussed in further detail in the following paragraphs.

Most of the examples have been found in the information technology and microelectronic, automotive and food and beverage and CPG industries. Multi-tier manufacturing processes characterize all these industrial sectors, and for this reason information and material flows are difficult to manage. Moreover, many initiatives exist in such industries to set process standards (e.g. Rosettanet, AIAG, VICS), and this proves the need to create process standardization to intensify collaboration, thus increasing the overall market responsiveness. All these portals adopt main standards currently existing in the specific industrial sector.

As a matter of fact, industry consortia manage the most of analysed portals. Such consortia usually gather almost all industry leaders, which provide high credibility to the initiative. An issue often arisen from the analysis refers to the huge experience of those partners in the specific industrial sector and their capability to set together industry standards in order to support effective and efficient collaboration within the trading community. Of course, this causes competition problems among the actors and it could be an inhibitor to the initiative (see Section 5.3).

Table 7.1 Examples of portals supporting collaborative markets

	Industry	Products	Typology	Property	Bias
E2open	Microelectronics	Direct	Vertical	Consortium	Neutral
Converge	Hi-Tech	Direct	Vertical	Consortium	Neutral
Covisint	Automotive	Direct	Vertical	Consortium	Buy-side
E-steel	Steel, Automotive	Direct	Vertical	Consortium	Neutral
Transora	CPG, Food&Beverage	Direct	Vertical	Consortium	Buy-side
CPGmarket	CPG, Food&Beverage	Direct	Vertical	Consortium	Neutral
WWRetailExchange	Retail, Food&Beverage	Direct	Vertical	Consortium	Neutral
Elemica	Chemical	Direct	Vertical	Consortium	Neutral
Chemconnect	Chemical	Direct	Vertical	Consortium	Neutral
RailMarketplace	Railways	Direct	Vertical	Consortium	Neutral
TradeMC	General spending	Direct / Indirect	Horizontal	Independent	Neutral
I-faber	General spending, Food&Beverage, Textile, Energy	Direct / Indirect	Horizontal / Vertcal	Independent	Neutral

Table 7.2 VAS and collaboration services

Category	VALUE ADDED SERVICES	I-faber	TradeMC	Rail Marketplace	Chemconnect	Elemica	WWRetail Exchange	CPGmarket	Transora	E-steel	Covisint	Converge	E2open
Payment, Financing	Electronic payments	X	X	X	X	X	X	X	X	X		X	X
	Funding	X	X			X						X	
	Legal and financial consulting	X	X	X	X	X		X	X	X			X
Marketing, Intelligence	Market research	X		X					X				
	Direct marketing - mailing list	X											
	e-intelligence	X	X	X	X	X		X	X				
	Sales force automation												
Information, Content	News and reports	X	X	X	X	X	X	X	X	X	X	X	X
	Products and services reviews	X	X		X	X	X	X	X	X	X	X	X
	Comparison matrixes						X						
	Newsgroups and forums							X	X	X	X	X	
	Experts consulting	X			X	X		X	X	X	X	X	X

Table 7.2 VAS and collaboration services (cont.)

COLLABORATION SERVICES	E2open	Converge	Covisint	E-steel	Transora	CPGmarket	WWRetail Exchange	Elemica	Chemconnect	Rail Marketplace	TradeMC	I-faber
Collaborative planning	X	X	X	X^1	X	X	X	X^1	X	X^1		X
Collaborative forecasting	X	X	X	X^1	X	X	X	X^1	X	X^1		X
Collaborative inventory management	X		X	X^1	X	X	X	X^1	X	X		X
Order management	X	X	X	X	X	X	X	X	X	X	X	X
Exception management	X				X		X	X	X	X		
Collaborative design	X		X							X	X	
Project management	X	X	X							X		
Product life cycle management	X	X	X				X			X		X
Private hub into the portal	X		X		X				X		X	

1. Only information sharing provided.

The need for competence in industry specific issues and relevant materials is also delineated by the fact that these portals are mainly vertical and manage mainly direct materials. As a matter of fact, transacted items are often complex to describe and critical to the manufacturing process and to the final product. Where materials are relatively simple, competence is needed to support effectively and efficiently the complex coordination process between customer and supplier (e.g. forecasting, planning, order management).

Some of the analysed portals are neutral, whereas others are biased facilitating buyers. This is related to the fact that big players' consortia firstly focused their attention into obtaining advantages over suppliers by aggregating their demand. In such a context, it is extremely difficult to create a collaborative environment. In the last year, however, this trend seems to be smoothed leaving space for more neutral initiatives (e.g. Transora).

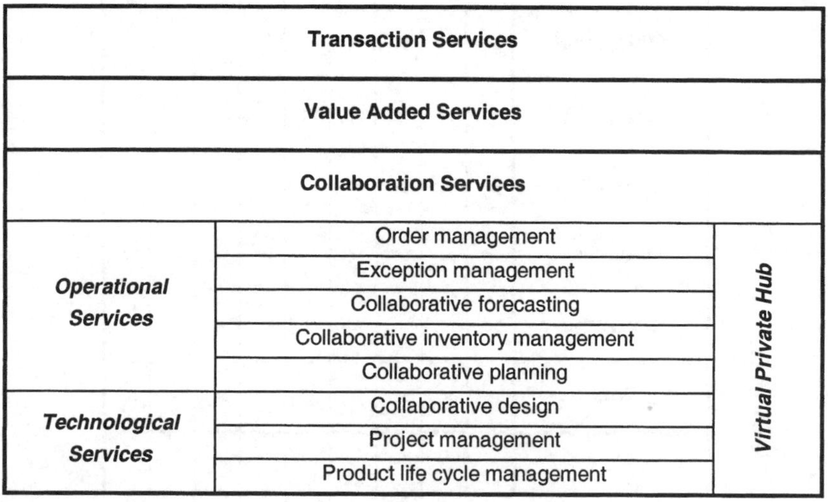

Transaction Services		
Value Added Services		
Collaboration Services		
Operational Services	Order management	*Virtual Private Hub*
	Exception management	
	Collaborative forecasting	
	Collaborative inventory management	
	Collaborative planning	
Technological Services	Collaborative design	
	Project management	
	Product life cycle management	

Figure 7.2 Portals supporting collaborative markets

There are two exceptions: TradeMC and I-faber (become 1city.biz in 2002). The former is simply a general hub managing mainly MRO materials, whereas the latter started as a horizontal marketplace, but now is deepening competencies in some specific industries (e.g. Food and Beverage and Textile); in these industries they started managing also direct materials. Both of them are managed by independent entities. These aspects, compared to the other examples, can be related to the mainly indirect products transacted.

All those marketplaces are characterized by three sets of services offered to companies (Figure 7.2). The first class consists of traditional transaction services (e.g. electronic catalogs, electronic liquid exchanges, and electronic auctions); the second class consists of the VAS (Value Added Services), which support, for example, market research studies, financial services, or community services. These first two sets of services are always present, and they are common also to many other marketplaces. The third class is the one characterizing portals supporting collaborative markets relationships; they are called *collaboration services* or *supply chain management services*.

Collaboration services might support either operational collaboration or technological collaboration (see Section 1.2). Such tools are dependent on the specific industry. On the one hand, where continuous innovation and time to market are critical factors, technological services are stressed (e.g. Automotive); on the other hand, where demand is more stable and process and technologies are consolidated, operational services are stressed in order to improve supply chain efficiency (e.g. Food and Beverage).

Operational Services
Within this category, there are five main services.
Order management tools support all the required activities to manage the order both on the customer and on the supplier side: order approval and generation, order fulfillment, order tracking and tracing, invoicing, and payment (also through a third financial party). This functionality essentially provides higher process efficiency both on the supply side and on the buy side, by matching the two concurrent needs.
Exception management supports emergencies occurred when a firm needs immediately to vary ordered quantities or to issue entirely new orders. Those tools communicate the exception directly to the involved supplier, and, if necessary, search for other potential suppliers basing on available quantity, distances, quality, price, and previous interactions with the customer.
Collaborative forecasting allows sharing and formulating final customer demand forecasts. Every actor involved in the specific supply chain might observe demand data, forecasts and, if necessary, contribute to their formulation. Processes sharing these kinds of data essentially refer to the CPFR methodology (Section 2.3). This functionality contributes smoothing demand signaling imperfections along the supply chain (see Section 1.3).
Collaborative inventory management evokes VMI (Vendor Managed Inventory) and consignment stock models (Section 2.3). Customers and suppliers can share information about reciprocal inventories and agree on stock management policies. Similarly to some vertical alliances, suppliers might even manage customers' inventories.
Finally, *collaborative planning* allows companies sharing information and collaborating on production and transportation schedules. Customers and suppliers might coordinate each other by observing quantities and production lead times. If necessary, also capacity planning and allocation decisions could be shared.

Technological Services

Within this category, there are three main services.

Collaborative design tools allow companies interacting in the product or process development phase, thus supporting co-design relationships (see Section 1.2). Both drawings and 3D virtual prototypes can be shared among actors involved. Moreover, new technologies will also support concurrent distant development, thus supporting real distant team working and facilitating postponement policies. However, such concurrent solutions are not mature yet and will be commercially available in the next future.

Project management tools might be also available. Through these services, it is possible to co-manage the planning and the execution phase of any project. Often, a workflow supports project activities across companies. Every actor involved is aware of its role within the project and the state of the activities, both in terms of time and budget.

Product life cycle management tools support longer-term decisions. These services allow companies sharing information across the whole life of the product, from its introduction to its decline. Such information regards volumes, new versions and releases, long-term forecasts, and returns management.

Both operational and technological services can be exploited either on the public portal, through obvious strictly security accesses, or on private annexes (Temkin, 2001). These annexes are virtual private hubs that offer collaboration services and could be used and designed by each company as its own private portal. The difference from ASP (Application Service Provider) is that using a virtual private hub, the company directly controls and manages its own data.

In this context, companies might collaborate without high systems integration costs and client-server infrastructures by leveraging their existing databases in sharing information in a peer-to-peer environment. Of course, databases would need standard interfaces allowing reciprocal communication. Strictly related to this, also specific investments into a private hub or extranet and associated risks are extremely reduced.

In collaborative markets, web-based technologies does not require data to be housed in specific proprietary repositories. It is possible to work across multiple application federations, support user- or event-driven publish/subscribe interactions, interface easily with different application domains using Enterprise Application Integration (EAI) adapters and Extensible Markup Language (XML), thus effectively eliminating information latency. This allows companies rapidly configuring and reconfiguring their supply networks to address new threats and opportunities, thus leading to dynamic supply networks. In managing 'border materials', those items in the proximity of the border in Figure 5.3, firms could assume an opportunistic behavior choosing the best supplier and sharing part of the risk with it in the short-term (Peterson, 2000).

Moreover, collaborative markets support industry-wide capacity optimization by matching effectively and efficiently demand and supply. In such a situation, any company can find ways to optimize inter-enterprise production, thus reducing costs and increasing service level.

Barriers to Collaborative Markets

The model of collaborative market relationships seems fabulous so far; nevertheless there are not many cases in place. This is due to the current presence of high barriers across all industries. Collaborative markets will not be firmly in place until these barriers exist. Main inhibitors identified from the field analysis by inquiring experts and practitioners are the following:

- trust issues;
- lack of process and communication standards;
- internal data and processes;
- learning effect issues;
- privacy and competitive concerns;
- data security.

The problem of trust between customers and suppliers is a big problem also in long-term vertical alliances (see Section 1.2). The risk of opportunistic behaviors is present in alliances and even more in collaborative markets; sharing strategic information in short-term relationships is even more risky. Hostages' theory (Williamson, 1983) finds more space in long-term alliances (e.g. complementary resources), but it can be valid also in collaborative markets: the reciprocal sharing of information might still be a deterrent for opportunistic actions. In any case, dealing with companies with high capabilities and reputation, sharing few but well defined common goals, and sharing risks and benefits are all factors that help in building trust, even in the short period. For these reasons, if collaborative markets emerge, then reputation will be even more important than today in relationships.

Another big problem is related to the establishment of common standards. Firstly, it is necessary that companies all 'speak the same language' in order to make possible collaborating with each other without huge investments. This essentially means agreeing on what kind of data, fields and format should be included in any shared document (e.g. orders, forecasts, and drawings). Although some global communication standards already exist (e.g. EDIFACT, XML), none of them is really established, and many different sub-standards are continuously emerging. Even more difficult is the establishment of process standards: if companies want to collaborate, they must share common interface processes and activities (e.g. order management, demand management, and product development) in order to know how interact with each other. Also in this field there are some industry specific initiatives mainly run by no profit consortia including major industry leaders (e.g. VICS/CPFR in the CPG industry, and Rosettanet/PIP in the electronic industry). If it is difficult to establish process standards within a specific industry, it is even more difficult to manage situations in which companies coming from different industrial sectors need to interact (e.g. high-tech companies interacting with logistics services companies). As proof of the difficulty in establishing common standards, it is possible to observe in the last years the proliferation of hundreds of industry standards. However, in order to face this problem, also *integration portals* are emerging. These marketplaces will provide the ability (through adapters, workflow and data translation services) to enable integration in such processes as planning and designing among participants using similar but not equal standards (e.g. UCCNet in the overall consumer goods and retail industry).

The third barrier is related to internal problems within each company. Adopting standards and dynamically collaborating with other companies implies a deep change into traditional organizational structures and processes, which were designed to cope with traditional arm's length transaction on the one hand or with vertical alliances on the other. Such change could be very painful for companies, which might prefer not facing such efforts. Moreover, hypothesizing companies' will to adopt a collaborative market relationship model, also data accuracy within each company is critical. In order to obtain valid results coming out from real time information and data sharing through web-based tools, such data and information must be correct and updated.

Within collaborative market relationships the switching costs deriving from changing from one relationship to another are surely lower than in vertical alliances; however they still exist, especially related to learning effects. Collaborating is not an easy task, and a satisfactory level of collaboration can be reached only after a certain period of *fine tuning* of the relationship between the parties. For this reason, the path along the collaboration learning curve could be an inhibitor to dynamically change allied.

Of course, also privacy and competitive concerns are a big barrier. In collaborative markets companies are asked to share information with other companies, which could be interacting with their direct competitors in the near future. The fear to disclose specific competitive capabilities leads many firms to create their own private web portal to interact with pre-selected and well-established actors (e.g. Wal-Mart with Retail-link and Dell). It is also true that this last solution is not as flexible as collaborative markets and that reputation issues smooth the disclosing risk when participating to a collaborative market relationship.

Finally, the less critical barrier, but still existing, is the security issue. Companies might be worried about sharing strategic data on the Internet because of the possibility of uncontrolled intrusion accesses. However, nowadays firewalls and security algorithms are sufficiently robust.

The highlighted barriers stress even more the fact that collaborative markets are still to come and will not be used in every relationship (e.g. for strategic and critical materials procurement), but might be a competitive factor if effectively used mainly for 'border materials'.

7.2   Examples on the Web

Tables 7.1 and 7.2 provide a synthetic description of analysed portals supporting relationships that can be considered close to collaborative markets. In the next pages, a more detailed description is given for each initiative through a table framework. Such frame summarizes the origins of the initiative, including founders, objectives and related products. Moreover, a synthesis of main services is provided. As far as collaborative markets are concerned, transaction and value added services are not described, whereas emphasis is given to proper collaboration services characterizing each case. Finally, where possible, examples of companies adopting such services are stated.

Portal:

www.e2open.com   (2000)

Origins:

E2open has been founded by Acer, Hitachi, IBM, LG Electronics, Lucent Technologies, Matsushita Electric (Panasonic), Nortel Networks, Seagate Technology, Solectron, and Toshiba. It is also supported by strategic partners: Crosspoint Venture Partners, Morgan Stanley Dean Witter, Mitsubishi Electric, Omron, Ricoh, Sanyo, and Sharp. Its mission is to be the leader portal in collaboration within the electronic industry among all the main OEMs.

Services:

In addition to common transaction services, there are two main groups of collaboration services: *product collaboration* and *supply chain collaboration*.

Product collaboration services support the creation of inter-company teams working together over the whole product life-cycle: development, planning, procurement, production, commercialization, and returns. Information is monitored and visible among all the actors involved. In particular:

✓   Project management tools and standard best practices repository.
✓   Information and document synchronization through versioning management tools, and searching engines among those documents through attributes and key words.
✓   Communication services (e.g. web meetings, instant messaging, publish and subscribe tools).
✓   Views customization for on-line documents.
✓   Possible integration with *supply chain collaboration* services and back-end systems.

Supply chain collaboration services support logistical flows within a secure and private community. Information is communicated real-time (as opposed to batch communication) with the aim of reducing actors' inventories, increasing synchronization, and streamlining the overall lead time. In particular the main functionality are all supported by EDI, XML, and Rosettanet standards:

✓   Forecasting, planning, and procurement workflow.
✓   Data 'translator' matching different codes among different companies.
✓   Exception management through reports and alerts.
✓   Forecast collaboration supports forecasts sharing and incoherence notifications. Forecasts are shared directly through the web, file transfers, or even enterprises' systems integration through standard interfaces.
✓   Inventory collaboration supports stocks visibility, thus providing a tool for VMI and JIT practices. Stock levels could be communicated on a weekly or monthly basis also through alert messages.
✓   Order collaboration supports the order cycle, by communicating the order itself, its status, invoice issuing, shipments notification, and track and trace services.
✓   Capacity collaboration provides the ability to monitor production planning and scheduling along the overall supply chain in order to support capacity planning and negotiation among partners.

Described Cases:

In 2001 Acer adopted e2open to integrate 10 of its suppliers. With these suppliers the collaboration occurs at the supply chain collaboration level, exploiting Rosettanet communication standards.

Portal:
www.converge.com (1999/2000)

Origins:
Converge is a global portal that provides collaboration services aiming at gaining supply chain efficiency in the High Technology industry. Main founders are: AMD, Agilent, Canon, Compaq, Gateway, Hitachi, HP, Maxtor, NEC, Samsung SCI Systems, Solectron, Synnex, Tatung, Western Digital.

Services:
Converge offers a number of value added services providing market information reports and trade or transaction activities. In addition, main collaboration services are as follows: ✓ 'Plan' is a service that supports demand and supply matching by consolidating and providing information coming from different systems in different companies. ✓ 'Design' is a tool supporting design and development phases in new products generation. In particular it provides prototyping tools, project management and reporting tools, design reviews supports, and communication services, all through specific workflows. ✓ 'Order' tool supports the order cycle, by communicating the order itself, its status, invoice issuing, shipments notification, and track and trace services. Also negotiation and collaboration on price and quantity definition is supported. ✓ 'Move' is a logistics tool, providing shipments visibility and supporting the ability to aggregate orders optimizing transportation and negotiating with carriers. ✓ 'Connect' is a technological habilitation service aiming at integrating internal information systems of companies with the portal.

Described Cases:
None

Portal:

www.covisint.com   (2000)

Origins:

Covisint was founded at the beginning of 2000 by DaimlerChrysler, Ford Motor Company, and General Motors. By the beginning of the next year, and after the cause with the Federal Trade Commission, also Renault, Nissan, and PSA Peugeot Citroen joined the initiative. Technical partners are Commerce One and Oracle. Major attention is given to procurement and transaction services (e.g. catalogs, auctions and RFx), and to collaboration services for product development in the automotive industry.

Services:

In addition to transaction services, developed essentially to increase procurement process efficiency of big players, also collaboration services have been gradually offered. As a matter of fact, in the automotive industry collaboration among supply chain partners is not a novelty at all; in addition to design collaboration services, which were the first to be developed, also supply chain synchronization services are now part of the portal.

Design collaboration services support the creation of virtual working teams with the aim of increasing innovation. Communication is made using main industry standards (e.g. AIAG, ASG). Such communication occurs on a platform called *Virtual Project Workspace*, which provides the following main services:

✓   CAD format drawings exchange.

✓   Forum discussion and videoconferencing.

✓   Documents management including versioning and retrieval.

Supply chain synchronization services aim at improving operations and logistics processes. Inventory reduction is pursued by adopting a Build-To-Order (BTO) approach by collaboratively communicating production plans. In particular, main services include:

✓   'Fulfillment' is a set of services supporting the sharing of direct material information such as inventory levels, forecasts, transit inventory, transportation scheduling.

✓   'Supplier connector' is a technological habilitation service that provides possible integration among partners by adopting EDI, XML, flat files, and spreadsheets.

Described Cases:

None

Portal:

www.e-steel.com (1998)

Origins:

E-steel is the major portal supporting supply chain activities in the steel industry. It was founded in 1998 by: Goldman Sachs & Co., Kleiner Perkins Caufield & Byers, Bessemer Venture Partners, GE Capital, Greylock, Amerindo Investment Advisors, Dofasco Inc., Generation Partners, Ispat International, Mitsui & Company U.S.A., Mitsubishi International and MC Capital Inc., U.S. Steel Corporation, Vulcan Ventures, and Dupont. Technological partners are WebMethods, Bea, Oracle, Sun Microsystem, Rational, Global Crossing, Java, and UEC. In 2001, an agreement occurred between e-steel and covisint on cooperation in direct material procurement in the automotive industry.

E-steel changed its name in NewView Technologies Inc. in November 2001.

Services:

As a matter of fact, main services provided by e-steel are mere transaction tools so far (e.g. catalogs, liquid exchanges, auctions). However, some visibility is provided at the operations and logistics level. Such information sharing occurs among partners in terms of orders, demand forecasts, and production plans visibility.

Some order management tools are in place in order to automate orders and payments, by integrating internal information systems.

Described Cases:

Ford has centralized its steel procurement process and exploits e-steel platform both for itself and its sub-contractors.

BHP Steel, one of the main steel producers in Australasia, has adopted e-steel in order to communicate with its main customers.

Portal:

www.transora.com   (2000)

Origins:

Transora is an initiative that has been founded by 58 companies. Its mission is to create linkages among all participants in the consumer packaged goods by overcoming companies' borders. Among those 58 founders, main enterprises are: Beiersdorf A.G., British American Tobacco, Campbell Soup, Colgate-Palmolive, Compania Cervecerias Unidas S.A. (CCU), Dannon Company, Eastman Kodak, Embotelladora Andina, H.J. Heinz Company, Heineken International, Johnson & Johnson, Kellogg, Kraft Foods (includes Nabisco), Mars, Morton International, Nestlé, Parmalat, PepsiCo., Sara Lee Corporation, Coca-Cola, Gillette, Pepsi Bottling Group, Procter & Gamble, and Unilever.

Services:

Common transaction services (e.g. catalogs) and value added services (e.g. customer service, content and community, and marketing on-line) are offered by Transora. In addition, a set of collaboration services on operations and logistics between producer and distributor is provided:

✓ 'Retail' services provide the possibility to communicate among partners through a forum.

✓ 'Order management' services support the procurement process with EDI standards.

✓ 'Inventory management' services provide stocks visibility to pre-selected partners and support jointly managed inventory (JMI) and vendor managed inventory (VMI).

✓ 'Transportation & Logistics' services aim at minimizing distribution costs by negotiating contracts, transportation scheduling, analyses and reporting, and transportation optimization.

✓ 'Collaborative Planning, Forecasting, and Replenishment' services support a standard process (CPFR developed by VICS) allowing customer and supplier collaborating on final consumer demand forecasts and on distributor orders forecasts. Once agreed on these two kinds of forecasts, producer can plan production together with the distributor. The overall objective of the process is reducing inventory levels and increasing service level to the final consumer.

Such services are exploitable either through Transora's hub or creating a direct private link among partners.

Described Cases:

None

Portal:
www.CPGmarket.com   (2000)

Origins:
CPGmarket was initially founded through a joint venture including Danone, Henkel, Nestlè, and SAP. By the beginning of 2001, other shareholders joined the initiative: Bahlsen & Co., Barilla, Fromageries Bel, Danisco, Delta Holding, Euroalimenti, Ferrero International, Firmenich International, Fulda Holding Stabernack JR Partner, Hero AG, L'Oréal, Madrange Group, Mahou, Maserpack, Mayr-Melnhof Packaging, Nutreco Holding, Pechiney, Pernod Ricard Group, Südzucker, Coca Cola, Tipiak, and Uniq plc. Technological providers are: Accenture, Hewlett-Packard Europe, and SAPmarkets.
CPGmarket is the main European portal in the consumer packaged goods, especially for what concerns food & beverage and make-up products.

Services:
CPGmarket aims at being a neutral marketplace linking main European actors in the CPG industry. Traditional offered services are 'e-sourcing' (suppliers search), 'e-requisitioning' (catalogs and order management), 'e-fulfillment' (shipment and payment), 'e-intelligence' (performance measurement). Moreover, it has recently started to offer some collaboration services:
✓   EDI emulation on documents exchange (e.g. products information, production plans, and inventory levels) through xCBL standard (extended Common Business Library).
✓   Planning, forecasting and inventory management collaboration through industry standard CPFR (see also Transora).
Those two main collaboration services are usable through the integration of companies' ERPs with the portal through WebMethods, whereas other traditional services are viable through a standard web browser.

Described Cases:
None

Portal: **www.WorldWideRetailExchange.org**   (2000)
Origins: 56 partners, mainly retailers, have founded WorldWideRetailExchange. In particular, its focus is on retail food & beverage industry. However, partners are planning to extend their competence also to general CPG and textile & apparel industry.
Services: WorldWideRetailExchange offers common transaction services (e.g. catalogs, auctions, RFx). In addition to those, some collaboration services are provided: ✓ 'New product development' services support the interaction between retailers and suppliers in private label products development. Actors communicate and collaborate on concept definition and product specifications.   ✓ 'Supply chain visibility' services provide full visibility on orders and shipments, also through reports and an alert system real time for exception management. The aim of such tools is reducing inventory levels and administrative costs on both sides.   ✓ 'Collaboration' services essentially cover the scope of CPFR process, supporting collaborative planning, forecasting, and replenishment (see also Transora).
Described Cases: None

Portal:
www.elemica.com   (2000)

Origins:
Elemica has been founded with the aim of improving collaboration along the supply networks within the chemical industry. Its 22 founders are: Air Products, Atofina, Basf, Bayer, Bp, Brenntag, Celanese, Chemcentral, Ciba, Degussa, Dow, DSM, Dupont, Mitsubishi Chemical, Mitsui Chemicals, Millennium Chemicals , Rhodia, Rohm Haas, Shell Chemical, Solvay, Sumtoma Chemical, and Vopak.

Services:
Elemica supports common transaction services, especially contracts and catalogs management. In particular, it also provides the possibility to customize contracts between different customers and suppliers, thus customizing the entire catalog. In addition to those transaction services and value added services, such as carriers negotiation and financial services, Elemica provides some collaboration services:

✓ 'Transportation planning' supports the optimization of shipments, by consolidating different needs coming from customers and suppliers.
✓ 'Supply chain planning' services provide the possibility to share information about demand forecasts, production planning, inventory levels, possibly supporting also VMI practices.
✓ 'Product technical information' services provide the possibility to access suppliers' databases in order to see and analyse product specifications.

These three main functionalities provide essentially visibility rather than proper collaboration. However, collaboration might occur through exception management services (then managed off-line), and efficiency improvement in the order cycle on both sides.

Described Cases:
None

Portal:
www.chemconnect.com   (1999)

Origins:
Chemconnect is one of the main portals in the chemical and plastic materials industry. From 1995 it is simply a reports repository to be diffused on the net; from the 1999 it started offering also additional services. Its founders are 42 major chemical companies, among which: Air Liquid, Basf, Bayer, Borden Chemical, Borealis, BP Amoco Chemical, Dow, Enichem, GE Plastics, Mitsubishi Corporation, Rohm and Haas, and Sterling Chemicals.

Services:
Chemconnect offers a number of services: 'Exchange floor' supports catalogs, bids, and offers; 'Commodities floor' essentially supports high volume commodities exchange also through liquid exchange; 'Corporate trading room' supports electronic auctions, and 'Envera' supports the real collaboration amongst partners.
Envera adopts XML translation servers in order to integrate different partners' ERP systems, including logistics and financing providers. This enables a *hub&spoke* model through its *clearing house* (the hub connecting all partners). This solution helps companies in streamlining process flows with complete security through a series of services:
✓ Automation of the complete order cycle on both sides (e.g. order placement, order acknowledgement, track and trace, shipment, payment, …).
✓ The possibility to build a centralized data warehouse aiming at sharing all relevant information along the supply chain.
✓ Collaborative forecasting and planning, highlighting peaks, throws, or future possible materials lacks.
✓ It is also possible to use appropriate *score-cards* in order to measure overall supply chain's and single partners' performances.

Described Cases:
None

Portal:

www.RailMarketplace.com   (2001)

Origins:

RailMarketplace was founded by the main actors in the railways industry in North America: Burlington Northern Santa Fe, Canadian National, Canadian Pacific Railway, CSX Transportation, Norfolk Southern, and Union Pacific. Moreover, GE Global eXchange Services is the technological partner managing marketplace technology. The mission of such initiative is to automate procurement process along the railways supply chain and to reduce inefficiencies in terms of transaction costs, purchasing and production costs, and lead times.

Services:

Traditional transaction services are offered on the portal (e.g. catalogs, RFx, liquid exchanges, and electronic auctions). Moreover, also some value added services are present (e.g. financial and marketing services).

In addition to those, also supply chain collaboration services are provided:

- ✓ 'Products and projects co-development' tools provide the possibility to share applications information, drawings, projects scheduling, and to manage documents real-time.
- ✓ 'Product life cycle' services support information sharing and marketing activities with a wider perspective, from concept design to commercialization and returns.
- ✓ 'Fulfillment status' consists of a set of tools providing inventory visibility and supporting possible VMI or JMI.
- ✓ 'Shipment' and 'purchase order status' services provide full visibility and coordination for what concerns transportation and order tracking and tracing.
- ✓ 'Schedule exception' tools support the management and resolution of urgent real time modifications in different partners' production plans.
- ✓ 'Sharing demand forecast' services support forecasts sharing aiming at planning requirements on the basis of known data.

Described Cases:

None

Portal:

www.TradeMC.com   (2000)

Origins:
TradeMC is an independent portal created by IBM and Fluor Corporation, one important company of engineering, procurement, and construction. The portal aims at improving cross-industry supply chains efficiency by reducing prices, lead times, and time-to-market. The initiative deals with both direct and indirect products in the chemical, pharmaceutical, mining, services, and oil & gas industries. Such products range from steel, valves, electrical equipment, pumps to office furniture, office supplies, stationery, and travel services.

Services:
TradeMC includes typical transaction services and value added services present on a horizontal marketplace. In addition, it offers process analyses, design, and implementation to companies willing to integrate their systems with the portal and to exploit collaboration services. Such services are as follows:
- ✓ 'Data warehousing services for market and supplier intelligence' allow analysing customers needs and creating forecasts basing on their demand and inventory profiles.
- ✓ 'Rollout' tools support customer and supplier synchronization in the procurement and order management process by integrating the two ERPs.
- ✓ 'Multi-enterprise collaborative design' supports virtual team working, by providing the possibility of closely interacting on the same objects.
- ✓ It is also possible to integrate one company's private extranet with the portal through a secure link, which can be also an interface with other marketplaces.

Described Cases:
None

Portal:

www.I-faber.com   (2001)

Origins:

I-faber was founded by Unicredito Italiano together with Oracle as technological partner. Initially it provided cross-industry transaction and value added services related to indirect products, ranging from stationery to personal computers. In the last year it has started to build competences in three vertical industries: textile&apparel, food&beverage, and energy. In 2002 it became 1city.biz and its main business is now based on electronic auctions.

Services:

The initial distinctive feature for I-faber was the richness and reliability of traditional transaction services (e.g. catalogs, auctions, and exchanges) and value added services. The latter includes numerous financial services, participant qualification and certification, and logistics services through shipment scheduling and carrier contract negotiation.

Initially, I-faber developed a suite of collaboration services; most important ones were:

✓ 'Collaborative supply planning' tools provide the possibility to automatically compare customer's demand with supplier's capacity in order to highlight either possible low capacity problems or possible opportunities for direct auctioning extra-capacity to other partners.

✓ 'Collaborative demand planning' supports forecasts comparing between customer and supplier.

✓ 'Collaborative inventory visibility and management' provides the full reciprocal inventories visibility amongst customers and suppliers, thus making also possible VMI and JMI practices through order points and security stock communication.

✓ 'Collaborative order promising' provides to the customer the possibility to search for specific quantities of specific products for specific dates among pre-selected suppliers.

✓ 'Collaborative product development' tools support the product prototyping process and its launch on the market, by tracing project status and delays of customers and suppliers development activities.

Described Cases:

None

Chapter 8

Conclusions

8.1 Main Conclusions

The presented research focused the attention on the role of the Internet adoption in customer-supplier relationships. In particular, three main research questions have been stated in Chapter 3.

The first main objective of the research is to clarify what are the motivations that should stimulate companies to adopt web-based technologies within their relationships with suppliers.

The second objective is to identify what are the appropriate Internet tools companies should adopt according to their specific goals.

Finally, the most relevant objective is to explain what are the implications on customer-supplier relationships related to the Internet adoption.

Motivations to the Internet Adoption

From case studies and survey analysis, clear motivations driving companies towards the Internet adoption were clarified, thus answering the first research question.

The first main motivation concerns the improvement of supply process efficiency. This priority regards the reduction of costs related to the internal ordering process, inventories, and leaning and automating most of the activities. Also the component of transaction costs related to proper transaction management process (e.g. control of shipment, control of quality, payments, possible compliance or breach of contract (Watson, 2000)) is included within this dimension. Moreover, supply process efficiency refers also to the improvement of supplier's delivery performance in terms of reliability, speed, and flexibility.

The second motivation refers to part of the variables considered in the transaction costs theory (Coase, 1937; Williamson, 1979; Watson, 2000). It describes the total cost sustained by the company to acquire the material, in terms of suppliers' search and selection, costs of negotiation and evaluation, and the proper purchase cost of the material. It does not include the operative or proper transaction management costs (see Table 1.2 in Chapter 1), as they are considered part of the first mentioned motivation.

Finally, the third main motivation refers to the improvement of supply process effectiveness both in terms of quality and service. In particular, it consists of new products time to market reduction, innovation enhancement, and quality improvement, all of which are related to a general concept of quality and innovation. Furthermore, this dimension includes also the reduction of stock-outs as a priority; this aspect is directly related to the level of service to the final customer.

The first two emerged categories of objectives pursued by companies adopting the Internet in their relationships with suppliers essentially cover two of main motivations highlighted in literature, respectively the procurement process efficiency, and the supply market efficiency. As far as the third motivation is concerned, things are different. In literature it is widely recognized that a third main objective driving the Internet use is to increase collaboration between trading partners. In reality, this aspect appears to be more an instrumental goal rather than a real primary objective. Such instrumental goal is aimed at pursuing either the first or the third mentioned motivations, respectively supply process efficiency and effectiveness.

Internet Tools Choice

As far as the second research question is concerned, analyses showed the contingent situations and effects on performances of some of the most known web-based tools (Figure 8.1).

Electronic catalogs are widely used by companies in the procurement of low-criticality and standard materials (e.g. indirect or MRO materials) with the objective of pursuing supply process efficiency. However, the analysed sample did not present significant effects on performances.

Electronic auctions, both reverse and direct, are adopted by companies in the procurement of relevant materials, both in terms of purchase volume and in terms of contribution to final product features (e.g. direct materials). The main objective, which also emerged from literature review, is reducing procurement costs in terms of suppliers' search and selection, contract negotiation, and purchase price. Analyses show that such objective is significantly reached, especially as far as reverse auctions are concerned.

Web EDI transactions have been mainly adopted to increase supply process effectiveness, regardless of a possible increment in procurement costs. This drawback might be due to the investments any supplier has to face when adopting EDI standards within its processes, thus increasing transaction costs. For this reason, web EDI transactions occur where the supply market is not complex at all, and suppliers are willing to face such investments in order to differentiate themselves from their many competitors. As a result, coordination through web EDI leads to higher efficiency and effectiveness in the supply process, even if procurement costs might be higher as well.

Team working tools are widely adopted by companies within the sample where supply market complexity is high; this might be due to the attempt of the customer to establish and consolidate good relationships where it is difficult to find the proper supplier. The main motivation to the use of team working tools, which emerged also as a reached performance, is the increment of supply process effectiveness (e.g. in terms of quality and innovation). Companies are willing to adopt such tools, regardless of a possible increment in procurement costs in a supply market which is rather complex in any case.

Horizontal portals are mainly adopted where the supply market is rather complex in order to reduce procurement costs, regardless of a possible loss in efficiency. As a matter of fact, procurement costs are significantly reduced, but supply process efficiency is lower. The adoption of horizontal portals is surely related to the typology of transaction tools they offer. In the analysed sample, horizontal portals offer mainly liquid exchanges and reverse auctions, which are typically tools adopted to increase market efficiency. On the contrary, vertical portals appeared to offer a wider range of tools, including catalogs and team working tools.

Customers prefer private exchanges where materials are critical and the supply market complexity is rather low. As a matter of fact, private portals allow managing securely and reliably customized or specific materials, even if supply market complexity should be as low as possible to allow customer contractual power inducing suppliers using customer's portal. Unfortunately, significant motivations and performances did not emerge, except for the fact that companies do not aim at reducing procurement costs through private portals, neither they actually do.

	Acquired material			Primary objectives			Results		
	Rel.	Crit.	S.M.	Effic.	PCR	Effec.	Effic.	PCR	Effec.
Sell-side catalog		−		+					
Reverse auction	+				+			+	
Direct auction	+				+				
Web EDI			−			+	+		+
Team working		+				+			+
Horizontal portal			+	−	+		−	+	
Private portal		+					−		
Supplier portal			−	+		+	+	+	+
Independent portal			+	−	+				+

Rel.:	Material Relevance	Effic.:	Supply Process Efficiency
Crit:	Material Criticality	PCR:	Procurement Cost Reduction
S.M.:	Supply Market Complexity	Effec.:	Supply Process Effectiveness

▨ The variable is positively related to the adoption of the specific tool
░ The variable is negatively related to the adoption of the specific tool

Figure 8.1a Adoption of web-based tools and relative results

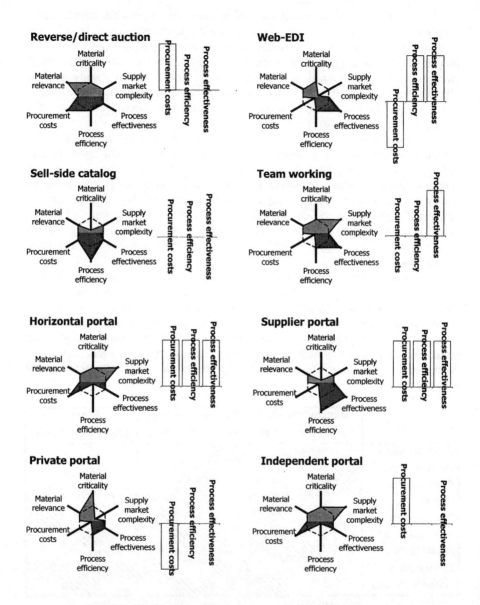

Figure 8.1b Adoption of web-based tools and relative results

Suppliers' portals have been mainly adopted for not critical materials in order to increase supply process efficiency and effectiveness. Generally speaking, critical materials procurement is managed more on privately owned and controlled initiatives rather than on other parties' initiatives. Data also show that procurement costs reduction, and increased supply process efficiency and effectiveness are all improved performances. Such initiatives assume, therefore, the nature of services offered by the supplier to the customer.

Finally, independent marketplaces have been used similarly to horizontal portals, which in fact are often independent. They work as intermediaries where supply market complexity is high, thus lowering the overall procurement costs. Companies do not consider process efficiency as a motivation driving to the use of independent marketplaces.

Also in the last three cases (i.e. private, supplier, and independent portals) the adoption is related to the typologies of the offered services. As a matter of fact, private initiatives present within the sample, either customer's or supplier's, offer a wider range of tools than independent or even consortium initiatives. These last portals are mainly focused on increasing market efficiency; therefore it is logical that companies adopt them in order to reduce their procurement costs.

Finally, empirical evidence shows clearly how companies prefer adopting private exchanges, either customer's or supplier's. As a matter of fact, using private initiatives guarantees higher control over the transaction, more customized services, and higher privacy and security.

Implications on Customer-Supplier Relationships

As far as the third research question is concerned, the effects of the Internet introduction within the procurement process has been analysed.

The research highlighted the twofold role of the Internet. On the one hand, new web based tools such as electronic auctions, liquid exchanges and public electronic catalogs emphasize market efficiency, thus making more convenient arm's length transactions among companies. On the other hand, the Internet, with its capability of standardizing communication protocols and supporting richer information sharing than before, provides the possibility to create deeper relationships based on higher coordination and collaboration than before. This context creates a clear divergence between pure market relationships and vertical alliances.

Such divergence can be explained by the shift of the efforts-integration trade-off, as discussed in Chapter 5 (Figure 8.2). Companies might build collaborative relationships on the market without investing as many efforts as they should have done in the past ('A' arrow in the figure). At the same time, companies might reach higher integration with equal efforts than before ('B' arrow in the figure). These opportunities are especially valid for those acquired materials that are placed in the proximity of the 'border' between market and alliance (e.g. bottlenecks and leverages in the Kraljic's classification - Kraljic, 1983).

In such a condition, a new form of customer-supplier relationship emerges: the *collaborative market*. A collaborative market relationship occurs where companies choose trading partners through a market-oriented approach, but new technologies allow them reaching high level of coordination and collaboration without big investments. These are short-term relationships with low initial costs, and therefore low switching costs: if the relation is not worthwhile any more trading companies can give it up and find someone else on the market. The existence of such relationships should allow companies competing on their businesses by leveraging their dynamic collaborating networks.

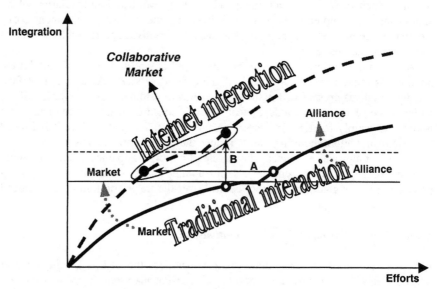

Figure 8.2 Integration-Efforts trade-off shift

The study also proposes a model for collaborative services exploitable through a collaborative market model (Figure 8.3). Those collaborative services are in addition to more traditional transaction services and value added services (VAS). Main collaborative services can be classified into two sets: operational services and technological services. On the one hand, operational services support collaboration on operational activities such as order management, exception management, collaborative forecasting, collaborative inventory management, and collaborative planning. On the other hand, technological services support collaboration in more technological and strategic activities such as collaborative design, project management, and product life cycle management.

Finally, the research study also recognizes that some barriers are still in place to the concrete emergence of collaborative markets. In particular, trust issues, lack of process and communication standards, current internal data and processes, learning effect issues, privacy and competitive concerns, and data security are all obstacles to be overcome in order to enable such a typology of relationship.

Transaction Services		
Value Added Services		
Collaboration Services		
Operational Services	Order management	*Virtual Private Hub*
	Exception management	
	Collaborative forecasting	
	Collaborative inventory management	
	Collaborative planning	
Technological Services	Collaborative design	
	Project management	
	Product life cycle management	

Figure 8.3 Portals supporting collaborative markets

8.2 Future Developments

Interesting future developments for further research arise quite spontaneously.

First of all, this research based the model of *collaborative markets* on a wide analysis mainly focused on vertical and consortium portals. Future research projects might aim at monitoring other initiatives and possibly creating new supply chain or collaboration services enabling coordination within customer-supplier relationships. The new emerging *web services* (see Chapter 5) are an example of new technology applied to a private network enabling collaborative market relationships without the presence of any intermediary.

Another interesting topic might be the standards achievement theme within different specific industrial sectors, a topic that is becoming more and more hot on managers and practitioners' agendas. As discussed within the work, standards are one of the biggest barriers, if not the biggest one, to the emergence of *collaborative markets*.

The entire research was based on a dyadic customer-supplier perspective and analysed the effects of the Internet introduction within such a relationship. This is only a first step necessary to analyse the effects on entire supply chains. Future research projects might enlarge the perspective by considering both upstream and downstream tiers, and, most of all, analysing portfolio strategies in managing complex networks of firms. In such a topic, companies are in relation with each other through a set of web-based tools different situation by situation. It becomes extremely important, then, to find the right balance among relationships, organizational structures, management practices, and technology tools.

Finally, it might be extremely interesting to analyse *collaborative market* opportunities within industries naturally characterized by possible short-term relationships between customers and suppliers. Some examples are the engineering industry or the construction industry where main contractors might present the need to create collaborative relationships with suppliers, but lasting only through the project life cycle. In such a context, *collaborative markets* tools might support numerous activities such as project management, collaborative design, project procurement, inventory management, and logistics and production scheduling. These activities could be performed in a collaborative supply chain environment, without high specific initial investments.

Bibliography

A.A. V.V., 2001, *Improving supply networks: development of skills and technological opportunities*, research report, MIP-Politecnico di Milano e Nomisma.

A.T. Kearney, 2000, *Building the B2B foundation: positioning net market makers for success*, report, www.atkearney.com.

Aldrich, Dubini, 1989, *Le reti e i processi di sviluppo delle imprese*, Economia e Politica Industriale, 64.

Ansari A., Modarress B., 1987, *The potential benefits of Just-in-Time purchasing for U.S. manufacturing*, Production and Inventory Management, 28.

Ansari A., Modarress B., 1990, *Just in Time purchasing*, New York, Free Press.

Baileys R. in Viganò S., Zagami G., a.a 1998-1999, *L'impatto delle tecnologie Intranet/Extranet sui processi aziendali: un modello di analisi*, Tesi di laurea in Ingegneria Gestionale, Politecnico di Milano.

Baker R. in Viganò S., Zagami G., a.a 1998-1999, *L'impatto delle tecnologie Intranet/Extranet sui processi aziendali: un modello di analisi*, Tesi di laurea in Ingegneria Gestionale, Politecnico di Milano.

Ballou R. H., Gilbert S. M., Mukherjee A, 2000, *New managerial challenges from supply chain opportunities*, Industrial Marketing Management, 29, 7-18.

Bartezzaghi E., Spina, G., Verganti R., 1999, *Organizzare le PMI per la crescita*, Il Sole 24 Ore, Milano.

Berry D., Towill D. R., Wadsley N., 1994, *Supply chain management in the electronics product industry*, International Journal of Physical Distribution and Logistics Management 24 (10).

Borders A.L., Johnston W.J., Rigdon E.E., 2001, *Beyond the Dyad: Electronic Commerce and Network Perspectives in Industrial Marketing Management*, Industrial Marketing Management, 30.

Bowles J., 1999, *E-procurement: the transformation of corporate purchasing. How the Internet is changing B2B Transactions*, The Custom Publishing Group.

Brynjolfsson E., Malone T:, Gurbaxani V., Kambil A., 1993, *Does information technology lead to smaller firms?*, unpublished manuscript (position paper), Massachusetts Institute of Technology, Cambridge, Massachusetts.

Brynjolfsson E., Smith J., 2000, *Frictionless Commerce? A Comparison of Internet and Conventional Retailers*, Management Science, Vol. 46, No 4, April, 563-585.

Burbidge J. L., 1961, *The new approach to production*, Production Engineer, December, 40(12), 769-784.

Busby, Fan, 1993, *The extended manufacturing enterprise: its nature and its needs*, International Journal of Technology Management, 8 (3-4-5).

Cagliano R., Sassatelli M., Savoldelli A., 1999, *Supply network reengineering: some evidence from the field*, Proceedings of the conference on SMEs, May 7th.

Carr N. G., 2000, *Hypermediation: commerce as clickstream*, Harvard Business Review, January-February.

Childe, 1998, *The extended manufacturing enterprise: a concept of co-operation*, Production Planning and Control, 9(4).

Chopra S., Dougan D., Taylor G., 2001, *B2B e-commerce opportunities*, Supply Chain Management Review, May/June, 50-58.

Chopra S., Van Mieghem J.A., 2000, *Which e-Business is right for your supply chain?*, Supply Chain Management Review, July/August, 32-40.

Christopher M.G., 1992, *Logistics and supply chain management*, Pitman Publishing, London, UK.

Cristopher M.G., 2000, *The agile supply chain: competing in volatile markets*, Industrial Marketing Management, 29, 37-34.

Clark K., 1989, *Project scope and project performance: the effect of parts strategy and supplier involvement on product development*, Management Science, 35.

Clark K., Fujimoto T., 1991, *Product development performances*, Harvard Business School, Boston, Massachusetts.

Coase R. H., 1937, *The nature of the firm*, Economica 4.

Cohen, Levinthal, 1990, *Absorptive capacity: a new perspective on learning and innovation*, Administrative Science Quarterly, 35.

Commons, 1934, in Scolaro A., 1998, Tesi di laurea. Università di Verona.

Cook T. D., Campbell D. T., 1979, *Quasi-experimentation: design and analysis issues for field settings*, Chicago: Rand McNally.

Cooper M.C., Ellram L.M., Gardner, Hanks, 1997, *Meshing Multiple Alliances*, Journal of Business Logistics, volume 18(1), 67-89.

Cooper M.C., Lambert D.M., Pagh J.D., 1997, *Supply chain management: more than a new name for logistics*, The International Journal of Logistics Management, 8(1).

Corbett C. J., Blackburn J. D., Van Wassenhove L. N., 1999, *Partnerships to improve supply chains*, Sloan Management Review, Summer.

Council of Logistics Management, 1986, *What is it all about?*, Oak Brook, Illinois.

Covill in Viganò S., Zagami G., a.a 1998-1999, *L'impatto delle tecnologie Intranet/Extranet sui processi aziendali: un modello di analisi*, Tesi di laurea in Ingegneria Gestionale, Politecnico di Milano.

Cronbach L.J., Meehl P.E., 1955, *Construct validity in psychological tests*, Psychological Bulletin, vol. 52.

Croom S.R., 2000, *The impact of web-based procurement on the management of operating resources supply*, The Journal of Supply Chain Management, Winter.

Croom S.R., Romano P., Giannakis M., 2000, *Supply chain management: an analytical framework for critical literature review*, European Journal of Purchasing & Supply Management (6).

Cross J. G., 2000, *How e-business is transforming supply chain management*, Journal of Business Strategy, March/April, 36-39.

Davenport T. H., 1993, *Process Innovation*, Boston: Harvard Business School Press.

Davidow W.H., Malone M., 1992, *The virtual corporation*, Harper Business, New York.

Davis, O'Sullivan, 1998, *Communications technologies for the extended enterprise*, Production Planning and Control, 9 (8).

Davis, O'Sullivan, 1999, *System design framework for the extended enterprise*, Production Planning and Control, 10 (1).

De Maio A., Maggiore E., 1992, *Organizzare per innovare. Rapporti evoluti cliente-fornitore*, Etaslibri, Milano.

De Toni A., Nassimbeni G., 1999, *Buyer-supplier operational practices, sourcing policies and plant performances: results of an empirical research*, International Journal of Production Research, 37(9).

Dean I., Carrie A., 1996, *The franchised factory: a new paradigm for manufacturing*, Proceedings of 3rd International Conference of EUROMA, London, 2-4 June.

Dillon W.R., Goldstein M., 1984, *Multivariate analysis: methods and applications*, Wiley, New York.

Dobrin D. N., Uchneat J., 1999, *Interenterprise computing enables supply chain synchronization*, www.ascet.com/ascet/wp/wpDobrin.html.

Dyer J. H., Kale P., Singh H., 2001, *How to make strategic alliances work*, MIT Sloan Management Review, Summer, 37-43.

Dyer J. H., Ouchi W. G., 1993, *Japanese-style partnerships: giving companies a competitive edge*, Sloan Management Review, 34, Fall.

Ellram L. M., 1991, *Supply chain management: the industrial organisation perspective*, International Journal of Physical Distribution and Logistics Management 21 (1), 13-22.

Ellram L. M., 1995a, *A managerial guideline for the development and implementation of purchasing partnerships (Honor Anniversary Article)*, International Journal of Purchasing and Materials Management, Spring.

Ellram L. M., 1995b, *Partnering pitfalls and success factors*, International Journal of Purchasing and Materials Management, Spring.

Eqos, 1999, *E-collaboration: enabling dynamic trade*, white paper, Eqos Systems Ltd..

Esposito E., 1996, *Le imprese ad alta tecnologia: il caso dell'industria aeronautica*, Cuen.

Etnoteam, 1999, www.etnoteam.it.

Feeny D., 2001, *Making business sense of the e-opportunity*, MIT Sloan Management Review, Winter.

Fine C., 2001, *Customer service operations analysis*, Sloan lecture material.

Fiocca R., 1982, *Account portfolio analysis for strategy development*, Industrial Marketing Management, 11, 53-62.

Fisher M. L., 1997, *What is the right supply chain for your product?*, Harvard Business Review, March-April, 105-116.

Flynn B.B., Sakakibara S., Schroeder R.G., Bates K.A., Flynn E.J., 1990, *Empirical research methods in operations management*, Journal of Operations Management, 9 (2), April.

Forrester J. W., 1961, *Industrial Dynamics*, MIT Press.

Frohlich R., Westbrook, 2001, *Arcs of integration: an international study of supply chain strategies*, Journal of Operations Management, 19.

Fujimoto T., 1997, *The Japanese automobile supplier system framework, facts and reinterpretation*, proceedings of the 3rd International Symposium on Logistics conference, Padova, July.

Fullerton R.R., McWatters C.S., 2001, *The production performance benefits from JIT implementation*, Journal of Operations Management, 19, 81-96.

Gartner Group, 1999, www.gartner.com.

Goldman S.L., Nagel R.N., Preiss K., 1995, *Agile competitors and virtual organizations*, Van Nostrand Reinhold, New York.

Grandori, 1989, *Reti interorganizzative: progettazione e negoziazione*, Economia e Management, 7.

Grossman S. J., Hart O. D., 1986, *The costs and benefits of ownership: a theory of vertical and lateral integration*, Journal of Political Economy, 94, 4.

Gulati R., Garino J., 2000, *Get the right mix of bricks and clicks*, Harvard Business Review, May-June.

Hair J.F., Anderson R.E., Tatham R.L., 1992, *Multivariate data analysis*, Macmillan Publishing, New York.

Hammer M., (1990), *Reengineering work: don't automate – obliterate*, Harvard Business Review, July-August.

Hammer M., Champy J., (1993), *Re-engineering the corporation: a manifesto for business revolution*, London, Nicholas Brealey Publishing.

Handfield R.B., 2001, *Before you build a B2B network, redesign your supply chain*, Supply Chain Management Review, July/August.

Handfield R.B., Krause D. R., Scannell T. V., Monczka R. M., 2000, *Avoid pitfalls in supplier development*, Sloan Management Review, Winter, 37-49.

Harland C. M., 1996, *Supply chain management: relationships, chains and networks*, British Journal of Management, 7, Special issue, s63-s80, March.

Hayes R., Wheelwright S. C., 1984, *Restoring our competitive edge: competing through manufacturing*, John Wiley, New York.

Hewitt in Cooper et al., 1997.

Holmstrom J., Hoover W.E., Louhiluoto P., Vasara A., 2000, *The other end of the supply chain*, www.mckinseyquarterly.com.

Houlihan J., 1984, *Supply Chain Management*, Proceedings of 19th International Technical Conference, BPICS, 101-110.

Ireland R., Bruce R., 2000, *CPFR: only the beginning of collaboration*, Supply Chain Management Review, 2000.

Jones T.C. and Riley D. W., 1985, *Using inventory for competitive advantage through supply chain management*, Int. Journal of Physical Distribution and Materials Management, 15(5), 16-26.

Kahl S.J., Berquist T.P., 2000, *A primer on the Internet supply chain*, Supply Chain Management Review, September/October.

Kalakota R., 2000, *Next-generation B2B solutions*, Supply Chain Management Review, July/August.

Kalakota R., Robinson M., 1999, *e-Business: roadmap for success*, Addison Wesley Longman Inc..

Kaplan S., Sawhney M., 2000, *E-hubs: the new B2B marketplaces*, Harvard Business Review, May-June, 97-103.

Kerlinger F. N., 1986, *Foundations of behavioural research*, Holt, Rinehart & Winston, New York.

Ketchen D. J. Jr., Shook C.L., 1996, *The application of cluster analysis in strategic management research: an analysis and critique*, Strategic Management Journal, Vol. 17.

Kopczak L. R., 1997, *Logistic partnership and supply chain restructuring: survey results from the US computer industry*, Production and Operations Management 6 (33).

Kopczak L. R., 2001, *Designing supply chains for the 'click-and-mortar' economy*, Supply Chain Management Review, January/February.

Kraljic P., 1983, *Purchasing must become supply management*, Harvard Business Review 61, 109-117.

Lambert D. M., Cooper M. C., 2000, *Issues in supply chain management*, Industrial Marketing Management, 29, 65-83.

Lamming R.C., 1993, *Beyond partnership: strategies for innovation and lean supply*, Prentice Hall, London.

Lamming R.C., Johnsen T., Zheng J., Harland C., 2000, *An initial classification of supply networks*, International Journal of Operations and Production Management, 20(6).

Lancioni R. A., Smith M. F., Oliva T. A., 2000, *The role of the internet in supply chain management*, Industrial Marketing Management, 29, 45-56.

Law A. M., Kelton W. D., 1991, *Simulation modeling and analysis*, McGraw-Hill, New York.

Lee A., 1991, *Integrating positivist and interpretative approaches to organizational research*, Organization Science, Volume 2, 342-365.

Lee H.L., Billington C., 1992, *Managing supply chain inventory: pitfalls and opportunities*, Sloan Management Review, Spring, 65-73.

Lee H.L., Ng S. M., 1997, *Introduction to the special issue on global supply chain management*, Production and Operations Management 6 (33).

Lee H.L., Padmanabhan V., Whang S., 1997a, *Information distortion in a supply chain: the bullwhip effect*, Management Science, vol. 43, n. 4, 546-558.

Lee H.L., Padmanabhan V., Whang S., 1997b, *The bullwhip effect in supply chains*, Sloan Management Review, Spring.

Lee H.L., Whang S., 2001, *Supply Chain Integration Over the Internet*, www.commerce.net/research/ebusiness-strategies/2001/01_01_r.html.

Lee H.L., Whang S., 2001, *Winning the last mile of e-commerce*, MIT Sloan Management Review, Summer.

Ljungdahl L.G., 2000, *What you need to know about the Internet-enabled supply chain*, Supply Chain Management Review, November/December.

Macbeth D. K., Ferguson N., 1994, *Partnership sourcing: an integrated supply chain approach*, Pitman, London.

Maddala G.S., 1992, *Introduction to econometrics*, Prentice Hall, Englewood Cliffs, New Jersey.

Malone T.W., Laubacher R.J., 1998, *Are big companies becoming obsolete? The dawn of the e-lance economy*, Harvard Business Review, September-October.

Malone T.W., Yates J., Benjamin R.I., 1987, *Electronic markets and electronic hierarchies*, Communications of the ACM, 30 (6). June.

Malone T.W., Yates J., Benjamin R.I., 1989, *The logic of electronic markets*, Harvard Business Review, May-June.

Manrodt K. B., Fitzgerald M., 2001, *Seven propositions for successful collaboration*, Suppply Chain Management Review, July-August.

Mariotti S., 1996, *Mercati verticali organizzati e tecnologie dell'informazione: l'evoluzione dei rapporti di fornitura*, Fondazione Adriano Olivetti.

Mariotti S., 2000, *Teaching Material of Industrial Economics Lectures*, Politecnico di Milano.

McCutchenon D., Stuart F.I., 2000, *Issues in the choice of supplier alliance partners*, Journal of Operations Management, 18, 279-301.

McKinsey in Rangone A., 2000, *Dispense del Corso di Strategia e Pianificazione Aziendale*, Politecnico di Milano.

Menard S., 1991, *Longitudinal research*, Sage Publications, Newbury Park, California.

Mentzer J. T., Foggin, J. H., Golicic S. L., 2000, *Collaboration: the enablers, impediments, and benefits*, Supply Chain Management Review, Sep-Oct, 52-58.

Merli G., Saccani C., 1994, *L'azienda Olonico-virtuale. Un'opportunità storica per la piccola e media impresa,* Il Sole24Ore.

Metz P. J.,1998, *Demystifying supply chain management*, Supply Chain Management Review, Winter.

Miles, Snow, 1992, *Causes of failures in network organizations*, California Management Review, summer.

Moakley G., 2000, *eCommerce requires intelligent supply chains*, Achieving Supply Chain Excellence Through Technology (ASCET), white paper.

Monczka R. M., Petersen K. J., Handfield R. B., Ragatz G. L., 1998, *Success factors in strategic supplier alliances: the buying company perspective*, Decision Sciences, 29 (3).

Moore K. R., 1998, *Trust and relationship commitment in logistics alliances: a buyer perspective*, International Journal of Purchasing and Materials Management, Winter.

Nakane J., Hall R.W., 1991, *Holonic Manufacturing: flexibility - the competitive battle in the 1990s*, Production Planning & Control, 2(1).

Nassimbeni G., 1996, *Factors underlying operational JIT purchasing practices*, International Journal of Production Economics, 3, 38-55.

Nassimbeni G., 2000, *The evaluation of suppliers' co-design effort: comparison between fuzzy, neuro fuzzy and OLS regression approaches*, First World Conference on Production and Operations Management POM, Sevilla.

Norusis M., 1993a, *SPSS for Windows. Basic statistics. Release 6.0*, SPSS Inc., Chicago, Illinois.

Norusis M., 1993b, *SPSS for Windows. Advanced statistics. Release 6.0*, SPSS Inc., Chicago, Illinois.

Norusis M., 1993c, *SPSS for Windows. Professional statistics. Release 6.0*, SPSS Inc., Chicago, Illinois.

Nunnally J., 1978, *Psychometric theory*, New York, McGraw-Hill.

O'Leary-Kelly S.W., Vokurka R.J., 1998, *The empirical assessment of construct validity*, Journal of Operations Management, 16, 387-405.

Oliver R. K., Webber M. D., 1982, *Outlook*, Booz Allen and Hamilton Inc.

Olsen R. F., Ellram L. M., 1997, *A portfolio approach to supplier relationship*, Industrial Marketing Management, 26, 101-113.

Patton M. Q., 1987, *How to use qualitative methods in evaluation*, Newbury Park, California: Sage.

Peterson K., 2000, *Collaborative Commerce: your path to e-marketplace optimization*, B2B e-marketplaces: competing and prospering in the world of online exchanges, Westin Copley Palace, Boston, Massachusetts, 6-8 November.

Phillips C., Meeker M., 2000, *The B2B Internet report: collaborative commerce*, Morgan Stanley Dean Witter, April, www.msdw.com

Platt J., 1992, *Case study*, American Methodological thought, Current Sociology, 40, 17-48.

Porter M. E., 2001, *Strategy and the Internet*, Harvard Business Review, March.

Porter R., 1998, *Managing the supply chain with internet based collaboration*, Logistics & Supply Chain Journal, November.

PWC in Rangone A., 2000, *Dispense del Corso di Strategia e Pianificazione Aziendale*, Politecnico di Milano.

Quinn, 1999, *Strategic outsourcing: leveraging knowledge capabilities*, MIT Sloan Management Review, 40(4).

Quinn, Hilmer, 1994, *Strategic outsourcing*, Sloan Management Review, summer.

Rangone A., 2001, *Verso i private exchange*, Il Sole24ore, 17 ottobre.

Rice J.B., Hoppe R., 2001, *Supply chain versus supply chain: the hype and the reality*, Supply Chain Management Review, Sep-Oct.

Rice J.B., Ronchi S., 2001, *Collaboration, alliances and the coordination spectrum: an introductory essay*, working paper, MIT.

Ronchi S., 1999, *Gli studi di caso: una metodologia di ricerca nel campo dell'Ingegneria Gestionale*, Research assignment, Politecnico di Milano.

Ross K., 1999, *Creating value from business to business integration*, www.ascet.com/ascet/wp/wpRoss.html.

Samson D., Terziovski M., 1999, *The relationship between total quality management practices and operational performance*, Journal of Operations Management, 17, 393-409.

Saunders M. J., 1995, *Chains, pipelines, networks and value stream: the role, nature and value of such metaphors in forming perceptions of the task of purchasing and supply management*, First Worldwide Research Symposium on Purchasing and Supply Chain Management, Tempe, Arizona.

Schonberger R.J., Gilbert J., 1983, *Just-in-Time purchasing: a challenge for U.S. industry*, California Management Review, 26.

Schwab D.P., 1980, *Construct validity in organizational behavior*, Research in Organizational Behavior, vol.2.

Scott and Westbrook in Cooper et al., 1997.

Seidel D., Mey M., 1994, *IMS - Holonic manufacturing systems: strategies Vol. 1*, IFW, University of Hannover, Germany.

Sheffi J., 2001, *Transportation procurement*, Course on Logistics & Supply Chain Management: Fundamentals and Thought Leadership, MIT, Boston, June 25-29.

Short J., 2001, *Dot.coms and the second generation of e-business: what's next?*, Next e-Business: the future as a business, Seminar ISVOR FIAT, Torino, Italy, 23rd January.

Simchi-Levi D., 2001, *Internet-based supply chain strategies*, Course on Logistics & Supply Chain Management: Fundamentals and Thought Leadership, MIT, Boston, June 25-29.

Simchi-Levi D., Kaminsky P., Simchi-Levi E., 2000, *Designing and managing the supply chain*, McGraw-Hill Companies, Inc.

Simon H.A., 1977, *The science of management decision*, (Revised ed.), Harper & Row, New York, 1977.

Smeltzer L.R., Carter J.R., 2001, *How to build an e-procurement strategy*, Supply Chain Management Review, March/April.

Smith B., 1999, *The future of supply chain management on the internet*, Logistics & Supply Chain Journal, February.

Spina G., Leandro L., 1998, *Il co-design nei rapporti cliente-fornitore*, MS thesis, Politecnico di Milano.

Spina G., Zotteri G., 1999, *The strategic context of customer-supplier partnerships: evidence from a global survey*, Managing Operations Networks, EUROMA Conference, Venice.

Sportoletti A., 2000, *e-procurement strategies*, PriceWaterHouseCoopers seminar.

Sterman J., 1989, *Modeling managerial behavior: misperception of feed-back in a dynamic decision-making experiment*, Management Science, vol. 35, n. 3, 321-339.

Stevens G. C., 1989, *Integrating the supply chain*, Int. Journal of Physical Distribution and Materials Management, 19(8), 3-8.

Stock G.N., Greis N.P., Kasarda J.D., 2000, *Enterprise logistics and supply chain structure: the role of fit*, Journal of Operations Management, 18.

Stuart I., Deckert P., McCutcheon D., Kunst R., 1998, *A leveraged learning network*, Sloan Management Review, Summer.

Tan K. C., Kannan V. R., Handfield R.B., 1998, *Supply chain management: supplier performance and firm performance*, International Journal of Purchasing and Material Management 34 (3).

Temkin B., 2001, *B2B success: going beyond e-marketplaces*, Supply Chain Management Review Global Supplement, July/August.

Thomas D. J., Griffin P. M., 1996, *Coordinated supply chain management*, European Journal of Operational Research, 94, 1-15.

Thorelli H.B., 1986, *Networks: between markets and hierarchies*, Strategic Management Journal, 7.

Trochim W., 1989, *Outcome pattern matching and program theory*, Evaluation and Program Planning, 12, 355-366.

Turnbull P., Oliver N., Wilkinson B., 1992, *Buyer-supplier relations in the UK automotive industry: strategic implications of the Japanese manufacturing model*, Strategic Management Journal, 13.

Umar R. in Viganò S., Zagami G., a.a 1998-1999, *L'impatto delle tecnologie Intranet/Extranet sui processi aziendali: un modello di analisi*, Tesi di laurea in Ingegneria Gestionale, Politecnico di Milano.

Upton, McAfee, 1996, *The real virtual factory*, Harvard Business Review.

Venkatraman V., 2001, *E-Business strategies: the next chapter*, Next e-Business: the future as a business, Seminar ISVOR FIAT, Torino, Italy, 23rd January.

Von Neuman J., Morgentern O., 1964, *Theory of games and economic behaviour*, New York, John Wiley & Sons Inc..

Voss C., 2000, *The impact of the virtual economy on logistics and manufacturing*, e-business seminar, Como, October.

Watson R. T., Berthon P., Pitt L.F., Zinkhan G.M., 2000, *e-commerce e impresa*, McGraw-Hill, Italy, Milan.

Wenninger J., 1999, *Business-to-business electronic commerce*, Current Issues in Economics and Finance, 5/10, June.

Whitaker J.D., Murphy M.D., Haltzel A.H., Dik R.W., 2001, *Private exchanges: the smart path to collaboration*, Supply Chain Management Review Global Supplement, July/August.

Wholey J., 1979, *Evaluation: performance and promise*, Washington, DC: Urban Institute.

Williamson O. E., 1975, *Markets and Hierarchies: Analysis and Anti-trust Implications. A Study in the Economics of Internal Organization*, The Free Press, New York.

Williamson O. E., 1979, *Transaction cost economics: the governance of contractual relations*, Journal of Law and Economics, vol. 22, 233-261.

Williamson O. E., 1983, *Credible commitments: Using hostages to support exchanges*, American Economic Review, 73, 519-40.

Wise R., Morrison D., 2000, *Beyond the exchange: the future of B2B*, Harvard Business Review, Nov-Dec.

Wolak R. in Viganò S., Zagami G., a.a 1998-1999, *L'impatto delle tecnologie Intranet/Extranet sui processi aziendali: un modello di analisi*, Tesi di laurea in Ingegneria Gestionale, Politecnico di Milano.

Yin R. K., 1994, *Case study research: design and methods*, Applied Social Research Methods Series, Volume 5, Sage Publications.

Appendix

The Survey Tool

The role of the internet in customer-supplier relationships

The aim of this research project is to identify what are the main trends in customer-supplier relationships across the supply chain. Although there are five pages, this questionnaire will take approximately 10 minutes to complete.

In answering the questions you will be asked to chose a particular material and a particular supplier for that material and describe the relationship before and after the internet adoption in the procurement process. If you have not applied any web-based tools in your procurement process, please complete only section 'A' and send the questionnaire back.

The questionnaire is divided into five sections:

A   General information about your company

B   Information about the selected material purchased by your company

C   Information about the relationship with the selected supplier before and after the internet adoption

D   Information about the internet adoption in the procurement of the material

E   Information about the performances in the procurement process after the internet adoption

Instructions – Electronic: This document is set up for you to respond electronically – you can answer the questions (both with mouse and keyboard), and send it back pressing the option button at the end. The questions are set up so you can indicate your answers by clicking on the check items and by writing responses in the fields provided.

Instructions – Fax: If you prefer, you can respond by preparing the document and faxing back to us at +1 617.253.4560 or at +39 02.2399.2720. If you elect to use this method, please let us know to look for your responses by sending an e-mail to Stefano Ronchi at <stefanor@mit.edu>.

All information you will provide will be kept anonymous and will not be disclosed in any way.

A comprehensive final report will be sent out to respondents. The report will trace the main trends observed in the e-procurment and will allow your company to make a comparison with other experiences.

Thank you in advance for your participation.

Stefano Ronchi

stefanor@mit.edu

+1 617 577 5612

SECTION A: GENERAL INFORMATION

Q A-1 Has your company applied any internet based tool in the procurement process?

Ye O   No O

If you answered "No" to this question, please complete only section 'A' and then send the questionnaire back using the option button at the end.

Q A-2 Company name:

Q A-3 Approximate number of employees:

Q A-4 Approximate revenues: Before procurement through the internet: After the internet:

Q A-5 Total material purchases amount: Before procurement through the internet: After the internet:

Q A-6 This question describes the location of your sourcing and sales activity. Please indicate the approximate split of sourcing and sales according to the following:

% of purchases from   % of sales to

	Locally	
	Within your economic area (NAFTA)	
	Outside your economic area (globally)	
100%		100%

Q A-7 Industry in which you operate:

Q A-8 Main products or product families:

Q A-9 Approximate market share (percentage):

Q A-10 Please identify whom you sell mostly your products to:

materials manufacturers O
product assemblers O
distributors O
end consumers O
others O

SECTION B: THE SELECTED MATERIAL

Please, select one of the materials for which you introduced the internet in the procurement process.

Q B-1 The material is: Direct to the product O   Indirect O

Q B-2 The frequency of the purchase is: | Just once ○ Occasional ○ Recurrent ○ |

Q B-3 Brief description of the selected material:

Q B-4 Purchase volume of the material: Before procurement through the internet: ___ After the internet: ___

Q B-5 Please indicate the extent to which the **material** responds to the following **characteristics**

Percentage of the cost of your product covered by the selected material (if direct to the product)	<5% ○ 5-10% ○ 10-15% ○ 15-20% ○ >20% ○

The material is relevant to your product features, performances or main characteristics	Low	○	○	○	○	○	High
Complexity in terms of number of parts (compared to the average purchase)	Low	○	○	○	○	○	High
Manufacturing process and involved technologies complexity (compared to the average purchase)	Low	○	○	○	○	○	High
Novelty (compared to the average purchase)	Low	○	○	○	○	○	High
The specifications of the material are difficult to formalize and communicate	Low	○	○	○	○	○	High
The material is customised for your company	Low	○	○	○	○	○	High
The supplier needs specific investments to supply the material to your companay	Low	○	○	○	○	○	High
Other characteristics (specify ___	Low	○	○	○	○	○	High

Q B-6 Please describe the **supply market** characteristics:

Number of potential suppliers: ___

Number of usual suppliers selected for the purchase: ___

Suppliers' power compared to other materials' suppliers	Low	○	○	○	○	○	High
Competition among suppliers	Low	○	○	○	○	○	High

SECTION C: SELECTED SUPPLIER BEFORE AND AFTER THE INTERNET

Please, select a supplier for the material you previously selected. You will be asked to describe the relationship before and after the internet adoption in the procurement process.

Q C-1 Brief description of the selected supplier (optional):

Q C-2 Length of the relationship:

Q C-3 Length of the contracts: Before procurement through the internet: ___ After the internet: ___

Q C-4 Volume of the material purchases from the supplier:

Before procurement through the internet: [ ]

After the internet: [ ]

Q C-5 Please indicate the extent to which the **relationship** responded to the following **characteristics** before the internet adoption and the extent to which it responds to them after the internet adoption:

	Before the internet adoption	After the internet adoption
Pure arm's length transaction pursuing market efficiency	None ○ ○ ○ ○ ○ High	None ○ ○ ○ ○ ○ High
Coordination in marketing activities (e.g. promotions, co-branding, ...)	None ○ ○ ○ ○ ○ High	None ○ ○ ○ ○ ○ High
Order tracking / tracing	None ○ ○ ○ ○ ○ High	None ○ ○ ○ ○ ○ High
Share information about production planning	None ○ ○ ○ ○ ○ High	None ○ ○ ○ ○ ○ High
Share information about the inventory levels	None ○ ○ ○ ○ ○ High	None ○ ○ ○ ○ ○ High
Share information about products specifications	None ○ ○ ○ ○ ○ High	None ○ ○ ○ ○ ○ High
Just In Time coordination	None ○ ○ ○ ○ ○ High	None ○ ○ ○ ○ ○ High
Collaborative planning and forecasting	None ○ ○ ○ ○ ○ High	None ○ ○ ○ ○ ○ High
Vendor Managed Inventory (your supplier manages your inventory)	None ○ ○ ○ ○ ○ High	None ○ ○ ○ ○ ○ High
Consignment stock (your supplier holds its own inventory in your sites)	None ○ ○ ○ ○ ○ High	None ○ ○ ○ ○ ○ High
Collaborative design in product development	None ○ ○ ○ ○ ○ High	None ○ ○ ○ ○ ○ High
Collaborative process and technology development	None ○ ○ ○ ○ ○ High	None ○ ○ ○ ○ ○ High
Other (specify [ ]	None ○ ○ ○ ○ ○ High	None ○ ○ ○ ○ ○ High

Q C-6 Please describe the **efforts** required **to manage the relationship** before and after the internet adoption, in terms of:

	Before the internet adoption	After the internet adoption
Time and resources spent into sustaining the relationship	None ○ ○ ○ ○ ○ High	None ○ ○ ○ ○ ○ High
Costs in Information and Communication Technology	None ○ ○ ○ ○ ○ High	None ○ ○ ○ ○ ○ High
Costs sustained for joint team working	None ○ ○ ○ ○ ○ High	None ○ ○ ○ ○ ○ High
Investments in tangible assets from both you and your supplier	None ○ ○ ○ ○ ○ High	None ○ ○ ○ ○ ○ High
Other (specify [ ]	None ○ ○ ○ ○ ○ High	None ○ ○ ○ ○ ○ High

SECTION D: THE INTERNET ADOPTION

Q D-1 What kind of **internet tool or tools** have you applied in the procurement of the selected material?

Electronic liquid exchanges (please specify the web-link or the software vendor)	☐	
Electronic reverse auctions (please specify the web-link or the software vendor)	☐	
Electronic direct auctions (please specify the web-link or the software vendor)	☐	
Sell-side e-catalog: the catalog is designed by the supplier (please specify the web-link or the software vendor)	☐	
Buy-side e-catalog: the catalog is designed by your company (please specify the web-link or the software vendor)	☐	
Vertical Market Place (please specify the web-link)	☐	
Horizontal Market Place (please specify the web-link)	☐	
Supplier's private portal or extranet (please specify the web-link or the software vendor)	☐	
Your company's private portal or extranet (please specify the web-link or the software vendor)	☐	
Portal run by a consortium (please specify the web-link)	☐	
Independent public portal (please specify the web-link)	☐	
Web-EDI	☐	
Team-working tools (please specify)	☐	
Others (please specify)		

Q D-2 For how long have you been using these internet-based tools?

Q D-3 Please indicate the **level of priority** you had in implementing the internet in the procurement process, in relation to the following objectives:

Objective	None					High
Reduce costs of suppliers search and selection	None	O	O	O	O	O	High
Reduce costs of negotiation and evaluation	None	O	O	O	O	O	High
Reduce costs of transaction management (e.g. control)	None	O	O	O	O	O	High
Reduce the cost/price of the material	None	O	O	O	O	O	High
Improve internal processes efficiency	None	O	O	O	O	O	High
Reduce inventory costs	None	O	O	O	O	O	High
Improve delivery performance (reliability, speed, flexibility)	None	O	O	O	O	O	High
Improve the quality of the material	None	O	O	O	O	O	High
Reduce stock-outs	None	O	O	O	O	O	High
Reduce the Time To Market	None	O	O	O	O	O	High
Enhance innovation	None	O	O	O	O	O	High
Other (please specify	None	O	O	O	O	O	High

SECTION E: PERFORMANCES IMPROVEMENT AFTER THE INTERNET ADOPTION

Q E-1　Please indicate the **performances improvement** reached through the internet adoption in procurement, where it is possible indicate also the improvement amount (e.g. %):

	None					Significant
Reduction of costs of suppliers search and selection	O	O	O	O	O	
Reduction of costs of negotiation and evaluation	O	O	O	O	O	
Reduction of costs of transaction management (control, contentious, ...)	O	O	O	O	O	
Cost/price reduction	O	O	O	O	O	
Internal processes efficiency improvement	O	O	O	O	O	
Inventory costs reduction	O	O	O	O	O	
Delivery performance improvement (reliability, speed, flexibility)	O	O	O	O	O	
Improvement of the quality of the material	O	O	O	O	O	
Stock-outs reduction	O	O	O	O	O	
Time To Market reduction	O	O	O	O	O	
Innovation enhancement	O	O	O	O	O	
Other (	O	O	O	O	O	

Send directly by e-mail to
<stefanor@mit.edu>

Index